HEA
MINUTES

HEALTH MINUTES

UP-TO-DATE INFORMATION ON TOPICAL HEALTH ISSUES FROM ABC NEWSRADIO

D<small>R</small> NORMAN SWAN

ABC Books

Published by ABC Books for the
AUSTRALIAN BROADCASTING CORPORATION
GPO Box 9994 Sydney NSW 2001

Copyright © Dr Norman Swan 2004

First published May 2004

All rights reserved. No part of this publication may be reproduced, stored in a retrieval system or transmitted in any form or by any means, electronic, mechanical, photocopying, recording or otherwise, without the prior written permission of the Australian Broadcasting Corporation.

National Library of Australia
Cataloguing-in-Publication data
   Swan, Norman.
   Health minutes.

   ISBN 0 7333 1353 1.

   1. Diseases – Handbooks, manuals, etc. 2. Medicine – Handbooks, manuals, etc. I. Australian Broadcasting Corporation. II. Title.

616

Cover design by Lore Foye
Back cover photograph by Warren Clarke/Oculi Photographers
Text design by Lore Foye
Typeset in 10.5/13.5pt Berkeley Book by Kirby Jones
Colour reproduction by Colorwize, Adelaide
Printed and bound by Griffin Press, Adelaide

CONTENTS

About This Book	vii
Asthma and Allergies	1
Babies and children	13
Bones, Joints and Bad Backs	27
Breasts	45
Cancer	55
Cars	65
Chronic Fatigue Syndrome	73
Dementia	77
Diabetes	91
Digestion	95
Drugs and Alcohol	105
Environment and Health	115
Exercise and sport	119
Eyes	127
Heart and Arteries	135
infections	167
Men's Health	183
Mental Health and Psychology	189
Nervous System	209

Pregnancy and Childbirth	215
Prostate	221
Sex	229
Staying Young	235
Weight Loss	245
Women's Health	253
References	263

ABOUT THIS BOOK

It's often been said that it's much harder to write succinctly than at length, which is why when ABC NewsRadio asked me to do a daily one-minute segment on the latest in health, my heart sank. I could sense the agony of forcing complex messages from medical research into two hundred words. The effort, however, has been worth it. None of us has time to spare these days – more's the pity – so a minute has been ideal for giving large numbers of people new information that can help them to make better decisions about their own wellbeing and that of their families. *Health Minutes* allows access to research that even many doctors don't have time to read.

So to extend their usefulness, we've put a selection from the last couple of years *Health Minutes* into this book. I've tried to group them under headings that hopefully correspond with the practical questions and needs you may have. At times you'll find I've updated the material to take account of the changing conclusions from newer studies. You see, while scientific research provides the best evidence you have for deciding what to do about your health, it isn't infallible and there's a danger in coming to definite assumptions based on single studies. Again, where appropriate, I've tried to give an idea of where the balance of current knowledge lies.

Almost every piece is referenced, so you know where I've got the information and you or your doctor can go and double check what I've said. A good place to find summaries of these papers is either the specific journal's website or the US National Library of Medicine. Just type in Entrez PubMed into a search engine, and it will take you there.

Dr Norman Swan

Asthma and Allergies

▼ Should you have a plan for your asthma?

A Victorian study of young adults with asthma found that despite many years of major education campaigns, a significant proportion of these people were having less than adequate care. Very few of them had a written plan from their doctor advising them what to do day to day, particularly if their breathing got worse. Of those who did have a written plan, in only a tiny number was it up to date.

This is significant because such plans do make a difference and do reduce the risk of a life-threatening attack. While doctors wouldn't look after someone with high blood pressure without measuring their blood pressure, it seems most are happy to ignore lung function in asthma when all it needs is a puff into a machine.

The question is whether anyone's coming to grief over this – but the statistics aren't detailed enough for us to know. It's hoped that new asthma programmes for GPs will improve the situation.[1]

▼ But is it actually the plan?

It makes sense to give people more control over their medical care, especially if they have a condition that can turn nasty quickly. One such situation is moderate to severe asthma. These are people who have symptoms frequently enough to require daily preventive medication, and at the severe end people may have their activities restricted by poor lung function.

For years, GPs have been told that what they need to do is write out an asthma action plan for patients so they can look after themselves more effectively. These days, GPs even get paid for doing it. But by and large the plans don't get written, despite plenty of evidence that they prevent hospitalisation and days off work.

The question is does it matter, if a doctor is already seeing you regularly and actively monitoring your asthma, teaching you about it and adjusting the treatment? The answer, according to a review of the international evidence, is no. The written plans and very active follow-up work equally well.

One key is to recognise the signs of worsening asthma, such as more wheezing and coughing on exercise, having a disturbed night's sleep and needing more reliever medication – that's puffers like salbutamol (Ventolin).[2]

▼ There's a lot of it about

Why's there so much asthma around? That's a question many mothers of wheezy children often ask.

The fascinating thing is that the poorer a country or region, the less asthma appears to occur. The theory is that it's a side effect of our hygienic lifestyle. Our immune systems have evolved to fight off parasites and infections in childhood, and when the white blood cells don't get that kind of training they go looking for trouble elsewhere – in this case creating the allergic-type inflammation in the airways that produces the cough, wheezing and phlegm of asthma.

It's a nice theory, but is there much evidence to back it up?

A group of German children were followed from birth to the age of 7. Children with two or more episodes of a runny nose during the first year of life were about twice as likely to develop asthma, eczema or hay fever as children with one episode or less.

Children who had a herpes infection – that's things like chickenpox, cold sores and a harmless fever with rash called roseola – before the age of 3 had a lower chance of having asthma by age 7.

So viruses in a child's early years may be protective.

What does that mean if you're a parent? Probably not a lot that's practical, except that the increased risk of viruses in childcare centres might not be something to be too worried about.[3]

▼ Lifestyle – or what?

Some research into Aboriginal children has complicated the story about early social circumstances and asthma.

There's not a lot of asthma among Aboriginal children living in remote communities, which seems to prove the point made above about our hygienic environment, because they've been exposed to an environment more suited to our evolutionary needs.

Research in two NSW country towns though found that Aboriginal children have high rates of asthma when they're not so remote — in fact the same rate as non-Aboriginal children. Theory proved, you might think. Well not so fast, because the Aboriginal children had lower rates of allergy and didn't seem to be allergic to the things the other kids were allergic to. What seemed to increase the risk for Aboriginal children was a chest infection in the first year of life.

So where does that leave the theory?

Well, the first thing to say is that the study wasn't perfect, so the conclusions could be wrong, but even if they're right, it may be that different infections have different effects.

What I want to know is why medical science is always messing up perfectly good stories with facts?[4]

▼ NEW THEORY ABOUT ASTHMA

Despite being common, there's still mystery surrounding what causes asthma and what happens in the lungs. Someone with asthma has inflammation of their airways, and rather than focus on why the inflammation occurs in the first place, researchers at the University of Cambridge have asked, why doesn't the inflammation go away? And the reason may relate to a very special kind of death.

Inflammation is the process of the immune system coming to attack an infection or remove a foreign substance such as pollen.

But once the white blood cells have done their job, the inflammation stops, largely because the cells are programmed to die. The theory is that in people with chronic asthma, this programmed cell death doesn't occur; the cells linger like bored toddlers with nothing to do — and you know what happens then. When the cells eventually do die, they do so unnaturally, spilling out toxins into the lung tissue.

It turns out that preventer medications for asthma, such as inhaled steroids, are very good at switching on this programmed cell death. So if the theory is right, we may have highly focused, safer medications for asthma — and perhaps for other inflammatory diseases, such as of the kidneys or joints.[5]

▼ Environmental prevention

Many parents of children with asthma look for ways to minimise their reliance on medications, and they're often told that one of the factors causing the wheezing is a little insect which lives in and on carpets, bedding, soft furnishings and curtains. It's called the house dust mite. Some families go to extraordinary lengths to eliminate the house dust mite, such as ripping up carpets and covering mattresses. But does it work?

Dutch researchers did a trial of anti-allergy covers for mattresses, pillows and continental quilts (duvets or doonas). The people taking part were adults and children with moderate to severe asthma who had already taken up or were prepared to take up the carpets in their bedroom.

The results showed a dramatic reduction in house dust mites, but it didn't make any difference to their asthma. The only change in symptoms was that they had less rhinitis and sneezing.

The message is that house dust mite reduction may not help if your asthma is well established, but it may be worth trying for your nose or for a child whose asthma is still mild.[6]

▼ Pets not necessarily bad

Children who are exposed to two or more cats or dogs in the first year of life have lower responses to a whole host of allergic substances when they're aged 6 or 7.

This news comes from an allergy study which followed hundreds of children from when their mothers were pregnant with them.

Exposure to two or more cats or dogs in the first year was associated with a significantly lower rate of positive skin tests to common allergy-causing substances such as house dust mite and pollens. That was after allowing for parental smoking and all sorts of other factors, including whether the parents had avoided pets because there was a family history of asthma or allergy.

Negative blood tests for allergy and better lung function were also associated with exposure to two or more dogs or cats in the first year, but only in boys.

High early exposure to animals may reduce allergy because of the bacteria the animals carry or because of an immune response to the fur, either of which might give cross-protection to other allergy-causing substances. Why girls may not be as protected as boys is a mystery.

It's probably not a good idea to take pet ownership as a public health message, but the research does give new insight into the causes of allergy and might even save a few pooches from being thrown out when the baby arrives.

A word of warning: this study was about preventing allergy. There are children who do have strong allergic responses to animal dander who may benefit from the pet's removal.[7]

▼ Spring cleaning – is it worth it?

Asthma, hay fever and eczema are a family of problems that go under the heading atopy – this essentially means they're allergies on top of a genetic susceptibility.

One of the sources of allergy is in the home – mostly from that wee beastie, the house dust mite. There's great debate about whether it's worth parents controlling the home environment by pulling up carpets, getting rid of pets, covering mattresses and pillows, spraying soft furnishings with a chemical that knocks off the mite and vacuuming often with a powerful machine.

One trial tested doing this during pregnancy and the first year of a child's life in families where there was a strong family history of atopy.

Only limited conclusions could be drawn because a lot of families dropped out, but the children may have had fewer wheezy attacks in the first year of life. It had no effect on eczema or other allergies.

The benefits later in life are still uncertain, particularly given the effort and considerable expense involved.

The cheapest environmental manipulation is to eliminate adult tobacco smoke, which is a well-known cause of respiratory problems in infancy.[8]

▼ Homeopathy for asthma?

One of the most popular complementary therapies around is homeopathy, with its attractive philosophy of treating like with tiny doses of like: where substances are diluted so much that there isn't a single molecule left in the water other than water.

The problem with homeopathy is that it becomes *alternative* rather than complementary medicine if it's used instead of something that's of proven effectiveness, such as immunisation or asthma prevention. So you need to be sure it works.

Some people who have asthma do benefit from desensitisation injections of the substance to which they're allergic. This is called immunotherapy.

Homeopaths also offer immunotherapy, but with ultra-diluted preparations of the allergic substance. Does it work in asthma? A study in the UK compared a placebo – a dummy preparation – with homeopathic immunotherapy for the house dust mite in more than 240 people with asthma and house dust mite allergy.

The results showed that a treatment regime like this does improve people's asthma significantly, but that it doesn't matter what's in the bottle. Homeopathy worked no better than the placebo, and whether or not a person was a strong believer in complementary medicine made no difference.

So why not try it for yourself at home? *Don't* stop any of your current asthma treatment; put some water in a sterile small container, shake it hard, get a clean dropper and put three or four drops on your tongue on three occasions over a 24-hour period, and see what happens![9]

▼ STICK WITH THE TRIED AND TRUE

In the last decade or so, asthma medications which are long-acting relievers (beta agonists) have come onto the market and have names like salmeterol. They open up the airways with only a couple of inhaled doses a day and can make a big difference to people with severe asthma.

But – and it's a big but – these long-acting beta agonists don't do anything for what's causing the asthma: the inflammation. Drugs which do that are preventive; most are corticosteroids, taken by inhaling. People are often wary of steroids, so the temptation has been to assume that because these long-acting beta agonists are effective, they can replace the steroid puffers.

Not so, according to two US studies. They found that long-acting relievers may allow you to reduce your dose of inhaled steroids, if they become your sole therapy, you are placing yourself at risk.

It reinforces the message that if you have asthma you need to have a plan of some kind from your doctor (see previous article), and have the cause addressed as much as the symptoms. As to worries about inhaled steroids, it is true that many people are put on doses which are too high; in some situations, those doses could probably be safely and carefully reduced in consultation with a doctor.

If you need more information, contact the Asthma Foundation in your state.[10]

▼ ONE GROUP OF MEDICATIONS OF LITTLE USE IN ASTHMA

There are two main groups of asthma medications. One is the reliever, for the times when you actually have a wheeze or difficulty breathing, and the second – the mainstay – is the preventer, to keep the asthma at bay.

With the relievers, almost all the medications fall under the category of beta agonists – Ventolin-like drugs which open up the airways by imitating, in a benign way, the effects of adrenaline on the lungs. There is another group of reliever drugs, though, which act by blocking the nerve messages that are sent to narrow the airways. They are called anti-cholinergics, and the most popular is ipratropium – one of the brand names being Atrovent.

Asthma specialists argue about the usefulness of ipratropium even though lots of people, especially children, are prescribed it. The question, in relation to using it for children, is whether it's worth taking in the long term. A review of the available trials in children over 2 years of age has found that there is very little difference between ipratropium and a placebo in the maintenance treatment of children with asthma.

So while there may be some small benefits, it's probably best to stick with the preventers if you need them and the beta agonists for relief.[11]

▼ But one preventer may be questionable, too

The main revolution in asthma treatment in recent times has been appreciating that what counts is prevention – far more than treatment. Prevention here means stopping the inflammation in the lungs that is at the core of the wheezing, coughing and sleep-broken nights of the person with moderate to severe asthma.

While inhaled steroids do this job very well, they have side effects, so for children, paediatricians have tended to use another preventer called sodium cromoglycate – Intal's the brand name.

But some have doubted that cromoglycate is worth the bother, and a review of cromoglycate trials suggests they could be right. Putting the evidence together, there didn't seem to be a benefit from cromoglycate over placebo, and it looked as though there were more unpublished negative results from trials than positive ones; this suggests that good news on cromoglycate has been more likely to see the light of day than bad news – a bias, as they say.

Where does this leave you if your child's on cromoglycate? Well there is evidence it's good for exercise-induced asthma. But either way, don't change anything till you've talked to your doctor about it.[12]

▼ Treatment in a bubble

Could a plastic bubble be an answer for acute asthma? Yes, suggests a study into non-life threatening attacks at Sydney Children's Hospital.

Over the last 25 years or so, the nebuliser has become a common sight in every Emergency Department around the nation and in many homes. It's an electrical pump which pushes air through a solution of anti-asthma drugs for a child (or adult) having trouble with wheezing. But research suggests that for most asthma attacks, a simpler, faster, cheaper and perhaps safer device is as good at relieving the attack.

It's a largish plastic bubble called a spacer. The asthma inhaler slots into one end and is pressed twice, and the person breathes in from the other side. The advantages are that no co-ordination is required, and because only small particles remain in the cloud inside the spacer, the drug gets to where it needs to be – the lungs – rather than to the mouth and throat, where it can have side effects.

The Sydney study got doctors and nurses to stop using the nebuliser when it wasn't needed and use the faster, less bothersome spacers instead – with excellent results.

Spacer devices are very handy to have at home for those on regular asthma medication. You can get more information from your state's Asthma Foundation.[13]

▼ THE IMPACT OF ASTHMA ON FAMILIES

The way families function affects asthmatic children's quality of life and how they perceive their illness, and may flow on to how well they accept treatment.

It might seem like the bleeding obvious, but in fact there hasn't been much research into this area that goes beyond anecdote and impression. If families really do affect asthma, then getting your mum, your dad, your brothers and sisters to deal with the situation better might pay off.

Adelaide-based researchers studied the extent to which children were bothered by their symptoms, comparing kids with similar levels of asthma severity. They also looked at how well these children's families functioned across a whole range of measures, including how they managed conflict, how supportive they were to each other and so on.

The poorer the family functioned, the worse the asthma felt to the child, even though it might not have actually been worse objectively. The key factor in families seemed to be how supportive they were and how much concern they showed for each other's welfare.

It's known that a sense of wellbeing can affect whether or not people take their medications, so the flow-on effect in terms of the asthma could be considerable. The next step is to see whether helping families to function better clears the air in more ways than one.[14]

▼ NEW ANSWERS FOR PEANUT ALLERGY?

Of all the foods that children and adults can be allergic to, peanuts are arguably the most dangerous. Peanut allergy can be induced by the tiniest amounts – even traces on a knife from making a peanut butter sandwich – and every so often there's a preventable death from the profound shock that can ensue.

Some British researchers have been following nearly 14,000 healthy children, trying to work out why some of them developed peanut allergy in the first place.

The factors which turned out to be associated with peanut allergy were drinking soy milk, having had a rash affecting the creases over joints, having a rash which oozed and crusted (you're not eating, I hope!) – and, interestingly, having used skin creams or lotions containing peanut oil.

The connection with soy and the eczema-type rashes could just indicate that the child already had allergic tendencies. But the peanut oil in the skin creams may be more causal: it may sensitise the child's immune system to peanut and prepare the ground for allergic reactions when peanuts are eaten.

All this has to be confirmed, and more work needs to be done to see whether or not these findings can translate into prevention.[15]

▼ Are you really allergic to penicillin?

Up to 1 in 10 people have an allergy to penicillin, but many more than that claim to be allergic. So how do you know whether you are or not?

It's important, because penicillin and its sister medications are important drugs for serious infections. In addition, the replacement medications often have more side effects and are expensive.

There are certain symptoms which are not penicillin allergy, and some which are unlikely to be.

Some people develop nausea or diarrhoea after penicillin, for example. Those are usually non-allergic side effects in the intestinal system.

Even many rashes aren't a sign of allergy. For example, antibiotics are often wrongly prescribed for viral infections and some viruses, and especially in children, they can produce a rash after 2 or 3 days. The classic one is an illness called roseola.

And if you've been given amoxicillin – Amoxil – and have glandular fever or another infection called CMV, a rash can also result. Again, this has nothing to do with an allergy.

The rash in these cases is usually flat with small spots, and there are rarely other symptoms with it. An allergic rash, however, tends to be raised and blotchy. And a severe reaction can interfere with breathing and cause swelling around the mouth.

One of the indications of a real allergic reaction is that it begins within an hour of taking the antibiotic. Allergies can be more common and more severe in people with HIV infection or who are taking beta blockers.

The advice from the experts is that if the reaction you had was just a touch of diarrhoea, it's okay to receive more penicillin. If you've had an Amoxil rash and the doctor's confident that that's what it was, then again it's probably okay. Skin and blood tests can be done, but they're not always very reliable.

If there's any doubt about the seriousness of the reaction, and particularly if the reaction occurs within an hour of taking penicillin, you should probably stop using penicillin. Luckily, there are plenty of alternative medications.

But the key is still making sure you only take antibiotics when they are truly needed.[16]

Babies and Children

▼ BREASTFEEDING NOT THE ANSWER FOR OBESITY

Breastfeeding is touted as a good thing for lots of reasons, from nutrition to protection against infection. One oft-touted benefit is that breastfed babies are less likely to become obese. In the interests of truth and honesty in advertising, though – and risking the ire of breastfeeding zealots everywhere – this may be one area where the magic of breast milk is overwhelmed by the realities of day-to-day living.

A study of more than 2600 3- to 5-year-olds in the US found that breastfeeding gave no protection against being overweight regardless of how long or fully they were breastfed. The variable that seemed to matter was whether or not the mother was overweight. The risk of becoming an overweight child tripled if the mother was overweight and went up four times if the mother was sufficiently overweight to be classified as obese.

The authors felt that if breastfeeding had an effect, it was swamped by things like lack of physical activity and dietary habits in their households.

Just to confuse matters, a paper in the same scientific journal did show less risk of being overweight among adolescents who were breastfed as babies – but the authors felt that maternal obesity was a factor because overweight women are apparently less likely to breastfeed their babies.

The obesity prevention idea has also taken a knock from two more recent studies. One is a follow-up of all male babies born in the hospitals of Pelotas in Brazil during 1982.

Eighty per cent of these young men were examined on entry to the army at the age of 18, and there were no consistent, statistically significant findings to indicate that having been breastfed reduced the amount of fat on their bodies in late adolescence. There seemed, though, to be some connection between breastfeeding between the ages of 3 and 5 months and a reduction in obesity – but not in just being overweight – with long duration breastfeeding. Both of these results are hard to explain. And of course they tell you nothing about women.

A British follow-up study of a group of children born in 1958 also found no significant relationship.

Another negative is that while breastfeeding rates have increased in recent years, so have obesity rates. Not a sign of protection.

But even if there is no proven correlation between breastfeeding and reducing obesity, that means the reasons for breastfeeding have only gone down by one – it's still the best food for a baby. What research like this does is remind us that our destiny is not necessarily fixed by a spot of mother's milk.[1]

▼ If at first you don't succeed, try again ...

That's the message for women who failed at breastfeeding first time around.

A small study in the UK was sparked by statistics showing that women who have difficulties with breastfeeding with their first baby and give up are less likely to even try it with later children. The study followed a group of 22 women through their first and second babies and measured the amount of milk they produced after one week and one month, with both children.

They found that for the second baby, the breasts appeared to have improved at their trade. About 30 per cent more milk was being produced at one week, and the increase was greatest in those women who'd had poor milk output with the first baby. The second baby also took less time to feed and put on more weight.

While some of this could also be explained by more experience, what's interesting is that at 4 weeks there wasn't much difference between first and second babies, suggesting that the benefit is in the start-up phase – getting the baby onto the breast successfully.

So while there are reasons not to breastfeed, if you fail first time around, don't give up when your next baby arrives.[2]

▼ Babies, cereals and diabetes

A US study has found that introducing cereals early or late in the first year of life is associated with an increased risk of juvenile onset, or type 1, diabetes.

Type 1 diabetes is an autoimmune disease where the immune system destroys the insulin-producing cells in the pancreas. Most people with the condition have a genetic profile that makes them vulnerable, but something triggers the disease. Certain viruses may be involved, an infant's diet could play a role in genetically susceptible children. Introducing cows' milk formula in the first 3 months might be a risk factor.

One study, which followed over 1000 at-risk babies from birth, found that cereal introduction before 4 months and after 6 months increased the risk of developing auto-antibodies to insulin-producing cells in the pancreas.

Babies who were breastfed had no increased risk, and the kind of cereal they ate didn't matter. A European study has made similar findings, which strengthens the case for there being a cause and effect link, but good explanations for the phenomenon still aren't easy to come by.

So hanging on till around the middle of the first year before introducing solids, and breastfeeding as long as possible, is still the best way to go.[3]

▼ BABIES AND DENTAL DECAY

Research on dental decay could put a merciful end to politicians kissing babies, and provide a warning about connecting with strange mouths.

Studies at the University of Queensland have been looking at dental decay as a transmissible infection. They've found, for example, that babies are born with perfectly clean mouths, but by as early as 48 hours of age they can be infected with decay-causing organisms that will sit and wait for teeth to come along.

Mothers with high numbers of these bacteria are more likely to pass them on to their children. Things which increase these oral germs in mothers include smoking (probably because of lower oxygen), poor dental hygiene and consuming soft drinks with lots of sugar and acid, especially black cola.

Adults and older children should avoid sharing food utensils with babies or sucking on a dummy to clean it.

The other thing they've found is that the bacteria in your mouth can change as you go through puberty and even later. As an adult, the changes might depend, for example, on who you kiss – presumably more profoundly than a peck on the cheek.

So if your partner can't work out why he or she is having extra fillings at the dentist, I'd keep very quiet if I were you and change the subject.[4]

▼ Babies who regurgitate

Reflux is the bane of many parents' lives. That's the baby who regurgitates milk and can become distressed by it. In its severe form it's called eosinophilic oesophagitis.

Eosinophilic oesophagitis is associated with food allergy, but just what foods is hard to diagnose. The condition seems to be increasing in the community; this could just be that paediatricians are getting better at recognising it, but one of the world leaders in this field feels that its numbers are truly going up.

His theory is that it may be doctor-induced – iatrogenic – by aggressive treatment of milk regurgitation. For this problem, doctors sometimes resort to two types of medication: one which moves food out of the stomach and one which reduces acid.

Professor Hugh Sampson, of Mount Sinai Medical School in New York, thinks that these medications may flush potentially allergy-inducing foods through into the bowel and then into the bloodstream, while at the same time reducing the chances for them to be destroyed by stomach acid.

Until this theory's been properly researched, perhaps doctors need to take some care with what they use on the refluxing baby.[5]

▼ Soy milk formulae

Soy milk formulae for babies have, from time to time, been rather controversial. They are artificial milk formulae made from soy protein rather than cows' milk. They're often used for cows' milk allergy and sometimes – perhaps unnecessarily – for babies who are a bit fussy and colicky.

Anyway, over the years, a concern that the phyto (plant-derived) oestrogens in soy formulae might affect the reproductive capacity of infants at a vulnerable stage of their lives has developed. A research group at the University of Pennsylvania School of Medicine in Philadelphia wanted to find out if that was true.

They followed up over 200 young adults in their 20s – most of them had in fact, as babies, been part of the original studies of soy milk formulae. The beauty of using these people was that the researchers could be sure how much milk they'd taken in the first year of life, and knew that at the time they had been otherwise healthy.

The study focused mostly on their reproductive health: it found no significant differences compared with a control group. There were also no differences in cancer rates, but it was probably too soon in their lives to pick that up.

The only abnormality was a slightly longer duration of menstruation in women who'd had soy formula as babies, but the researchers didn't think that was a statistically significant finding. Which means that so far the news is good on soy formula if a baby needs it.[6]

▼ Sweet drinks make kids fat

While it seems obvious that sweetened drinks make children fat, the evidence to back this up is actually patchy, and relies on less than adequate ways of working out the real intake. The other gaps in our knowledge relate to trade-offs: when a child is taking a fruit drink or lemonade, what nutrients are being missed?

A group of US researchers decided to fix up some of the possible errors by measuring intake in an environment where the food could be controlled and observed more closely: a summer camp. Children were offered a range of drinks, including milk, and their food intake was measured carefully.

The findings confirmed what everyone had suspected, namely that children consuming sweetened drinks had a higher-calorie diet – up to about 250 calories per day more – put on more weight and (particularly girls) consumed less milk. This lower milk is a concern because it relates to future risk of osteoporosis.

Interestingly, the amount of sweetened drink didn't affect the food consumption one way or other.

So the message for parents, schools and marketing regulators is to reduce the availability of such drinks to children.

Mind you – that's easier said than done. You can't spend your life at camp.[7]

▼ WATCH VITAMIN A IN CHILDREN – TOO MUCH IS A PROBLEM

Two case reports from the Royal Children's Hospital in Melbourne give a salutary warning to parents who are keen on giving their children extra vitamins. The cases were about potentially life-threatening complications resulting from inadvertent vitamin A consumption via naturopathic preparations.

The first was a 2-year-old girl who was off her food, wouldn't walk and had pains in her legs. The paediatricians thought she had cancer. Her bone scan showed suspicious inflammation and her skull bones were separating because of raised pressure in the brain. All the cancer tests were negative, though, and eventually they discovered that she'd been on a naturopathic preparation with a high vitamin A content. In fact the parents had even been giving it to her in hospital.

When the child stopped taking the mixture she got better – but the specialists reckoned she wouldn't have survived if it had gone on much longer.

The second child was a 4-year-old boy with a very similar story – also on a so-called natural remedy from a naturopath. This little boy wasn't so lucky. He was going blind because of the vitamin A toxicity, and has been left with permanent damage to his vision.

So buyer beware: the main message is that it's a good idea to let your GP know if you or your child are taking a natural preparation in case there are issues he or she needs to be aware of.[8]

▼ SLEEPLESS BABIES – THE BANE OF MANY A FAMILY'S LIFE

A large study in Victoria has found – surprise, surprise – that when sleepless babies are trained to sleep through the night, their depressed mothers feel better. A survey of normal healthy mothers found that nearly half of them complained that their babies either wouldn't get off to sleep at night or woke up too much, and that was the factor which had the highest chance of predicting whether a woman was likely to be suffering from postnatal depression. In other words, having a sleepless baby beat all the other known risk factors, such as a history of depression, marital discord and so on.

So the researchers at the Royal Children's Hospital then carried out a trial where one group of mothers received training and assistance in how to get their babies to go to sleep by themselves, rather than needing rocking or a dummy. The commonest technique was controlled crying, where the baby is allowed to cry for longer and longer periods till he or she gets the message. The 'placebo' group just received general advice.

The results showed that the sleep training worked, and many of the babies started sleeping better – plus the mothers' depression ratings fell significantly compared with the control group.

Other common advice for teaching babies how to get themselves to sleep includes getting the baby into a routine, slowly reducing night feeds, and removing the dummy or pinning it to the baby's jumpsuit so there's no crying when it falls out – all these things help teach babies that they can fall asleep by themselves. Unanimity of purpose between mother and father was important too. It doesn't help when one of you cracks. One or two fathers had to wear earplugs to stop them going in to the baby.

After 2 months there were no differences between the control babies and the group who'd had the intervention, which is probably confirmation that most infants, if you wait long enough, will sort themselves out.

The question now is how you can get such help to new mothers en masse, rather than in a research project.

That will probably mean GPs and community nurses being taught the skills.[9]

▼ Sleeping babies on their backs

One of the great discoveries in the past few years has been that putting babies to sleep on their backs significantly reduces the chances of cot death. Before that, doctors and parents believed that sleeping on their fronts was better; it was associated with less regurgitation and perhaps even with avoiding pneumonia from inhaling some milk.

This might be a reason why some parents still resist the sleep-on-the-back advice.

Well, they needn't worry – a survey of nearly 4000 babies up to the age of 6 months has found that these concerns have no basis. Babies who sleep on their backs are more settled and have fewer episodes of fever, cough, stuffy nose, regurgitation, admissions to hospital, diarrhoea and ear infections.

The only side effect of sleeping on the back is a slightly misshapen noggin, which will usually remodel itself as the child grows up.[10]

▼ Stop babies smoking

The smoking epidemic has taken such a hold among women that while they may quit or reduce cigarettes in pregnancy, once they've had their babies, they often return to the habit. Quitting is a tough ask, especially if life's a struggle. Smoking cessation programmes haven't worked very well with this group.

Instead of focusing on quitting, it may be more sensible to concentrate on reducing passive smoking among these women's children, because these kids are significantly more likely than those in non-smoking households to develop respiratory disease and middle ear infections.

A US trial in low-income households had success by actually going into women's homes and measuring the levels of nicotine in the air and then giving advice on how to cut that down. In some homes the levels were the same as those in a smoke-filled pub.

This tended to motivate the women to change, and they were given a few choices about what they could do. Stopping smoking or a self-imposed ban on smoking in the home were most effective at reducing environmental tobacco smoke.

Interestingly, when that ban only applied to the room in which the child happened to be – and allowed smoking in another part of the house or flat – the ambient smoke actually increased.[11]

▼ KIDS COVERED BY MMR VACCINE

One of the aims of immunisation is to ensure that a high percentage of the population is covered, so that the disease either disappears or is driven down to very low levels.

Measles, for example, could be eliminated if there were mass coverage. The main measure is the Australian Childhood Immunisation Register, and it seems to show that 5-year-olds are not well covered for measles. So a research group has looked at 5-year-olds and assessed how big the gap actually is for the measles, mumps, rubella vaccine: the MMR.

What they found was good news. A large proportion of children not on the register had been immunised, which suggests that at least at the age of 5 the coverage isn't too bad. There may, however, still be vulnerable people, such as those in their late teens and young adults who need an MMR booster. The same group could also benefit from a whooping cough booster; one way that could be done is by giving them these vaccines when they travel overseas.

In case you weren't aware, the MMR booster is now given at 4 years old, not pre-school. And being allergic to eggs is not a contraindication.[12]

▼ POLIO LANDMARK

Just over 50 years ago, something momentous occurred. A US researcher called Jonas Salk published a paper announcing he'd developed an effective vaccine against polio.

It's hard to overestimate the impact of what became known as the Salk vaccine. In 1953, Australia had just come through its worst-ever polio epidemic. At its peak, about 10,000 people a year – mostly children and teenagers – were coming down with polio. There was no treatment for this virus, which caused paralysis by 'cruise missile' targeting the nerve cells in the spine which control muscles.

Australia started using the vaccine 2 or 3 years later, and by the end of the 1950s, we'd almost eliminated the disease.

The Salk vaccine isn't given today because one of Salk's colleagues, Albert Sabin, came up with a better, cheaper immunisation using a live form of the virus given by mouth. However, Salk's needle saved millions.

Now, only 50 years after the first vaccine, polio is on the verge of being completely eliminated from the world. That'll be only the second time this has happened in human history; the other disease eradicated was smallpox.[13]

▼ VACCINE INFORMATION ON THE NET - TAKE CARE

Health information is one of the most common reasons people use the Internet, but there is always a question about reliability. A group at the University of Sydney has had a longstanding interest in the activities of the anti-immunisation movement, so they decided to see what the Net had to offer.

They chose 7 leading search engines and typed in immunisation (with an 's' or a 'z') and vaccination. About half of the search results which came up in the first 10 were actually anti-immunisation sites. And on Google, *all* of the first 10 results opposed vaccination.

The sites found had the trappings of science: they sometimes gave themselves fancy, scientific sounding names, and they dressed up anecdotes as reliable research. Emotion played a bigger role than facts and the net effect, to use an unfortunate pun, for someone seeking unbiased information could have been to undermine the intention to have their child immunised.

The message is to avoid health information if it's based on anecdote, watch out for bias – especially commercial – and try to use respected sites such as the National Library of Medicine in the US.

And, of course, ours: abc.net.au/health.[14]

▼ CHICKENPOX VACCINE AND SHINGLES

Shingles is a painful rash which usually erupts in adult life and is caused by the chickenpox virus, for which there's now a children's vaccine.

There are, however, unanswered questions about it.

For example, no one knows for sure yet that the chickenpox vaccine in childhood will prevent shingles later on, although there is some evidence that that will happen. The second question is, what should we do till the vaccinated children grow up? And is there a case for vaccinating adults in the hope of stymying shingles even in those who've already had chickenpox?

A study in London has come up with what might sound like a surprising argument in support of this. They have results which suggest that adults are less likely to develop shingles if they've been in contact which children with active chickenpox. Perhaps the live virus is tickling up their immune systems. This could mean that a side effect of childhood chickenpox immunisation will be increased shingles among adults, because they're no longer re-exposed to the infection.

So now researchers need to find out whether adult immunisation in people who've had chickenpox will prevent shingles.

Nothing's simple, is it?[15]

▼ THE GROMMET EPIDEMIC

Just how necessary is the medically induced epidemic of making holes in children's ears? The operation is the insertion of grommets – tiny plastic tubes – for a condition called glue ear, a collection of fluid in the middle ear cavity (the space between the drum at the end of the ear canal and the inner ear, next to the brain).

It's the commonest operation performed on Australian children, but according to a study published in the US, it can safely be delayed to see whether or not the child really needs it.

The usual reason grommets – or tympanostomy tubes – are put in is because of the fear that the child's hearing might be affected if glue ear is allowed to persist, and poor hearing could delay language and intellectual development.

It's not a worry if you hang on for a few months, the US study concluded. This large study followed over 6000 healthy babies and toddlers at the Children's Hospital of Pittsburgh. Parents of babies with glue ear were allocated either to an immediate grommet operation or to a group which waited for 6 months.

The results showed that only a third of the waiting group needed to have the operation at all after the 6 months, and when the children's language, intellectual development and behaviour were measured at 3 years of age, there were no differences between the groups.

So it's safe to watch and wait, and in many instances, it seems, nature will take care of the fluid itself.[16]

▼ Febrile fits

One of the things that can scare parents of young children (and, of course, the children themselves!) is a febrile seizure – a convulsion when the child has a fever. Doctors have long debated what should be done when this happens: do you check for meningitis; do you put the child on anticonvulsant drugs; what indicates a high risk of another seizure; and what advice should parents be given?

The statistics are that about 1 in 25 otherwise healthy children will have a febrile fit between the ages of 6 months and 5 years. The vast majority of these seizures last less than 15 minutes, are generalised – in other words involve the whole body – and only happen once in any 24-hour period.

If the seizure doesn't fit that description – it involves just one arm or one side, or lasts longer than 15 minutes, or the temperature isn't very high, or there's more than one fit in a day – then it's not a simple febrile convulsion, and it may indicate a risk of epilepsy.

But when it is more straightforward, what should you do?

During the fit the child should be placed on his or her side until the fit is over. There is a small chance of meningitis, so you do need to see a doctor pretty much as soon as possible, but if the doctor can't find any meningitis symptoms, a lumbar puncture isn't necessary.

There's no point in giving anti-epileptic drugs routinely, because there's no evidence they'll prevent another episode – and by the way, having another episode is more likely the younger the child is and if there's a family history of febrile fits.

Some people recommend that parents be supplied with diazepam (Valium) suppositories for the child in case of another fit. It does help, but the child is very groggy afterwards; so you might want to discuss that with your doctor.[17]

▼ A child's memory – some myths debunked

There's a common belief that a child's earliest experiences are critical, and can be an indelible blot on his or her future. An eminent child psychologist at Harvard University, Professor Jerome Kagan, has long criticised that view, saying how can that be, if a baby has no long-term memory?

He and a colleague have done some more work on this. They took babies at 9 months, 17 months and 2 years and got them to imitate some actions, such as putting a ring in a bottle in a certain way and shaking it to get a sound. They then followed them up 4 months later to see whether they could remember the sequence.

The babies who had been 9 months old at the start had no memory of the action, but the older ones did.

The reason for this, the researchers think, is that the frontal lobes of the brain are still developing even in the second year of life, and it's these which assist the ability to retrieve such past events.

There are two messages here: a technical issue about brain development, and a reminder that experiences a bit later in childhood (after the first year, say) are probably more significant for the child's future than earlier experiences.[18]

▼ AN UNDER-RECOGNISED SYNDROME

Just when you thought it was safe to go out, someone's found a new syndrome in children. Well, actually, they found it about 25 years ago, but many doctors and certainly parents are still to hear about it, even though it's almost as common as Down's syndrome.

These children are often late to speak, and when they do it's very nasally, due to a hidden cleft palate. They can have heart defects, mild intellectual delay, and as teenagers may develop a serious mental illness, similar to schizophrenia.

The name for this is Velocardiofacial syndrome (VCFS), and it's often missed because none of the defects may be severe and the children appear fairly normal apart from a longish-looking face.

VCFS is caused by a defect on chromosome number 22, affecting about 25 genes. The diagnosis is easy from a blood or tissue test, but the doctor has to suspect VCFS first.

For many parents it gives a welcome name to problems they've been having trouble pinning down; it gives schools guidance on how to help the child and it allows doctors to search for treatable abnormalities (in the heart, for example).[19]

Bones, Joints and Bad Backs

▼ Strong muscles, stronger knees

One of the most common and most disabling places to have arthritis is your knee. The sorts of people who develop osteoarthritis of the knee include women, people who are overweight and those who've stressed their knees (often in sport or occupations like farming).

Unfortunately, arthritis drugs – even the new expensive ones – have side effects, and knee replacement surgery has a way to go before it's as good as hips. So non-drug ways of controlling the pain and stiffness would be welcome. There's no mystery about what works.

Strengthening the muscles in the front and back of your thigh – the quadriceps and the hamstrings – stabilises the knee, reduces pain and stiffness and increases mobility. The question is how people who avoid exercise because their knees hurt, and for whom the thought of going to the gym is anathema, can do this effectively.

A group in Boston has trialled a 16 week home-based strength training programme that used progressively increasing weights plus exercises of the legs, including stepping. The results showed significant reductions in pain and depression and improvements in mobility and confidence which seemed to last long after the initial programme.

The question is how applicable this is on a mass scale.[1]

▼ What about exercise in general for the knees?

At least 10 per cent of people will develop arthritis of the knee, which results in stiffness, pain, a clicking sensation called crepitus and difficulty kneeling, climbing stairs and getting out of chairs. Arthritis of the hip is also a major public health and personal problem, causing at least as much disability.

Some people say you shouldn't exercise if you have arthritis because you'll wear out the joint. Others say you have to exercise, especially against gravity, otherwise your muscles will waste away, you'll become less fit and fatter, and a vicious cycle will set in.

Who's right?

A group of researchers has recently looked at the world literature on land-based therapeutic exercise for people with osteoarthritis of the hip or knee to see whether or not exercise designed to help the problem actually does help.

There haven't been many trials on arthritis of the hip but there were more data on people with knee problems.

And there was good news. Exercise using gravity (as opposed to exercise in water) was helpful, whether it was done in classes or with one-to-one supervision. There was less pain and greater mobility. However, just which exercises were best, and how long and how often they needed to be done for the benefits to be realised wasn't clear.[2]

▼ RISK FACTORS FOR KNEE ARTHRITIS

One mystery about arthritis of the knee is why twice as many women as men suffer from it. British researchers have done a pilot study comparing women aged between 50 and 70 who were waiting to have an artificial knee joint with those of the same age who had healthy knees.

The factors associated with arthritis were: being in jobs requiring a lot of lifting, kneeling and bending, obesity and smoking. Obesity was the big stand-out, so to speak, especially in women who were overweight by the age of 40. Sports participation wasn't a factor.

The researchers also looked at the extent to which women had worn high heels, because some people have thought that was a risk factor due to the stresses high heels place on the legs. All stiletto-wielding women will be delighted to hear that their fashion sense isn't destroying their knees.[3]

▼ WASH AND BRUSH UP FOR YOUR KNEES?

Arthroscopy for osteoarthritis has been quite popular for osteoarthritis of the knee. The technique involves looking inside the joint, cleaning up any rough spots on the cartilage and washing out the joint. But a trial studying this treatment came up with mixed news. The bad news was that arthroscopic (keyhole) surgery for this common form of arthritis doesn't work. The good news was that it turned up fascinating information about the placebo effect; information which could be used to benefit all of us.

The operations tested were two kinds of knee arthroscopy: just washing out the joint fluid or washing out the fluid plus sanding down the arthritic knee cartilage. There was a placebo group who just had a general anaesthetic: cuts were made in the skin around the knee but nothing else was done.

The people were followed for up to 2 years, and there was no benefit from the operations. In fact, those who'd had the so-called debridement – the sanding, if you like – tended to be worse off. The people who came out best in terms of pain and mobility were those who'd had the strongest belief that the procedure was going to help them.

This was probably the result of what is an almost universal trait among orthopaedic surgeons: having absolute, unshakeable confidence in their skills. The researchers are now trying to bottle that to see if it can make effective therapies even more effective.[4]

▼ STRAPPING REDUCES KNEE PAIN

The fun-run season is never-ending. Baby boomers in their thousands get out to pound the pavement, pathetically pretending they're 20 years younger than they are. As their knees clap out at kilometre 12, they discover that you can't beat the years indefinitely. But a group of physiotherapists in Melbourne seem to have a solution that might keep ageing try-hards going a little longer.

They did a 3 week trial of continuous knee taping in people with osteoarthritis of the knee. One group got active taping: it aimed to make the kneecap move straighter and closer to the midline and to relieve pressure below the joint. It involved therapeutic strapping above and below the kneecap. A second group got strapping in a similar position but without the effect on the kneecap, and a third group got nothing.

The active strapping was associated with a significant reduction in pain. That group had seven times the benefit of the control group and about twice the benefit of those who'd had the dummy strapping. The effects seemed to last after the trial, although the two taped groups came closer together over the 6 week follow-up.

It's a relatively cheap treatment which avoids the possible side effects of medication – but no one knows why it works.[5]

▼ CROSS-KNEED

The way your knees point may affect your chances of developing arthritis.

If findings from the US stand up, fixing knee alignment with podiatry, say, could become a major industry. It may all be related to whether you're knock-kneed or bow-kneed – whether your knees go in or out.

The researchers examined people who already had osteoarthritis of the knee. They found that the more knock-kneed a person was, the more likely they were to experience worsening arthritis on the inside – or medial side – of the knee joint. If they were bow-legged, the pressure and the arthritis was worse in the outer – or lateral – part of the joint. It makes sense, because that's where the lines of pressure would be at their most severe.

The next step is to see if taking pressure off the side of the knee which is being pressed can prevent the arthritis from getting worse. Things like shoe inserts could work – but proper trials are needed to see. Aren't they always?[6]

▼ AND IF YOU ARE GOING TO HAVE A JOINT REPLACEMENT ...

The whole business of blood transfusion in the era of AIDS, Hepatitis C and Mad Cow Disease has become fraught.

This in turn has driven a trend for people undergoing certain kinds of planned surgery, like a hip replacement, to donate two or three units of their own blood ahead of time. It means that if they need a transfusion it can be autologous – from themselves. But findings from a 12 month study in Melbourne suggest that autologous donation is not necessarily worth doing.

The results showed that about a quarter of the blood collected was not used, and – here's the interesting statistic – that if you gave your own blood you were more likely to be transfused. Findings from overseas research suggest that this isn't because the surgeon is more relaxed about transfusion or more careless during the operation. It's because if you've donated your own blood, you're more likely to be anaemic and actually need it back again.

So given that if you have a good surgeon the chances of needing a transfusion are low, and that the blood supply is by and large safe, donating your own blood might well be a waste of time and money.[7]

▼ ... AND MAKE SURE THEY KEEP YOU WARM IN THEATRE

If you're heading for an operation in the near future, there's a question you should ask your surgeon: 'How cosy am I going to be in theatre?' Because there's growing evidence that if they unintentionally let you become cold, the risks of all sorts of things go up.

In one trial, people whose temperature fell just under 1.5 degrees had three times the risk of heart problems either in theatre or just after. Another study showed a doubling or tripling of wound infection rates with a fall of 2 degrees.

People who were hypothermic (had lower than usual body temperature) during hip replacement surgery lost more blood, and in general this group stayed in the post-operative recovery ward longer and were in hospital nearly 3 days longer overall than those kept warm.

Some operations, especially on the heart, need hypothermia, but when it's unnecessary, there are ways of staying warm – from heated intravenous solutions to specially warmed blankets.

After all, it's not the sort of place to wear your ski gear.[8]

▼ MEDICATIONS: ARE THE NEW ONES MUCH COP?

There's considerable debate about new anti-inflammatory drugs for arthritis. In case this is news to you, and in case you think, I don't have arthritis, why should I care?, just remember that these new medications are costing you and me, as taxpayers, many millions of dollars a year – on the basis that they're safer than common or garden anti-inflammatories.

They're called selective Cox 2 inhibitors, and include celecoxib (trade name Celebrex) and rofecoxib (trade name Vioxx). The older anti-inflammatories are medications such as ibuprofen and naproxen.

The theory is that Celebrex and Vioxx are more targeted drugs, and therefore spare the stomach from potentially serious complications such as ulcers, ulcer perforation and gastric bleeding.

But there is another theory, too: that because of the way they work, these new drugs may mask the symptoms of an ulcer and delay its healing, making complications more likely over, say, 12–15 months.

The first report from the Celebrex study which was supposed to answer that question showed an advantage for Celebrex, but it only presented 6 months' worth of data. When the study was analysed in terms of its full 12 month impact, which had been the original idea, there were few, if any, benefits. A trial of Vioxx did show that it was safer, but there are quibbles over that work as well.

It's also true that in the Celebrex trial the dose given was higher than normal. However, the fact is that most doctors are prescribing Celebrex on the basis of the findings of the first study.

Anyone on these medications can be reassured that they are at least as safe as the regular anti-inflammatories, that they work just as well – and there's some evidence they could be safer.

The question for the government is whether that's worth the extra cost?[9]

▼ ... AND ONE OR TWO OTHER THINGS BESIDES

Another warning about Cox 2s emerged a couple of years ago and hasn't been conclusively nailed down. Some experts believe it's an issue, some don't.

The problem, if there is one, comes from the fact that Cox 2s block an enzyme which does more things in the body than affect the inflammation associated with, say, arthritis. Blocking the Cox 2 enzyme may make arterial disease more risky and, according to an editorial in *The Lancet*, could in theory affect women's fertility. This idea isn't new – the older anti-inflammatories may do this as well.

Studies with rofecoxib have suggested that the problem may be a delayed release of the egg from the ovary. When the women came off the medication, their ovulation returned to normal, so the effects weren't permanent. If the phenomenon is real, the women this is most likely to affect are those with rheumatoid arthritis who take Cox 2s because they may have a lower risk of side effects. There's no cause for panic: it may just mean going on a lower dose (not stopping the medication altogether) if they want to fall pregnant. They should discuss this with their doctor.

The bottom line if you have osteoarthritis is that there are several options. Paracetamol is effective in many people at the right dose, for instance. And traditional non-steroidal anti-inflammatory drugs (NSAIDs) which are just as good as Cox 2s for pain relief may also be okay, especially if you use them at the lowest possible dose and don't forget non-drug treatments such as exercise.[10]

▼ ACHILLES HEEL FOR ANTIBIOTICS

Over the last few years it's been noticed that a relatively new group of antibiotics, called the fluoroquinolones, seem to increase the chances of a ruptured Achilles tendon. The Achilles tendon is the one at the back of your heel.

You can recognise fluoroquinolone antibiotics because their *generic* names end in 'floxacin' – for instance ciprofloxacin (trade name Ciproxin) or norfloxacin (Noroxin). They're often used for urinary infections or STDs (sexually transmitted diseases), and 'cipro' got a lot of publicity after September 11 as a treatment for anthrax.

No one's too sure why these antibiotics might cause Achilles tendon problems – pain and rupture – but it's possible that the medications are toxic to collagen. The other thing no one was too sure about was the real risk of this complication.

A study of over 46,000 people taking floxacins delivered some answers.

They found that people likely to have an Achilles heel rupture tended to be over 60, have had steroid treatment and/or gout, and/or be obese. When you factored in the antibiotics, the extra risk of a tendon disorder if you were over 60 was threefold; and less than twofold if you were under 60.

Reassuringly, the risk seemed only to be raised while they were actually taking the antibiotics. It returned to normal afterwards. In absolute terms, the risk is really low. For every 1000 person years of use, 3 people may develop Achilles tendinitis or a rupture who wouldn't have otherwise.

So if you really need these antibiotics, unless you're over 60 and on steroids, or have had tendon problems in the past, you should probably just go ahead and take them.[11]

▼ Hard mattresses no cure for back pain

The days of lying on a rock-hard mattress if you have a bad back seem to be over. For years doctors, chiropractors and physios have recommended mattresses which are so hard they give you bone pain on contact.

In a randomised trial, a group of Spanish researchers handed out firm or medium-firm mattresses to people with lower back pain and assessed them after 3 months. The participants didn't know which mattress they had and most believed that firm ones were good for you.

Everyone had a reduction in pain and disability, but the difference was greater, especially in daytime back pain, for those who'd had the medium mattresses. Furthermore, those sleeping on firm mattresses were more easily able to detect their mattress type, whereas those on medium mattresses could not. This only strengthens the findings, since personal beliefs could have had a placebo effect.

It wasn't clear why the medium mattresses were better, but it probably had something to do with posture in bed. More people slept in the foetal position on the softer mattresses.

So there's no need to lie back and think of England – go for comfort.[12]

▼ Driving and your back

It's been long believed that people who drive for a living are at particular risk of slipped discs. It's important, though, to be clear what we're talking about.

There's no doubt that when you have a sore back, driving can be agony. Speaking personally, I can usually do with a chiropractor to get me out of the driver's seat after a long trip. But that's different from whether driving *causes* a bad back in the first place. An interesting study from Finland suggests that it doesn't.

The study looked at middle-aged, male, identical twins and rated them according to how many years of occupational driving they'd done. They then took those who'd had significantly different exposures to driving and compared their rates of back problems, and performed MRI scans of their backs. The results showed that occupational driving had made no difference to the state of their backs.

Now this might leave me stranded in the street – or on it! – but the message for taxi drivers and other drivers is that if you have a bad back, it's probably for the same (mysterious) reasons as the rest of us.[13]

▼ COULD A BAD BACK BE IN YOUR GENES?

A Finnish study took people with back pain bad enough to need medical or surgical care, and who had a prolapsed disc (proven by scanning), and compared them with a control group of people who didn't have a back problem.

The people with back pain had sciatica, meaning pain radiating down the leg to below the knee, and their disc problem was in the lumbar area – the lower back. So they weren't feeling too flash. The whole group was then tested for a newly discovered genetic abnormality in the production of collagen – the tissue at the heart of a spinal disc. People with disc problems were two and a half times more likely to have the abnormal gene than the controls; correspondingly, if you carried this gene, you had triple the risk of lumbar disc disease.

The reason may be that the gene defect results in the disc drying out – it doesn't hold water as well as it should. But the other finding is that many people carry the gene but have no back problems, which probably implies that more than one gene is at work when you're on your back with your back.

What does this mean when you're bent crooked and in agony? Well, you now have something else to swear at: namely, the genes your parents gave you. The more sinister side of this research is that insurance companies could get interested in it: if you can blame genes for your bad back, they may try to wriggle out of paying workers' comp claims – or insist on gene testing before providing cover.[14]

▼ A PAIN IN THE BACK

A review of the international scientific literature on bad backs by a group of Australian research physiotherapists has found that the medical profession may be labouring under some myths.

If you've had an acutely painful back, you may well have been told by your GP that you'll be completely better within 4 to 6 weeks, but apparently there isn't a lot of evidence to back up that confident assertion. The review did find that about 6 out of 10 people with a bad back had radically less pain and disability within a month of the initial episode, and that soreness continued to decline for another 3 months.

What won't surprise any back sufferers reading this is that despite what the quacks tell you, for many people the pain didn't disappear altogether, and nearly three-quarters had another bout of acute lower back trouble within a year.

There was no reliable way of deciding at the beginning which people were going to do badly and which would do well, but the degree of disability may be a guide. And all this was independent of the treatment given. With acute back pain, there isn't a lot of evidence that 12 months out, one therapy is better than another.[15]

▼ X-RAYS DON'T USUALLY HELP

Should you have a spinal X-ray if you have a bad back? And by 'bad back', I mean the usual sort of thing: lower back pain, maybe with some pain going down one leg, and with no other things going on (weight loss, infections such as HIV or TB or medications such as steroids) which might make the bones frail.

Back X-rays are a big-ticket item in our health budget, partly because they often lead to unnecessary CAT scans, and these days also to even less necessary MRIs – magnetic resonance image scans. Even chiropractors order them.

In Britain, more than 400 people who had had simple lower back pain for more than 6 weeks and less than 6 months were randomly either given a back X-ray or not given one. The results confirmed previous findings that back X-rays by and large make no difference to treatment; however, people who had them were more satisfied with their care.

Ironically and inexplicably, even though the selection was random, the ones who received an X-ray were also those who had more pain and disability in the short term. But in the long run, the two groups did equally well. So the challenge now, as one commentator has said, is to find out how we can be happier about our back care without needing X-rays fired at our spines.

So what is the right treatment for common or garden lower back pain? Don't lie down and give in to it. Try to keep going (gently) with it, using painkillers as necessary, and make sure you get checked by your GP. There is some evidence that physio and chiropractic can speed recovery.

And remember, most people with a bad back get better no matter what – it's a matter of time.[16]

▼ THE BAD NECK

Manipulation of the neck (the cervical spine) is quite popular among chiropractors and manipulative physiotherapists. ('Manipulative' refers to their professional preferences, by the way, not their personalities.)

Cervical spine manipulation is used for all sorts of things, from stiff painful necks to recurrent headaches, and involves moving your neck to the end of your normal range of movement then doing a slow or quick thrust.

Unlike manipulation of the lower back, there really isn't much evidence of benefit from manipulating the neck. But, also unlike the lower back, the neck is much more vulnerable to accidental injury during the procedure. In the worst-case scenario this can mean serious damage to arteries supplying the brain, causing a stroke.

The Medical Journal of Australia published a review of the available evidence from around the world on injuries from cervical spine manipulation.

The author found 42 examples in the literature, 18 of which were arterial injuries producing strokes.

But given that the total number of cervical manipulations performed each year is probably quite large, and that there's patchy reporting of adverse events, it means that this study doesn't help to assess the real risk of such an event occurring. It's almost certainly low, but the event can be devastating when it occurs.

The procedures may be less risky with milder thrusts, but no one really knows, and since there's no good evidence to indicate that you should expect significant benefit from it, the question for consumers is, why take a chance in the first place?[17]

▼ WHAT ABOUT A MORE GENTLE APPROACH?

A group in The Netherlands took nearly 200 people who'd had neck pain for 2 weeks with no serious underlying cause and compared manual therapy – various ways of loosening up the muscles without using manipulation – with physiotherapy exercises and standard care from a GP, which included practical advice, heat and exercise.

The results suggested that manual therapy was associated with the fastest recovery over a 7 week period, and was also cheaper. The benefit was sustained for 6 months, but there was no difference between treatments after a year.

So now you know where to tell pains in the neck to go.[18]

▼ COULD IT BE YOUR PILLOWS?

All sorts of bodily symptoms can affect you in the morning when you wake up.

The commonest are probably aches and pains in the upper arms, shoulders or neck. A South Australian physiotherapist surveyed the population of Port Lincoln to see how common they were. She found that nearly 1 in 2 adults were affected.

Her suspicion was that pillows were to blame, but it's not at all clear what it is that makes a difference: thick or thin, feather or synthetic, one or two.[19]

▼ A WORD OF WARNING ABOUT MORNING STIFFNESS

There are, however, some serious symptoms on waking that you do need to see the quack about fairly quickly. Morning headaches are quite common in migraine sufferers, but if they're something you've never had before and they seem to be getting worse, they can be a sign of raised pressure in the brain and need to be sorted out.

And if you find yourself with *really* severe stiffness and pain in your neck, shoulders and hips in the morning, and it takes you quite a while to get going, you could have a condition called polymyalgia rheumatica. It is treatable and should be diagnosed early, because it is associated with a dangerous form of headache called temporal arteritis.

So just when you thought it was safe to get up in the morning, you opened this book ...

▼ TENDINITIS – THE WRONG NAME?

Some researchers are arguing that many health professionals have got it wrong when it comes to people with painful tendons. They're usually treated as if they have tendinitis – inflammation – when, the authors say, there's no evidence of that and it should be called tendinopathy. The implication of this different diagnosis is that treatment should change.

The problem is often found in people involved in sports and exercise programmes and people whose work involves overuse of a limb. In sports involving jumping, for example, there can be pain in the tendon which attaches the kneecap to the leg. Tennis elbow is similar, as is pain in the Achilles tendon at the back of the ankle in runners.

While doctors, and indeed physiotherapists, often treat people with these problems as though they have an inflamed tendon, it seems that whenever the problem is studied, researchers are unable to find evidence to support that diagnosis.

What appears to be happening is damage to the tendon and pain which is sometimes hard to explain. Anti-inflammatory medications don't seem to help, and steroid injections probably only give temporary relief.

Unfortunately, no one has the answer about the right treatment yet, but careful physio – often to correct abnormal ways of compensating for the pain (in the way you move your arm or walk, for instance) – can help. However, the timeframe is usually weeks and months, not days, and the recovery time depends on the severity of the damage.[20]

▼ No magnetic cure for pain in the sole

Apparently lots of us love the idea of magnets to cure our ills. It's been estimated that about $7 billion has been forked out on things which will generate magnetic fields therapeutically. It's an ancient treatment, and originates in the idea that maybe magnetic fields suck out the disease. Nowadays the idea is that the fields influence molecular systems. Sometimes the magnet produces a static field; sometimes it's what they call bipolar, which is more dynamic.

There isn't much, if any, evidence that magnetic therapy works, and a recent trial won't have helped the marketers. It looked at a condition called plantar fasciitis, a sharp pain going along the sole of the foot from the heel bone forward. They tried bipolar magnetic insoles compared with placebo insoles. Both groups improved as a result of the treatment, which is good, but magnetic insoles performed no better than the placebo ones.

So save money and buy a simple cushioned insole and you won't have to worry about picking up stray metal as you plod along.[21]

▼ The low-down on bunions

One of the conditions you don't see in societies where people go barefooted is bunions. A bunion is an inflamed, painful protuberance where the big toe joins the rest of the foot, and occurs when the big toe is angled towards the second toe. As anyone with a bunion will tell you, they can be murder to walk on.

There are all sorts of reasons for bunions, but the commonest is self-induced. They're more frequent in women who wear narrow, high-heeled shoes. So what's the best way to treat them?

Podiatrists can offer relief with shoe advice and inserts called orthotics, and orthopaedic surgeons can operate to re-align the toe. A trial in people with painful bunions has compared these two forms of treatment with doing nothing.

In a 12 month period of follow-up, those who'd had the operation did best. They had less pain, found it easier to walk and wear shoes, and the foot had a better appearance than those who'd had nothing or the orthotics.

Orthotics from a good podiatrist are probably still best for mild bunions, and when it comes to surgery, the type of operation is critical – there are some which can cause significant problems. The one in this study was called a chevron osteotomy.

So if you're considering having a bunion operation, make sure you use an orthopod who's particularly expert in the tootsies.[22]

▼ OSTEOPOROSIS: VITAMIN A MAY MAKE IT WORSE

Women who take high amounts of vitamin A in their diet or as supplements may double their risk of a hip fracture due to osteoporosis.

Vitamin A is one of the so-called fat-soluble vitamins: this means that excess amounts are kept in the body and stored in places such as the liver and in fat. That explains why nutritionists are more twitchy about these vitamins – it's much easier to suffer toxic effects from them, because they linger in the body.

Vitamin A is important for the eyes, for the immune system and for controlling the division of cells. Vitamin A toxicity includes making the bones thinner.

Anyway, one study followed the health of over 72,000 post-menopausal, mainly white women in the US and found that those with the highest intake of vitamin A – 2000 micrograms or more per day – had nearly double the risk of hip fracture over an 18-year period. There was no added risk from beta carotene, which is a compound the body can use to make vitamin A; it was vitamin A itself.

Multivitamin supplements were the main source of vitamin A, though milk and breakfast cereals (both of which are often vitamin-fortified in the US) were also important.

If a woman was taking hormone replacement therapy, it seemed to reduce the effects of vitamin A. The message for Americans is that they may have to think hard about whether or not they continue to fortify foods with vitamin A. For Americans *and* Australians, it's more confirmation that we should be getting our nutrients from food rather than from supplements.[23]

▼ But vitamin D might be a different story

Nothing whets the appetite of pharmaceutical companies – and generates alarm in the Federal Treasury – more than a common disease. If you find a good medication for one of these it can be an El Dorado, but someone has to pay, and it's usually us taxpayers.

And so it is with osteoporosis – bones thinning with age. A lot of people are going to get it, suffer fractures and become disabled as a result. But there are so many people with thinning bones that it will be impossibly expensive to treat everyone. So are there cheap and effective ways of preventing bone loss?

Vitamin D helps to build calcium into bones, but whether it's worth taking if you're otherwise healthy has not been clear. To help find out the answer to this question, nearly 2700 British men and women aged over 65 were given vitamin D or a placebo four times a year for 5 years. Yes, just four times a year.

It was safe, and there were significant reductions in the risk of fractures in those taking the active capsules. There was also a trend to lower death rates.

To help decide whether it's worth doing, the figures translate to 250 people having to take Vitamin D once every 3 months for a year for 1 fracture to be prevented.[24]

Breasts

▼ Breast cancer and fat

Knowing what to do to prevent breast cancer is hard. There are risk factors which are impossible to change – like having a sister or mother with breast cancer, not having children or having your first pregnancy later in life, or starting your periods earlier than average.

There is modest evidence that alcohol intake increases breast cancer risk, and there are conflicting results from studies about saturated fat. Animal studies suggest that saturated fat intake counts. Some specialists actually put at-risk women on extremely low-fat diets in an almost evidence-free hope that they will help.

The dilemma remains, though, because large studies comparing the diets of similar women with and without breast cancer have failed to implicate saturated fat.

The answer may be that the studies haven't measured women's diets well enough. To save money, shorthand techniques for dietary measurement may have fallen short on the fat front when week-long food diaries – a more expensive but possibly more accurate test – would have come up trumps.

So the fat and breast cancer jury's back out till the researchers get their act together.[1]

▼ Smoking might not be great, either

There's a debate going on about whether or not cigarette smoking increases the risk of breast cancer. Rates have gone up since World War II, when large numbers of women started to smoke, and there's laboratory evidence that carcinogens in tobacco smoke can be toxic to the breast. On the other hand, smoking might actually *reduce* breast cancer, because female smokers have earlier menopauses and lower levels of oestrogen.

Research in this area hasn't been terribly convincing.

But a study of nearly 1500 women sheds some light – albeit tentatively. The researchers looked separately at pre-menopausal and post-menopausal breast cancer. Women were at increased risk of pre-menopausal breast cancer – up to seven times the risk – if they'd begun to smoke within 5 years of starting their periods or had smoked 20 a day for 20 years.

With post-menopausal breast cancer, though, some women who didn't start to smoke until after having their first baby actually had a reduced risk. But this is a very small group of women, because most start smoking in their teens.

The theory is that smoking while the breast is still developing is a really bad idea and can cause damage which will reap a nasty harvest later in life.

However, better studies are still needed.[2]

▼ Unfruitful for the breast

Fruit and vegetables don't seem to prevent breast cancer.

An unlikely link anyway, you might say – but in fact several studies have suggested a benefit. The theory is that green vegies such as broccoli have anti-cancer compounds in them. One study has criticised the previous work, though, saying that the research relied too much on memory and looking back.

They didn't do any new research; they simply re-analysed existing data by combining the findings from eight studies which had involved monitoring women's diets and observing them over several years to see who developed breast cancer: 352,000 women were followed, of whom over 7000 developed breast cancer. No association was found between breast cancer and total fruit consumption, total vegetable consumption or combined fruit and vegie consumption. This study even looked at individual greens and fruits and couldn't find anything there.

The only finding was that women on the very lowest intake levels might – just might – have a slightly increased risk, but they were really trawling to come up with that statistic.

So while fruit and veg help reduce the risk of heart disease and almost certainly do the same for colon cancer, don't rely on them to reduce the risk of breast cancer.

At the moment there really isn't any good prevention other than exercise, an anti-oestrogen drug called tamoxifen if you're at very high risk, and regular mammography if you're in the right age group.[3]

▼ To self-examine or not to self-examine

When news of a Canadian study recommending that doctors and nurses stop teaching women to perform breast self-examination (BSE) broke, the media responded with emotive stories of women who claimed they'd found their tumour themselves and would be dead if they hadn't.

The Canadians had reviewed evidence from trials of BSE which aimed to reduce the death rate from breast cancer. Three large studies found that teaching breast self-examination to women aged between 40 and 69 did not improve their chances. They also found good evidence of what they termed 'harm' – unnecessary diagnostic procedures and anxiety.

It's important to appreciate that what they assessed was the results of the teaching, not the results of the doing. Their research was mainly related to the expenditure of resources for breast cancer prevention.

The findings don't imply that women should stop noticing changes in their breasts or avoid seeing their doctor if they feel a lump. That's all still important. The research just confirmed what many suspected, which is that you can't depend on regular systematic breast self-examination to detect early cancer; you need a mammogram every 2 years if you're between 50 and 69 (or over 40, if you choose).[4]

▼ The great mammography debate

There's been a debate for some years about whether mammographic (X-ray) screening for breast cancer in women really saves lives and is therefore worth the money.

The argument is that while scientifically conducted trials of mammographic screening in ideal circumstances may show a 30 per cent reduction in the chances of dying from breast cancer, the real world, with all its imperfections, is different.

A review of the evidence by some Danish researchers suggested that there was actually no benefit, and that led to an enormous bunfight about statistics and the quality of the analysis. Now another review seems to have provided some clarity.

Over 16 years, a group of women in Sweden were invited to attend mammographic screening. Note that I said 'invited'. That doesn't mean they turned up for it; this gave the research a real-world flavour, but it also meant that the benefits of screening were diluted for the group, because there were no-shows. Anyway, as a group, these women had a 21 per cent lower risk of dying of breast cancer than women who weren't invited for screening. The benefit took about 4 years to show up, peaked at 10 years and was sustained after that.

It wasn't dramatic, though. Since breast cancer isn't a large cause of death in women – compared with heart disease or stroke, which are the big killers – the impact of mammographic screening on women's overall chances of dying of *any* cause prematurely is only 2 per cent. In fact, from years of follow up of between 1.6 and 1.8 million women, there were 511 deaths from breast cancer in the screening group and 584 deaths in the control group. The women who benefited most were in their 60s.

Because of the public confusion, in March 2002 the International Agency for Research into Cancer (IARC) in Lyon formed a large expert working group to look into this further.

They concluded that 'trials have provided sufficient evidence for the efficacy of mammography screening of women between 50 and 69 years. The reduction in mortality from breast cancer among women who chose to participate in screening programmes was estimated to be about 35 per cent. For women aged 40–49 years, there is only limited evidence for a reduction. The quality of the trials that were used to make these evaluations was carefully assessed. The working group found that many of the earlier criticisms were unsubstantiated, and the remaining deficiencies were judged not to invalidate the trials' findings.

'The effectiveness of national screening programmes varies due to differences in coverage of the female population, quality of mammography, treatment and other factors. Organised screening programmes are more effective in reducing the rate of death from breast cancer than sporadic screening of selected groups of women.

The working group also concluded that there is insufficient evidence that clinical breast examination or self-examination reduce mortality from breast cancer.[5]

▼ IN THE FAMILY

Many women whose mothers, sisters or daughters – what's known as first-degree relatives – have had a diagnosis of breast cancer live in fear of getting the disease themselves. While it's true that having a first-degree relative with the disease does put you at extra risk, the question of how much has been uncertain.

While a small minority of women have a recognisable genetic defect which means their chances can be more easily identified, the vast majority of women have so far had to rely on pretty uncertain information.

A new study of over 150,000 women has offered a better idea. Comparing women with breast cancer with similar women without the disease, they were able to assess the influence of having a first-degree relative who'd had the diagnosis.

If you have one first-degree relative with a breast cancer diagnosis, the risk doubles for you; it triples for two first-degree relatives and nearly quadruples for three. If the relative is diagnosed young, your risk is higher – it doesn't matter whether the relative is a mother or a sister.

That sounds dreadfully dramatic, but it becomes much less so when the figures are translated into the average risk for an individual woman: most women who have a first-degree relative with breast cancer won't get the disease themselves, and if they do it will mostly be after the age of 50.

And your lifetime risk is actually only raised a small amount: by just over 5 per cent with one relative and 13 per cent with two. That means that if an Australian woman has, say, a 1 in 12 chance of developing breast cancer in her lifetime, then if she has one relative with breast cancer that risk will go up to about 1 in 11.5; with two relatives it will go to about 1 in 10.5. So it's not a cause for panic – it is reason for extra vigilance and regular mammograms.[6]

▼ THE PILL AND BREAST CANCER

Are women who take the oral contraceptive pill at increased risk of breast cancer? The answer is no, from a well-conducted study.

Over 4500 women with breast cancer, aged between 35 and 64, were compared with the same number of women without breast cancer.

The results showed that regardless of the age they started taking the pill, regardless of the time they'd been on it, regardless of the type of pill, regardless of whether they'd used it in the past or were still on it at the time of diagnosis, and regardless of whether there was a family history of breast cancer, there was no increase in risk of breast cancer from oral contraception.

What did raise the risk was a family history of breast cancer and having a first baby at an older age, both of which were already known. The other good news about oral contraception is that it significantly decreases the chances of both ovarian and uterine cancer.

This is not to say that the pill is completely safe. There's still a slightly raised risk of blood clots, heart attacks and strokes in certain women – and, of course, unprotected intercourse makes STDs more likely.

However, breast cancer can almost certainly come off the list.[7]

▼ CHEMOPREVENTION

If you're a woman at high risk of breast cancer (because you have a strong family history or you've already had breast cancer), you'd like a way of reducing your chances of getting the disease.

One possible solution is chemoprevention – using a medication. One such drug is tamoxifen, which affects the way the breast responds to oestrogen.

The trouble with tamoxifen is that it can cause blood clots which can then be thrown off into the lungs. Given that we're talking about healthy women staying healthy, you have to be sure that the good has to outweigh the harm before you could say that tamoxifen is worth taking.

Probably the most reliable study of tamoxifen to date involved over 7000 women who were given tamoxifen for 5 years and then followed for another 4 years.

The good news was that the risk of breast cancer fell by a third. About 111 women had to be treated for one case of breast cancer to be prevented. The bad news was that for every 28 women taking tamoxifen there was one episode of blood clot, and that episode was usually associated with surgery.

The bottom line is that tamoxifen will only help a small proportion of women at high risk, and they clearly need something a lot better. Luckily there are some candidates being tested.[8]

▼ Vale radical mastectomy

The nail has finally been driven into a rather troubling episode in medical history.

There's a lot of evidence that with many forms of cancer, if the surgeon removes a tumour completely the outcome is much better. In breast cancer this belief took the form of a radical mastectomy, where the breast, the chest muscles and the lymph nodes in the armpit were all removed.

But doctors introduced the operation without scientific testing and continued to use it despite evidence that it wasn't working. This led some surgeons to conclude that even more radical surgery was warranted; others said that perhaps less severe procedures followed by radiotherapy would be just as good and less disabling.

It took till 1971 for a proper trial to be conducted. This trial showed that there was no extra benefit gained from radical mastectomy, compared with just removing the breast with or without radiotherapy. Believers clung on, though, saying, 'Just you wait; you'll find that the radical operation will be better in the long term.' But now an analysis of the 25-year results has confirmed the earlier findings – radical mastectomy offers no significant benefit.

For women, it's reassurance that less mutilating operations are not jeopardising their chances.[9]

▼ Male breast cancer

While breast cancer in men is rare, it's becoming more common in men under 40, and no one knows why. Also, compared with women, the disease in men is more likely to be life-threatening.

That's because breast tumours are nastier in men than women to begin with. Not only that, but they're also detected later in the course of the malignancy, usually when the man is older – even though, according to US statistics, it seems to be affecting a growing number of younger men.

One of the breast cancer genes – called BRCA2 – does increase the risk in men. Other factors include ethnic background (it's more common in Jews), a strong family history of female breast cancer, and having had problems with your breasts or testicles in the past.

The other thing which is not really known at the moment, because male breast cancer is so rare, is whether or not the treatment given to women works for blokes.

According to an editorial in the *British Medical Journal*, the facts (such as they are) suggest that the treatment ought to be the same – yet men don't always receive potentially beneficial chemotherapy, hormone therapy and radiotherapy, and the reasons for that aren't clear.

The symptoms, by the way, include a lump, breast pain and/or nipple problems such as puckering, bleeding or discharge.[10]

CANCER

▼ Preventing colon cancer

I reckon the world's divided into two types of people: those who love talking about their bowels and those who don't. Someone who does is a bowel surgeon in Perth, Dr Michael Levitt, who's written a handbook for people like you and me called *The Bowel Book*.

Michael Levitt reckons we've been brainwashed into believing bowel motions should be soft and happen every morning, when actually the range of what is normal is huge, and when we don't conform to expectations we become anxious.

He also thinks that many people have overshot on fibre, and the result – you're not eating, are you? – can be leakage and itching.

What you *should* be concerned about is a change of bowel habit from your normal pattern, or bleeding of any kind. That needs to be sorted out by your GP; you could have a benign polyp, and these can be removed before they turn nasty. You also need to touch base with your GP if you have a family history of bowel cancer or polyps.

If you have a strong family history, colonoscopy – a look inside with what's cruelly called the long black snake (if you're a patient) or the golden snake (if you're a gastroenterologist) – is the way to go. Just what constitutes enough of a family history is controversial. Some would say just having one first-degree relative (a parent, sibling or child) with colorectal cancer or polyps is enough for colonoscopy; the National Health and Medical Research Council (NHMRC) says it's at least one first-degree relative diagnosed under 55 years of age or two first- or second-degree relatives on the same side of the family.

Most people who develop colorectal cancer don't have a family history of it, and colonoscopy of the whole population is too expensive considering the number of people who'd benefit and the risks (small, admittedly) of the procedure.

Another way is for people over the age of 50 to look for blood in the poo, because most of these early tumours bleed. However, the bleeding is so slight that you can't detect it with the naked eye; you have to test for it – it's called faecal occult blood testing. The problem is that brushing your teeth can also cause bleeding, and test results can be affected by having a rare steak the night before. So it has taken a while to get the technology and the technique right, not to mention the price of administering a scheme involving hundreds of thousands of people smearing some poo on a card then sending it into a lab. (Sorry – you're not still eating, are you?)

There's pretty solid evidence that mass faecal occult blood testing saves lives. An 18 year study of nearly 50,000 50–80-year-olds in Minnesota who were given the test every 1 or 2 years found that there was a gain of about 20 per cent in protection with either annual or biennial screening. This amounts to a reduction of 7 cancers in every 1000 of the population.

If you're over 50 and have no symptoms and no family history, and haven't been offered screening, you should still talk to your GP about organising an annual faecal occult blood test, to check your poo for microscopic bleeding.

You can go back to eating now.[1]

▼ Is it possible to take something to ward off cancer?

Cancer chemoprevention, as it's called, is an active area of research – there are lots of suggestions but not many answers yet. A review of the evidence is hopeful, though.

Various drugs are being tried in people at high risk, anti-inflammatories for people at risk of intestinal tumours, for example – and there's already evidence that tamoxifen, an oestrogen blocker, can reduce the risk of breast cancer recurrence. Hepatitis B vaccine is probably the best of all so far, preventing hundreds of thousands, if not millions, of people from developing liver cancer.

However, medications don't have the attraction of natural substances from food. A diet high in fruit and vegetables – especially vegetables – does lower cancer risk, and this has set people off to test the thousands of natural chemicals in plants.

There are various compounds that in the test tube seem to control the growth of cells: genistein from soy, and diallyl sulphide from garlic and onion, for instance. But when they're tried in humans, the results have sometimes been disappointing.

There's a mixed picture with vitamins. Vitamin C in high doses might actually promote cancer; vitamin E may lower the chances of prostate cancer; and folic acid seems good for the colon.

Some minerals, especially selenium, also have potential.

Since cancer comes on over many years, huge numbers of people need to be followed for a long time if we are to get answers. In the meantime, keep eating your vegies – especially the red ones with lycopene.[2]

▼ CAN YOU AVOID QUITTING SMOKING BECAUSE YOU THINK YOU HAVE GOOD GENES?

We all know of someone who lived to the age of 90 and smoked a packet a day from the age of 14; if you're looking for reasons to not give up the cancer sticks, you might say, 'That could happen to me.'

Research in London has looked closely at whether genes really can protect you against smoking. They followed over 3000 middle-aged men whose genetic status for a particular gene, called ApoE, was known. ApoE affects the metabolism of the bad form of cholesterol LDL, and is affected by cigarettes.

ApoE comes in four varieties, a couple of which are good for you and one of which – ApoE4 – is definitely not good for you. The results showed that whatever your genetic status, smoking doubled (on average) your chances of a heart attack, and it tripled the risk for people who carried the ApoE4 gene.

The clear message is don't rely on your genes to save you – sometimes they might help to send you on your way … leaving a plume of smoke behind you.[3]

▼ ANOTHER ANGLE ON NICOTINE

Can nicotine be tarred with the same brush as … well … tar?

That's the suggestion coming from research which has found that nicotine stimulates blood vessels to grow. You might think that that's a good idea, that it would counteract the shortage of blood in smoking-induced heart disease, but you'd probably be mistaken.

Malignant tumours need blood vessels that grow and spread so that the tumours can also grow and spread, and if nicotine actually makes that easier, then cancer growth might be easier too. And there's some evidence to say that this is exactly what happens in lung cancer.

In mice, nicotine seems to do two things: it may help restore blood supply to a blood-starved limb, but it also seems to speed up the growth of lung cancer and, as it turns out, atherosclerosis – arterial blockages. The reason for this may be that the process of atherosclerosis itself needs a blood supply.

Some people are trying to use nicotine therapeutically, but this mixed bag of effects might make them think again. Such caution might also be merited since it appears that when the body metabolises – breaks down – nicotine, carcinogenic compounds are released.

What does all this mean for the nicotine replacement therapy (patches and gum) used to help people quit smoking? If these findings are right, the patches or gum should only be used for a limited period, not forever.

But even if nicotine in cigarettes did only good, you couldn't take comfort – there are 4000 other chemicals in each stick to do you in.[4]

▼ COPING AND CANCER – NO WORRIES

If I were to ask you, 'Does the way a person cope psychologically with a diagnosis of cancer make any difference to how well they do?', it's quite likely you'd say, 'Of course.'

We have a deep-seated belief (supported by media coverage) in the power of the mind.

The unspoken question, though, is which coping style actually works? Is it anger and wanting to fight the disease? Is it determination to ignore the cancer and get on with life? Is it someone who's filled with peace? And is someone who feels hopeless just condemning themselves to a poor outcome?

A group in the UK has looked at as many studies as they could lay their hands on, and they came up with the following.

The quality of research to date has been very poor. Studies which have shown an effect from coping styles have been small and unreliable. There was no good evidence suggesting that the way someone copes with cancer has any significant effect on their outcome.

More recent research from Melbourne has failed to find any relationship between a person's sense of optimism and how well or badly they fare.

Which means a lot less guilt for people with cancer (at least until better research is done), and a lot less pressure to keep smiling.[5]

▼ Stress and the return of cancer

Since unwelcome stress (as opposed to self-induced stress on those horrible rides at theme parks!) is such an unpleasant experience, it's tempting to believe that through the brain-body connection it could influence disease – and there's some evidence that it could.

Women with breast cancer, however, may be able to take stress off their list of possible causes of cancer recurring.

There have been suggestions that stressful life experiences may increase the chances of a breast tumour returning. 'Stressful life experiences' are events such as divorce, separation, the death of a partner or losing your job, or long-term situations such as having a handicapped child.

A British study followed about 170 women diagnosed with breast cancer. They carefully monitored both their mental health and the stress in their lives over several years, adjusting their figures for other influences on how well or badly the women fared.

The results were that stressful life experiences in the year before diagnosis had no effect on breast cancer recurrence. Nor did depression. Those women who'd had one or more severely stressful experiences in the 5 years *after* diagnosis, however, actually had a *lower* rate of tumour recurrence – it almost halved.

It's the opposite result of some other studies, but this one was better designed and almost certainly more reliable.

So if bad things happen to you in your life and you've had breast cancer in the past, you shouldn't worry about it making the malignancy return.[6]

▼ Cancer growth after surgery

There's a common story you may have heard: it's of the person with cancer who was fine till the surgeons opened them up, then the cancer ran wild.

Is it anecdote or is it real?

Well it turns out to be real, though probably not very common or dramatic, and it could be a hidden cause of cancer relapse. The good news is that there may be an explanation and solution.

Research in Italy investigated this phenomenon in women with breast cancer, and found that those suffering an early relapse after surgery were more likely to be positive for something called the HER2 receptor. If you're HER2 positive, your tumour is more likely to be stimulated by substances called growth factors.

That's the possible link with surgery.

These growth factors are released naturally when wounds heal. The irony is that healing in one place may provoke cancer cells in another, which means that non-cancer surgery or injury could cause relapse as well. This may also apply to other tumours, such as colon cancer – and perhaps with other receptors. The good news, if these findings are confirmed, is that there's an antibody available – at least for HER2.[7]

▼ Cannabis and cancer

There is still a debate about the medicinal uses of cannabis. In theory, there are a few potential benefits: the first is that cannabis stimulates the appetite; the second is that cannabis relaxes you when life's pretty miserable; the third is pain relief; and the fourth is cannabis' anti-nausea effect.

The question is whether cannabis – or medications made from it – can really deliver. Reviews of research into pain and nausea have been published and the news is mixed.

A group from the UK looked at all the studies on pain and cannabis that had been performed throughout the world, and sifted the reliable ones from the shakier work. First, they found that there were no randomised studies of smoked cannabis – only trials of cannabis-derived medications that are taken by mouth. When these were analysed the results showed that cannabis-type compounds do relieve pain but no more effectively than codeine – and at the cost of significant side effects, including clouding the mind, disconnected thoughts, blurred vision, disorientation and dizziness.

The group then did the same analysis for nausea induced by chemotherapy, and by and large the results were more positive. Cannabis compounds were more effective than most of the usual anti-nausea drugs used, with about 1 in 6 people getting complete control of their nausea and 1 in 8 getting complete control of their vomiting.

People often preferred cannabinoids to regular medications, even though the side effects were similar to the ones on the pain trial. Again, smoking a joint wasn't trialled.

So keeping your nausea at bay may be the main use until more specific derivatives of cannabis are found which have fewer side effects. More recent work has confirmed that cannabis has only small effects on pain.[8]

▼ Could cannabis – or something derived from it – become a treatment for cancer?

As noted above, cannabis is already being used to alleviate the nausea associated with chemotherapy, but this issue is different.

Cannabis works on our brains by locking onto receptors on nerve cells. In fact our bodies produce substances which stimulate these receptors naturally. It's thought that the pleasurable effects of chocolate, for instance, may work in this way.

These so-called cannabinoid receptors exist outside the brain as well, and experiments done 30 years ago suggested that the active chemical in marijuana – tetra hydro cannabinol (THC) – slowed down the multiplication of cancer cells.

Like everything in science, there are contradictions here: marijuana smokers have a *higher* incidence of lung cancer – but that may be the carcinogenic smoke rather than the cannabis doing the damage.

In any event, there's tantalising evidence that THC can slow the growth of brain cancer cells in the laboratory, and in Spain doctors have approval to try THC injections directly into malignant brain tumours to see what happens.

So THC, or drugs similar to it that are already used for chemotherapy-induced nausea, may turn out to be chemotherapy themselves.[9]

▼ X-rays and cancer

Professor Eric Hall, from Columbia University in New York, has spent much of his career studying the impact of environmental radiation, especially from diagnostic X-rays. The figures he uses extrapolate from what's known about the radiation exposure of Hiroshima and Nagasaki survivors and their risk of cancer over the past 50 years or so.

In developed countries, there has been a small increase in the numbers of people developing cancer beyond what would otherwise have been expected, and the question is why?

It turns out that the lowest radiation doses experienced after the A-bombs were dropped in Japan are similar to those you'd get from a whole-body CAT scan, and in the A-bomb survivors, these exposures were associated with a few additional cancers.

So given the controversy already over whole-body CAT scanning, the thought that you might as well have stood on the edge of Hiroshima in early August 1945 should give pause for thought.[10]

▼ Hodgkin's disease and breast cancer

Hodgkin's disease is a cancer of the lymph system. It is highly curable with chemotherapy and radiotherapy, which means there are lots of healthy survivors.

The problem is that those who've been treated for Hodgkin's disease are at risk of second cancers. In women the issue is breast cancer, and one study assessed 4000 women diagnosed with Hodgkin's disease when they were aged 30 or under.

When breast cancer did occur, it was about 18 years later, and the risk was linked to whether they'd had radiotherapy to the chest through the breast area. Women given chemo alone, or who had radiotherapy to the pelvis involving the ovaries, actually had reduced chances of breast cancer, since the chemo and the ovarian radiation would have lowered oestrogens.

The message for specialists is that they need to be careful about how radiotherapy is given.[11]

▼ Height and the pancreas

Cancer of the pancreas is often nasty. It's usually found too late, and the surgery to remove the tumour from behind the abdomen requires great skill and delicacy. As a result, pancreatic cancer is in the top five causes of cancer deaths. Since treatment is so difficult, prevention is the most realistic option.

Not much is known about the risk factors for cancer of the pancreas, though – except that smoking, height and diabetes are all on the list. The smoking one is self-explanatory, but tallness is less clear – and while you can quit smoking, it's hard to give up those extra centimetres.

The third known risk factor helps to explain the height conundrum. People with diabetes have about double the risk of pancreatic cancer; the thought is that the pancreas is overworked squeezing out more insulin.

And what does that have to do with height? Well, obese people tend to be taller, which means that greater height may reflect times, especially in childhood, when the person was too fat. In other words, it's possible that among the tall population there's a greater likelihood of finding people with a history of being overweight. Obesity is also implicated in what's called insulin resistance, where the pancreas doesn't respond to the sugar-lowering effects of insulin, and just keeps producing more of the stuff.

A group at Harvard Medical School focused on obesity as perhaps the first link in the chain, and they did find that obesity almost doubles the risk of pancreatic cancer. Physical activity in overweight people (but not in normal-weight individuals, interestingly) can almost halve the risk.

So the answer for that fat tummy – exercise – may be just what the pancreas needs.[12]

Cars

Cars are dangerous weapons, and the cause of a huge numbers of lost years of healthy living, so they are probably worth defining as a health issue.

▼ Teens in the driver's seat

If there's an image designed to strike terror into the hearts of most parents, it's a teenager at the wheel of a motor car.

While heart disease is what's most likely to kill you and me, the big killer in adolescence and the early 20s – especially of males – is the automobile. In the US, several states have tried to combat the problem by introducing what they call graduated licence schemes. These are where the young person has to go through quite a lot of hoops before getting a full licence.

It's more than anything we do in Australia, and research has shown a significant reduction in road deaths.

The schemes vary a bit, but they generally involve classroom lessons, compulsory driving school lessons, and after they've passed their test, considerable restrictions on their driving. The main ones are limits on the number of teenage passengers they're allowed to have. Teenage passengers multiply the risk of a fatal accident up to five times, depending on the number in the vehicle.

Their night driving is often limited to the early evening.

There's little evidence that Australian restrictions during the P-plate years save lives, but on the evidence of the US studies, our authorities should at least be considering restricting the numbers of teenage passengers P-plate drivers can have in the car, and possibly their night driving as well.

Who wants to go through all that agony in the teen years to have it end up round a lamp post?[1]

▼ Sleeping at the wheel

A fair amount of money is spent each year telling drivers that they need regular naps when driving long distances, and that they shouldn't get behind the wheel when they're tired.

It's very hard to assess the contribution that driver fatigue makes to bad road crashes, where a person is killed or seriously injured.

There are ways to work it out, though – the police use a variety of information sources, ranging from interviews at the time of the accident to the location of the crash. A smash on an open road with no junctions or hazards, for instance, would make police very suspicious that someone's fallen asleep behind the wheel.

Estimates of the actual proportion of road crashes where sleepiness is the main cause vary. In the US they think it's around 3 in 100, in France 1 in 10 and Australia 1 in 3. Since such figures are usually adjusted for distance travelled and car density on the roads, there's some doubt about their accuracy.

A New Zealand study has tried to fill in some of the gaps by comparing the sleepiness of drivers involved in accidents where there's serious injury with drivers who haven't had such accidents.

Drivers who had fewer than 5 hours' sleep in the previous 24 hours were at nearly 3 times the risk; if they were driving between 2 am and 5 am they had nearly 6 times the risk; and if they identified themselves as sleepy they had 8 times the risk.

Overall, sleepiness seemed to lie at the heart of about 1 in 5 serious accidents in New Zealand. All this was allowing for alcohol, other drug use, age, speed, gender and other factors which might affect crash risk.

So the message is that there's a 20 per cent potential reduction in serious accidents available if you could prevent people driving when they're tired, or in the wee small hours.[2]

▼ ... AND WITH ALCOHOL

Some people say that fatigue can equal alcohol in its detrimental effects on driving – but what about the *combined* influence of drinking while you're tired? This is important, because you could be *under* the limit, yet at very high risk of killing yourself or someone else on the road.

A study in France looked at the combined risk of alcohol and fatigue, and found that if you add the two together, the chance of a fatal accident was 7 times higher than in *non*-alcohol related crashes. In fact if someone had been drinking, fatigue was what made the difference between a non-fatal and a fatal accident.

For daytime crashes with no alcohol involved, driver fatigue was the single biggest factor.

So even though you're just having one drink – if you need a kip, don't get behind that wheel.[3]

▼ AIRBAGS – NOT ALWAYS A GREAT SELLING POINT

Safety features are always a big part of the sales pitch for new cars, and offering more and more airbags seems to be *de rigeur*. Airbags at the front, at the side, in the rear – goodness knows where they'll think of next.

There are some salutary stories about airbags, though. The first thing to say is that *seatbelts* make a big difference to car occupants in road crashes, and while airbags have been of benefit, their benefit has been smaller than the benefit of buckling up. Airbags reduce serious injury – especially to the head and neck – by about a third and fatalities by about 13 per cent for people wearing seatbelts.

While the equation is in favour of airbags, the list of injuries caused by the bags themselves is fairly long. Cuts and bruises are quite common, as are light burns, because the gases used to inflate the bag (which is done at around 160 km/h) are hot. Eye injuries and even ruptured oesophaguses and blockage of the carotid artery in the neck can occur.

The greatest risks are to small people in the front seat and drivers who sit too close to the steering wheel.

Broken necks from being too close to the bag or too low in the seat are a real problem, and several deaths of children have been recorded.

Asthma attacks can also be triggered by the gases.

The best advice is to keep children and small people out of the front seats. And if you've been in an accident involving airbag deployment, have your eyes checked in case there's been damage that might have gone unnoticed.[4]

▼ BELT UP FRONT AND REAR?

If you've ever wondered whether rear seatbelts are worth the effort, some Japanese research is quite convincing, especially if you're riding in the front seat.

Clearly, wearing a seatbelt wherever you are in the car stops you rocketing around in an accident, but what about the danger to the people in front of you if you're sitting in the back without a belt?

The group in Tokyo looked at over 100,000 front seat passengers and drivers injured in road crashes where there were back seat passengers – belted or unbelted.

If the rear seat passengers were unbelted, the risk of someone in the front seat dying or being seriously injured in the crash was doubled or tripled. In a head-on collision, the risk was far higher.

The theory is that if you are in the front with an unbelted person behind you, you stand a chance of getting crunched both ways in a crash.

So when you're sitting up front, it pays to insist on a spot of buckling up at the back before moving off.[5]

▼ WHIPLASH – WHAT NOT TO DO

In the bad old days, when you got hit from behind and your neck was forced back painfully, the first reaction of hospital staff was to stick a neck collar on you.

It took them a while to realise that this made things worse. The neck seized up, the muscles stopped working and in general the whole thing often got on the freeway to disaster – disaster being what they call chronic whiplash syndrome. This might be good for compo, but it's not great for quality of life.

It turns out that once you're sure there isn't anything dramatically wrong – nothing broken or dislocated – you should get down to some mobilisation exercises, moving the neck through its range several times an hour in a planned way, beginning within 96 hours of the injury.

If you do that, your chances of being pain-free and disability-free are really high. The other good news is that it probably means lower payouts for whiplash and less upward pressure on our car insurance premiums.[6]

▼ LET'S BLAME PEDESTRIANS

Is there nowhere that it's safe to be legless these days? In the revenge of the motorist, last year the NRMA in NSW came out and said that drunk pedestrians are their own worst enemies, and sometimes even kill innocent drivers.

There is, however, another group of pedestrians who are at risk of being struck down – while sober – and that's the elderly.

One theory of traffic management is that if you mark out a crossing place for pedestrians, you make things much safer. Makes sense, doesn't it?

Nope!

A study in the US has found that elderly pedestrian collisions with motor vehicles are over twice as likely to occur on marked pedestrian crossings as on a common or garden stretch of street. The crossings that caused almost all of this excess risk were those which didn't have traffic lights or stop signs. The figures in the study allowed for traffic flow, time of day and numbers of pedestrians out and about.

More research is needed to be sure of these findings, but if they're real, the reasons are probably a combination of a false sense of security and the disdain of some drivers for older pedestrians (can you believe it?).[7]

▼ HEAD INJURIES LINGER

Each year, up to 2000 (mostly young) men have a serious head injury, and most of these occur in road crashes. The result is often coma and months in hospital being treated and rehabilitated.

Because of medical technology, they survive, but that means at any one time there are tens of thousands of such people living in the community. They're often disabled physically and psychologically, although no one's sure how much, because they haven't been followed up very well – at least until now.

A 10 year study from the Epworth Hospital in Melbourne has discovered that a decade after their head injury, the problems these people face are still major. The findings were that a decade out, people's problems were social and psychological rather than physical: they had only half the rate of marriage of the general population; they were more likely to be socially isolated, with compromised memory and thinking ability; and many had dropped out of employment after initially getting back to work.

This all points to the need for long-term help for people with head injuries, and in terms of prevention, to the need to try harder to reduce the number of road accidents involving young men.[8]

▼ Booking to prevent road deaths

Each year, 25 million people are disabled for life because of road crashes, and 1 million – mostly young people – die. So in terms of being responsible for useful years lost to the community, driving is right up there.

Governments try to reduce this carnage with drink driving laws, random breath testing, speed limits, probationary driver rules, roadworthiness testing and safer roads. Another important ingredient, though, is how actively traffic laws are enforced; this can act both as a deterrent and as a way of making individual drivers safer (after they've been booked).

Which is what a recent Canadian study has looked at: the protective effect on a driver of a conviction. They compared 9000 drivers involved in fatal accidents with all drivers who had traffic convictions. The aim was to see what factors predicted involvement in serious accidents or protection from them. And it turned out that traffic convictions made a difference. The results showed that in the month after a conviction, the chances of a fatal crash were cut by a third – but the figures had reverted to normal after 4 months. Penalty points were particularly potent.

These figures translate to 1 life saved for every 80,000 convictions, and 1 visit to an emergency department avoided for every 1300 convictions. Although that doesn't sound dramatic, the authors say it's more cost effective than all the vehicle improvements over the last 50 years.[9]

Chronic Fatigue Syndrome

Chronic Fatigue Syndrome (CFS) is such a medical conundrum, and reduces the quality of life of so many people, that it seems worth a chapter in its own right.

CFS is arguably one of the worst-cared-for conditions by doctors – and indeed most other health practitioners.

First of all it's often confused with just plain tiredness caused by burning the candle at both ends – especially in women who have a job and a husband like me.

CFS, though, is very different. The sense of fatigue is not really tiredness. It's more about how the brain perceives the outside world: it's a kind of fogginess. It's also associated with headaches, muscle aches and difficulties with sleeping – which emphasises that we're not talking about normal fatigue here.

Other problems include tender lymph nodes, sore throats and inability to concentrate.

▼ A TREATMENT?

No one knows what causes CFS. Lots of things have been suggested, but nothing has survived scientific inquiry so far. Many treatments have been tried, with mixed success. A review of the available evidence found 350 studies in all, but only 44 treatment trials that were good enough to draw conclusions.

The two treatments which showed positive effects were cognitive behavioural therapy – a talking treatment aimed at changing a person's perception of problems and thinking processes – and graded exercise programmes, meaning slowly and steadily getting people back on their feet and active again.

Both may be working by changing the way the brain neurologically perceives the rest of the body, but like so much with this condition, no one's too sure.[1]

▼ GUIDELINES FOR DOCTORS

The Royal Australasian College of Physicians has a set of evidence-based guidelines for doctors looking after people with CFS. They've been well received in the UK and other countries.

The main thrust is to convince sceptics that this condition is real and not a figment of people's imaginations or a result of psychiatric illness. The diagnosis is based largely on the nature of the fatigue, which is different from the fatigue people experience in other circumstances. It's profound and long-lasting, often associated with disturbed sleep and trouble concentrating as mentioned before. The only tests worth doing are those which exclude other causes of fatigue, such as anaemia, kidney or liver disease. Looking for viral infections is probably not productive, as persistent viruses do not seem to be the problem.

CFS is often stereotyped as an incurable hopeless condition, when in fact many people, especially adolescents, recover very well.

The guidelines confirm that: the only treatments which trials suggest work are carefully tailored exercise programmes and cognitive behavioural therapy which helps people get out of the understandably negative thinking that can often follow the fatigue. What's needed from doctors is support, not judgment.[2]

▼ LINK WITH BLOOD PRESSURE DROP AND BEING DOUBLE-JOINTED

Studies from Baltimore in the US have found that a significant proportion of young people with CFS have an excessive fall in blood pressure when they stand up.

The researchers also made a chance discovery in the children and adolescents attending their clinic, which is that about 6 out of 10 patients they see with CFS are double-jointed – they have lax ligaments, which allows their joints to over-extend. To test for this they see how far back you can extend your little fingers, your elbows and your knees, and whether or not you can put your palms flat on the floor while keeping your legs straight.

The theory is that perhaps there's a genetic problem making the blood vessels lax as well allowing blood to pool in the lower limbs when the person stands.

The question now is, what should we do about it?[3]

▼ Post-viral Fatigue

Fatigue is an incredibly common symptom. Most of us feel knackered from time to time; women more than men. Knackeredness isn't fairly handed out, because we blokes tend to have it easier – at least that's what I keep getting told.

But some people experience a profound sense of long-lasting fatigue, often with other symptoms, which is hard to treat. For many years it was blamed on glandular fever, but good studies have shown that the glandular fever virus is *not* a lot more common in chronic fatigue sufferers than anyone else.

But it is true that certain viral infections, such as hepatitis and glandular fever, do increase your risk of having prolonged fatigue, and a group in London have tried to find out what makes one person experience long-term fatigue, say 6 months post-virally, when another person doesn't.

They focused on glandular fever – also known as infectious mononucleosis – and compared it with ordinary upper respiratory infections.

It wasn't a great study, partly because a high proportion of those who could have taken part didn't, which means that the people involved may not have been typical.

Anyway, the risk factors for fatigue at 6 months were a confirmed diagnosis of infectious mono by blood test, lower physical fitness, enlarged lymph glands in the neck and a longer time in bed with the illness. The findings were not very conclusive about whether depression made the fatigue worse or whether the bed rest was the result of a more severe illness or a certain personality type. The poor physical fitness may be from de-conditioning at the time of the illness, and may mean that it's a good idea to get up and exercise as soon as possible after a bout of glandular fever.[4]

Dementia

There are possibly as many as 300,000 Australians with diagnosed and undiagnosed dementia, with a flow-on to families and carers making a total population affected of perhaps as many as 1 million.

Each year you can add around 18,000 individuals to those with serious thinking and memory problems. Alzheimer's is the commonest cause, but by no means the only one.

Since people with dementia can live for years, the burden on them, their families and the nation is huge.

▼ IS IT PREVENTABLE?

About 10 years ago, French researchers went into the homes of healthy people in southwest France aged in their late 60s and over. They asked all sorts of things, including documenting what they ate. Over a 7 year follow-up, those who ate fish had a significantly lower risk of developing dementia. The more fish, the lower the chances, starting at one marine meal per week. Meat eating, on the other hand – just to cheer you up – didn't increase the risk.

The thing about the fish eaters, though, was that they tended to be better educated, and there are a few studies now which show that the further you've gone in your education, the later in life you develop thinking problems. It's probably a result of having more useable grey matter in your tank.

Even so, the researchers believe that fish and their oils have an effect on the brain, but it's still to be proven.

The key to this, of course, is remembering what you need to eat in order to remember everything else.[1]

▼ ... AND ALCOHOL?

Should you drink to forget? Maybe, just maybe, you should drink to remember!

There's evidence from Bordeaux in France that the more wine you drink, the lower your risk of dementia – but they *would* come up with a result like that, wouldn't they?

Holland, however, doesn't have the same conflict of interest. They've been following the health of thousands of people, whom they first saw about 10 years ago when they were about 55 years old, when none had dementia. Over 5000 of them gave good information on their alcohol intake, and after 6 years the figures for those who'd developed dementia and those who hadn't were analysed.

About 200 had some form of dementia after this time; mostly it was Alzheimer's disease, but some had vascular dementia, where the blood vessels were involved, and there were a few where the problem was Parkinson's disease.

Anyway, regardless of the type of dementia, light to moderate drinkers had around a 40 per cent reduction in the risk of any form of dementia and about a 70 per cent reduction in vascular dementia. Light to moderate drinking is 1 to 3 standard drinks per day of any form of alcohol: beer, wine, spirits, sherry – and yes, they still drink sherry in The Netherlands. Men had a bit more benefit than women, but several other possible influences – the person's age, whether or not they smoked, and how well educated they were – turned out to make no difference at all.

The results could be because of either the benefits of alcohol on arteries or even perhaps an anti-oxidant effect from alcohol.

The key to light alcohol drinking and dementia, of course, is remembering when to stop.[2]

▼ Brain teaser

Does exercising your brain reduce your chances of getting Alzheimer's disease, or are people who do a lot of activities requiring thought at less risk of dementia for other reasons?

A 5 year study of about 800 Catholic nuns, priests and brothers measured the amount of thinking activities they carried out and then followed them to see who developed dementia.

There were 7 activities which were believed to require thought: watching television (not sure what TV the researchers watched to think that), listening to the radio, reading newspapers, magazines and books, playing games requiring problem solving, and going to museums. They were also scored for how often they did this.

Eliminating those with any signs of dementia already, and controlling for the person's age, gender and educational level, the results were that the more thinking activities you do, the lower your risk of Alzheimer's disease.

In fact for every extra point of thinking activity, the person's rate of decline in thinking ability was slower by nearly half, in memory by more than a half, and in speed of processing information by about a third.

This doesn't prove cause and effect, because it is possible (but unlikely) that there were signs of dementia which weren't detected, and that keeping up these activities was secondary to their mental state. It also wasn't a normal population, as the people concerned were celibate and lived in unusual circumstances.

But since when has listening to ABC Radio done you any harm? So for the sake of your brain, keep it on![3]

▼ ALZHEIMER'S DISEASE – CLOSE TO THE HEART?

There's more and more evidence that Alzheimer's disease – the commonest form of dementia in Australia – has a very strong environmental component in its cause.

Finding that out hasn't been easy. And there's a growing belief that the risk factors for heart disease seem to predict added risk of Alzheimer's. A rather clever study from Africa and the US has fuelled the debate.

They surveyed what they believed were genetically similar populations – West Africans in Nigeria and African Americans in Indiana. Using the strictest criteria available, age for age, West Africans in Ibadan have half the rate of Alzheimer's of African Americans in Indianapolis.

It wasn't because the Nigerians had died before they could get the dementia: the researchers door-knocked and found people of the same age in the two communities.

They also looked at one of the genes which increases the risk of Alzheimer's, but it wasn't the explanation. What did stand out was the lower level of coronary risk factors such as cholesterol in Nigerians.

So while the world worries about aluminium pots and Alzheimer's, the problem may actually have more to do with what's cooking inside the pot.[4]

▼ Is Alzheimer's disease really what it's cracked up to be?

There's evidence that it's not. The risk factors for this form of dementia have traditionally been old age, a family history of dementia and a head injury in the past. Most other risk factors – such as aluminium in food or water – have fallen by the wayside.

With increasing regularity, high blood pressure and high cholesterol levels, especially in middle age, are being linked with Alzheimer's disease.

One study came from Finland, where researchers followed up about 1500 people whose health had been checked about 21 years beforehand. Those with either high blood pressure or a cholesterol reading of above 6.5 in middle age – between 45 and their late 50s – had about double the chance of getting Alzheimer's disease in their late 60s and 70s. The risk became even more significant – over 3 times higher – if they had both hypertension and high blood fats.

The numbers developing Alzheimer's were relatively small, so there could be errors in the conclusions, but other research, such as that in the previous story, has made similar findings.

The implications are that Alzheimer's disease may be more than one condition, and it could involve a mix of arterial and nerve damage. The most tantalising prospect is that coronary prevention might also protect your brain.[5]

▼ Lessons from Sweden

Studies following healthy people to see what happens to them are the best way of finding out possible causes of dementia – and indeed protective factors.

One of the most comprehensive such projects is in Sweden. It's been following the entire population aged over 75 on one of the islands that make up greater Stockholm. They're actually a pretty healthy group of people, but those who are ageing well have various things in common.

They tend to have high-quality social support from friends and family – in other words contacts which are more than a call once a week. Leisure activities of almost any kind seem to be protective, and that's allowing for the fact that if you're healthier to start with you're going to be more active.

People who have not had problems with blood pressure and cholesterol in mid life seem to be better off, and good folic acid intake seems important as well.

There are also some indications that pain relievers called non-steroidal anti-inflammatory drugs (NSAIDs) may be protective, but that's still controversial (see below).

So until the evidence firms up, it seems sensible to keep healthy in your early years, stay active, eat leafy greens and be nice to the people around you so they're there when you need them. The last one's probably the hardest work of all.[6]

▼ SILENT STROKES

Lots of information is emerging to indicate that there's more happening in the brain in Alzheimer's disease than was previously thought, especially when it comes to the state of your blood vessels.

It looks as though there's a group of people who have lost bits of their grey matter without knowing it. Silent strokes or brain infarcts are what these events are called.

Dutch researchers brain-scanned a group of 1000 relatively healthy people aged between 60 and 90, then watched what happened to them over the next 3 or 4 years, re-scanning most of them along the way.

About 1 in 5 showed evidence of having already had a silent stroke when they were scanned at the start, which was more people than expected. If someone did have a silent infarct, their thinking ability was likely to be worse than the average for this group, it declined faster, and the risk of dementia doubled. If they had a new silent stroke during the follow-up, the chances of developing dementia were even higher.

The assumption is that these tiny strokes help to cause dementia. An alternative explanation is that they're just a sign of rotten arteries. Either way, it adds to the growing evidence that lowering your cholesterol and blood pressure might help keep your head clear.[7]

▼ Making the diagnosis

Now that there are medications to slow Alzheimer's disease if you catch it early enough, there's more incentive to find out whether someone's heading down the dementia track. The question is whether there's a cheap and effective way of detecting dementia when it hasn't blossomed into full forgetfulness.

A group in Sweden evaluated a fairly fast way of assessing a person's thinking ability, brain functioning and memory. They gave the tests to nearly 1500 elderly people (aged between 75 and 95) who had no dementia, then followed them for 3 years to see whether the test results predicted brain decline.

They found that having abnormalities in all three measures was a predictor of dementia, but of all those who developed dementia, fewer than 1 in 5 had bad scores on the combined tests. So the tests missed 80 per cent.

Having complaints about your memory was a better predictor, but it may be a comfort to know that you shouldn't worry too much if you're having trouble remembering thingummy's name – you know, thingummy, whom you've known since you were 10. A large proportion of such people do not seem to be on a path to dementia any more than anyone else.[8]

▼ What do you do if someone close to you is developing dementia and you want to make their life and yours easier?

Step one is to get a proper assessment from a psychogeriatrician and his or her team. They're people who are expert in the diagnosis; most importantly, they can make sure the person doesn't have something else that is highly treatable, such as depression, anaemia or thyroid disease.

There are drugs for early Alzheimer's, but there are also lots of things that can be done at home to make things easier. Most of these aim to keep the person oriented in time and space. Strategies include making sure the person's vision and hearing are OK, keeping up general activity, ensuring that there are clocks, calendars and lots of familiar objects around, and making sure it's easy to get around the house. Sources of relaxation, such as television and music, can help too.

One of the most important things, though, is looking after yourself as the carer – it's a long haul. There are carers' associations in each state who can advise on things like respite care and general support.[9]

▼ Anti-inflammatories for Alzheimer's

There is some evidence from different parts of the world that people taking anti-inflammatory pain-relieving drugs – so-called non-steroidals (NSAIDs) – have a reduced risk of developing Alzheimer's disease.

For instance, a few years ago a large study from The Netherlands reported on their analysis of pharmacy records of people over 55: they compared the medications taken by those who developed Alzheimer's disease with those taken by people who didn't.

Over about 7 years, those who took long-term NSAIDs – these are commonly taken for arthritis, and include medications such as ibuprofen – had about an 80 per cent reduction in their risk of Alzheimer's disease. The researchers defined 'long term' as use lasting at least 2 years.

Interestingly, the effect was only on Alzheimer's disease, not on vascular dementia, where the brain damage is the result of arterial problems.

There is a sting in the tail of this. First, taking NSAIDS increases your risk of gastric haemorrhage – so they're not benign drugs. Second, the people on whom they seemed to have an effect were taking them before they had any symptoms of dementia. And third, this wasn't an experiment testing NSAIDS; it was what they call an observational study, and it can be dangerous to generalise from these.

But giving NSAIDs makes sense in theory, because Alzheimer's disease involves inflammation around the nerves in the brain. So a group of researchers performed a reasonably sized controlled trial of two NSAIDs in people with Alzheimer's disease, to see if the NSAIDs slowed the decline in thinking ability and memory.

The two NSAIDs used were naproxen, one of the older medications, and rofecoxib, a newer type that works in a different way and is supposed to have fewer gastric side effects. The results (after a year) were disappointing.

There was no difference in cognitive decline – in fact if anything, rofecoxib may have reduced thinking ability. Side effects weren't really significant.

It is possible that you need larger doses to gain any benefit, but that will need another study, as will the question of whether or not these anti-inflammatories protect people without Alzheimer's but who are at risk.[10]

▼ VITAMIN B12 AND DEMENTIA

Vitamins are all the rage for dementia and its prevention. Ask your geriatrician – I bet most are swallowing vitamin E in the hope that it will prevent their brain rotting. There's a little evidence in support of that.

Another vitamin that's had attention is B12. Vitamin B12 is found in fish, egg yolk, milk and some cheeses, and having none – or very low levels – can cause damage to the nervous system. For instance there's a condition called pernicious anaemia, where B12 isn't absorbed because of problems in the stomach.

Vitamin B12 deficiency can cause tingling, numbness, loss of balance, loss of smell and even changes to the personality, and since low B12 levels are common in older people, some have wondered whether giving B12 could help dementia.

Unfortunately, the evidence doesn't support this hope. There have only been a couple of small trials of decent quality, which showed no significant effect on thinking ability and memory. And there seem to have been no trials related to prevention.

Vitamin B12 is pretty safe. The main danger – and it's low – is that giving B12 blindly may mask pernicious anaemia, which needs to be watched because a stomach malignancy is a risk in that condition.[11]

▼ GINKGO FOR ALZHEIMER'S

Wouldn't it be nice to be able to buy something over the counter that will improve your memory and keep the dreaded Alzheimer's at bay?

That's what's been touted for a herbal medicine extracted from leaves of the maidenhair tree, *Ginkgo biloba*. Ginkgo is thought to dilate blood vessels and be good for people with arterial disease. From there, some have made the jump to the brain – they claim it prevents dementia, and there have been some trials that suggest it does lead to an improvement in memory.

Often the benefits have been very limited, and the trials have been carried out with people who already have dementia. However, Ginkgo is sold to people who don't have dementia, so the question is, what might it do for them?

One trial had disappointing results. Over 200 people with no dementia aged over 60 had a battery of memory and thinking ability tests and then took either Ginkgo or a placebo for 6 weeks. Unfortunately, there were no benefits on any of the measures assessed, which included ratings from the person's partner, family and friends. The authors say that while it's still possible that Ginkgo works at higher doses than the manufacturers recommend, it does not work with the amounts currently recommended.[12]

▼ AROMATHERAPY: MIGHT HELP, WON'T HARM

Aromatherapy is a popular complementary treatment which uses essential oils – concentrated oils – from plants such as lavender, sandalwood or rosemary. Some are synthetic.

The therapist chooses the oil to suit you and then can apply it in various ways, such as massage – the essential oil is usually diluted with almond, grapeseed or coconut oil. Another technique is inhalation: heating the oil in a small bowl or putting some into a hot bath. There's little scientific evidence that aromatherapy works, but it's possible these essential oils can act like medications when absorbed into the body.

Aromatherapy is used in some aged care facilities with people who have dementia. The belief is that it relieves agitation, helps sleep and perhaps makes them less apathetic. Apathetic in this context, means lack of motivation or drive to follow requests or become involved in activities, or to simply be active. This kind of apathy is a big problem for carers of people with dementia.

A research group surveyed the international literature and found that there's been only one semi-decent trial of aromatherapy, and it showed some benefit. There were problems with the study, though, and more work is needed.

Meantime, if you think a spot of aromatic massage or incense in the air will help, use it – it's unlikely to cause any harm, and perhaps at least the carers will feel better.[13]

▼ PAGERS AND DEMENTIA

How often have we been at the pictures or the theatre and annoyed by a pager going off?

Well, perhaps we need to be more tolerant, because pager technology is being used to compensate for memory problems.

A group in the UK has used a centralised paging service to send people with memory loss reminders like: 'Have you unlocked the door so the meals on wheels lady can get in?'; 'Have you actually *locked* the door before going to bed?'; 'Have you taken your pills (perhaps ironically, the memory pills)?'; 'Remember to take your money and keys when going to see the doctor today', and so on.

These researchers did a trial to see whether the pager helped people live a more independent life and whether they needed it forever or could be weaned off it.

It was a mixed group in the trial: some had Alzheimer's, but most had brain injury. The researchers found that the pager system allowed most of the people to take on more everyday activities, and that this improvement occurred in people of all ages with various degrees of memory loss. Some had to be reminded for a while what the pager sound was – but when they had learned that, they got the benefit. Interestingly, after around 7 weeks of use, some people had improved so much that they no longer needed the device.

And it definitely reduced stress in carers. So perhaps a pager should become the fashion accessory of the future for dementing baby boomers.[14]

▼ Preventing wandering

Once a person has dementia, there are certain behaviours that can drive carers over the edge: aggression and difficulty with feeding, for example. One of the most scary and frustrating is wandering, and this one often results in the person being institutionalised.

People with dementia can wander for miles and get into all sorts of strife, and this behaviour doesn't necessarily stop if they become disabled and are confined to a wheelchair. Even then they try to move around.

The fact is that not a lot is known about wandering in people with dementia, but some findings over the years offer clues. First, the worse the dementia, the worse the wandering. Second, the more active and outgoing the person was before they became demented, the more likely they seem to be to wander. Third, if they used to be easily stressed and showed it, that might express itself as wandering after the Alzheimer's has set in. Fourth, noisy, crowded, complicated environments don't help. And fifth, sometimes the person may just be hungry, and go wandering, presumably in a search for food.

People try all sorts of tricks to stop wanderers wandering, from fencing to Coke cans strung around the bed, to netting around the veranda, to designing simpler, quieter, more friendly living environments for these people to live in.

▼ Alzheimer's and survival

The number of years someone with dementia survives is about half what most experts have until recently assumed.

The general view is that a person diagnosed with dementia has a life expectancy of about 6 years, but a Canadian group of researchers weren't so sure about this because of a fairly well-known phenomenon in studies of survival (with any condition): unless you're careful, people with severe forms of the disease which lead to rapid death can be missed, simply because they don't live long enough to get into the study.

So it was in a large group of elderly Canadians with dementia who were being followed. When the researchers corrected their figures for people with rapidly progressive forms of dementia, the life expectancy dropped to around 3.5 years.

This doesn't mean that dementia is suddenly dramatically different. It's just a recognition that some people decline very quickly with it. It may be that that's because dementia isn't just one disease – it's probably many, most of which are yet to be discovered.

Another question is, why would you think that someone might die of dementia at all? Most people feel that having dementia just raises the risk of dying of any cause – with things like pneumonia perhaps being a bit more common. The reality is that no one knows for sure what people with dementia actually die of.[15]

Diabetes

Type 2 diabetes, the form which usually comes on in adulthood, is going to be the epidemic of the 21st century.

It's by and large *not* caused by a deficiency of insulin – the hormone that helps glucose to move from the bloodstream inside our cells for energy – but by a resistance to insulin's effects.

Adult onset diabetes is rising rapidly, and people are getting younger when they develop it: more and more teenagers are being diagnosed, for example, especially in Aboriginal and Torres Strait Islander communities.

And diabetes is toxic. People with diabetes are up to 4 times more likely to develop heart disease, and when they do have heart disease, they're more likely to have a heart attack, and if they have a heart attack, they're twice as likely to die. If they survive the heart attack they're at very high risk of heart failure. Damage to arteries in the legs is similarly higher, and the risk of having a stroke can go up *ten*fold. Diabetes also increases the risk of nerve damage and blindness – and virtually across the board, it's worse in women.

The treatment is weight loss, exercise (especially resistance exercises with weights), drugs and/or insulin.[1]

▼ IDENTIFYING RISK

If there was a way of identifying people at risk of type 2 diabetes, it'd be helpful. There's a pre-diabetic condition which is called the metabolic syndrome, or syndrome X, which includes high blood fats, being overweight or obese (especially round the middle), high blood pressure and high insulin levels. Family history is also important. If both parents have type 2 diabetes, the risk is very high in their offspring.

Another indicator in women may be their menstrual cycles.

A study which followed the health of a large number of women for over 10 years found that those who had long cycles – 40 days or more rather than around 28 days – had about double the risk of developing type 2 diabetes. That was also true if they had really irregular periods – so irregular, in fact, that they couldn't say what their cycle was.

Long cycles are also associated with obesity, but even when the statistical effects of obesity were removed, the higher risk from longer or very irregular periods remained.

No one knows why this should be so. But if you fit that description you should probably have a thorough check-up so that something can be done ahead of time.[2]

▼ Lifestyle changes

While intuitively it makes sense that if lifestyle can *cause* the problem, it can also *prevent* it, there hasn't been very good evidence to back that up.

A study was carried out with 900 Finnish men and women aged about 55 who were overweight, and who already had some abnormalities in sugar metabolism without being diabetic. They were put in a trial that involved weight reduction, a low-fat, high-fibre diet and increased physical activity.

Compared with the control group, the ones given the programme did better. They were about 2.5 kilograms lighter, 3 centimetres less in waist circumference and had half the rate of developing diabetes over a 4-year period: 1 in 10 in the intervention group compared with 1 in 5 in the control group.

The researchers felt confident that the lifestyle changes and the benefits were cause and effect. The really dramatic finding was that none of those who reached 80 per cent of their lifestyle goals developed diabetes during the 4 year follow-up period, suggesting that the closer you get to your ideal weight and fitness level the better, in terms of diabetes.

Very few people dropped out of this programme, which indicates that if you know you're at risk, the motivation to save yourself overcomes the inconvenience of the changes.[3]

▼ Nuts and peanuts could become weapons against diabetes

There's evidence that mono or polyunsaturated fats give some protection against diabetes, perhaps by increasing the body's response to insulin and ... getting to the kernel of this story ... those are just the kinds of fats in nuts and peanuts.

Sure enough, a 16-year study of 90,000 women has found that when everything else was equal, those consuming 28 grams of nuts

5 or more times per week were 30 per cent less likely to develop diabetes. The effect was similar for the peanut butter equivalent.

Because this study wasn't a randomised trial – it just observed the women – it doesn't guarantee that nuts will help, and the authors warn that if you don't want your shell to grow, the nuts should replace carbohydrate or meat.

The other answer is to buy whole nuts and count the calories expended cracking the things then scrabbling around the floor looking for them.[4]

DIGESTION

▼ Long-term abdominal pain

There are lots of reasons for people having long-term abdominal pain, from inflammation of the pancreas or the large bowel to infections to ulcers.

In many people, though, there's nothing to be found, and they soon find themselves on the medical merry-go-round, going from test to test and specialist to specialist, hoping the next one will have the answer. They usually don't – although they often want to have another stab at the problem ... occasionally literally.

Some surgeons believe that chronic abdominal pain can be caused by adhesions – sticky tissue gluing stretches of intestine together. So they look inside with a laparoscope, through a keyhole incision, and cut adhesions when they find them. It's a controversial approach and has been studied in a reasonably systematic way, comparing having a look with a laparoscope and doing nothing regardless of what's there, with having a look and then snipping.

It turned out that cutting the adhesions made no difference.

That doesn't help if you have chronic abdominal pain, I know. Probably the best favour you can do yourself is to decide – with your GP – to get off the medical merry-go-round before it speeds up.[1]

▼ Extinguished appendices

Could appendicitis be going the way of the long-nosed potoroo: extinction because of human activity?

It seems possible. The trend around the developed world is that the inflamed appendix is becoming rarer. The idea is that our hygienic lifestyle has changed the microbiological fellow travellers in our bowel, making appendicitis less likely to occur.

Even though appendicitis is disappearing, overseas experience has been that surgeons keep on removing lily-white (not inflamed, that is) appendices, in the belief that they're better out than in, when someone has a history of abdominal pain, or even when the surgeon's in the vicinity, so to speak, during another operation. The problem is that there are probably more long-term complications – such as bowel adhesions – resulting from discretionary appendicectomies than from emergency ones.

Western Australia is the only state in Australia which can follow the health of its citizens properly, because it links medical records and can track you through the system. They've looked at appendicectomy rates and found that they've fallen dramatically in the last 15 or 20 years. Two reasons may explain it. One is a fall in appendicitis itself. The other is better diagnosis, using techniques such as ultrasound, which means that surgeons are more sure when they go in that the appendix is inflamed. The other good news is that 'routine' appendicectomies – for things like chronic abdominal pain, where there's no evidence it's useful – seem to be dropping.

The problem is that the fall hasn't been so dramatic in rural areas; perhaps this is because the new diagnostic technology isn't so available there. Now the challenge is to allow more rural Australians to keep one of their appendages.[2]

▼ Might as well be extinct

Could it be that your appendix has far more importance than anyone has thought? Doctors have long assumed that the appendix is a useless dead-end piece of bowel down in the right-hand corner of your tummy, whose only function is to cause sleepless nights for surgeons.

But maybe there's more to it: research in Queensland has found that for some people, removing the appendix can have wider ramifications.

They studied Inflammatory Bowel Disease – that's Crohn's disease – and Ulcerative Colitis, both of which can be quite nasty. About 23,000 people in Australia are affected. People who'd had their appendix out earlier in life had up to 50 times less chance of developing Ulcerative Colitis or Crohn's. If they did develop these diseases, they were milder, or occurred later in life. No one knows why, but it's possible the appendix affects the way the gut's immune system works.

They're now testing whether or not appendicectomy can actually be a treatment for people with a certain form of Ulcerative Colitis.[3]

▼ Indigestion

Up to 1 in 2 of us gets indigestion from time to time. In the vast majority of us, the cause is unknown – there's no ulcer or acid problem. The name given to this by the specialists is non-ulcer dyspepsia.

It covers a range of symptoms, from fullness to burping to discomfort.

Before I get to treatments, what about diagnosis? Your GP should be able to tell from your history, but most experts would say that if you're getting gastrointestinal symptoms for the first time in your life in your mid to late 40s, then you should have an endoscopy done to make sure that there's nothing serious going on.

Assuming you're clear, what treatments works?

Half of the people with non-ulcer dyspepsia get better by themselves, so it's reasonable to do nothing and wait. If you want to take something, the best available evidence suggests that medications which make the stomach and upper bowel propel food more effectively – so-called prokinetics – may, just may, do better than a placebo, as might acid-reducing H2 receptor antagonists such as ranitidine and cimetidine. Antispasmodics don't do much good.

So if you feel some hot air coming on – either sit back and relax and think of your favourite politician, or discuss one of these treatments with your doctor.[4]

▼ Heartburn in the genes?

About 1 in 5 people suffer from gastro-oesophageal reflux disease. You and I know it as common or garden heartburn – burning in the upper abdomen and lower chest and acid which comes back sometimes as far as the throat. We blame many things for it, from coffee to stress, though obesity and smoking are probably more important. But how much is in your genes?

This was studied in a large number of identical and non-identical twins. Given that identical twins share the same genes and non-identical twins only share half, any differences in reflux rates will partly be due to genetics.

The results suggested that about 40 per cent of the blame for heartburn can be laid at the door of our genes. Since reflux is in almost epidemic proportions, though, environmental factors such as obesity, smoking and others yet to be discovered are very powerful as well.

The sting in the tail is that a dangerous form of cancer of the lower end of the gullet seems to be following the heartburn epidemic. The risk of cancer can be detected at endoscopy in some people who have pre-malignant changes called Barrett's oesophagus. So if you're over, say, about 45, or have severe symptoms, you should probably have an endoscopy done to check.[5]

▼ THE REFLUX AND CANCER LINK

The tumour associated with reflux is adenocarcinoma of the oesophagus, and its rate is increasing more rapidly than any other cancer of a lining tissue.

While its incidence is increasing, oesophageal cancer is still pretty rare and it's hard to calculate an individual's risk of developing it if they have a history of heartburn.

All that's known is that when you study a group of people who already have the tumour, about 8 times more of them have a severe reflux history than of similar people without the cancer. Researchers believe that the link is causative, and that long-term chemical irritation from the stomach can induce malignant changes.[6]

▼ REFLUX TREATMENT – WILL IT PREVENT CANCER?

The two main treatments are acid-reducing medications and surgery. The operation involves tightening the valve at the lower end of the oesophagus to stop the regurgitation of stomach contents. There are two questions about this: which is better for people with severe disease – drugs or surgery? – and is one more effective than the other in preventing malignancy?

In one US trial, several hundred people with quite bad reflux had drug treatment or surgery, and were followed up for nearly 11 years. While almost all those in the medication group were still on their medication, 60 per cent of the surgical group were also still taking drugs. There was no difference between the groups in the percentage of people who developed malignancies: they occurred at a rate of 1 person in 1500 every year. If those figures are accurate, it means that if you live for 50 years with *severe* reflux you have a 1 in 30 chance of oesophageal cancer at some time. In reality it's probably a lot less than this.

Those who'd had a pre-malignant lining in their gullet (Barrett's) had about a 1 in 200 chance of cancer every year, and there was no evidence, unfortunately, that treatment of any kind was better at cancer prevention than no treatment at all. The issue here, when it comes to treatment choice, is which best relieves your discomfort.[7]

▼ REFLUX, OBESITY AND OESTROGEN

Obesity is thought to raise your chances of having reflux disease, and in women, it's been suspected that female hormones may also have a role. Both suggestions have been road-tested in a survey of 65,000 Norwegian men and women.

And yes, the fatter people were, the more likely they were to have gastro-oesophageal reflux disease, but the relationship was stronger in women before the menopause. In post-menopausal women, heartburn was more likely if they were on hormone replacement therapy.

Why oestrogen is involved is unknown, but it's interesting to note that pregnant women also often suffer from heartburn. It may be that the hormone loosens the valve where the oesophagus joins the stomach, allowing acid to slosh back.

Good but boring news was that losing weight did help.

As for blokes and male hormones, well they are probably what the women blamed their heartburn on.[8]

▼ COULD SOME TREATMENTS BE ENCOURAGING SOME ULCER GERMS?

Are there more ulcer germs than we ever imagined?

It's quite a few years since Perth-based researchers discovered the ulcer germ, *Helicobacter pylori*. Their discovery allowed a revolution in ulcer treatment, by adding antibiotics to acid-reducing medications.

The treatment doesn't work in everyone, though, and recent research suggests that that might be because there may be more ulcer bacteria than *Helicobacter*.

The story revolves around acid in the stomach, which seems to have important roles in addition to aiding digestion. It may defend the stomach against bacteria. *Helicobacter* is actually resistant to acid attack, but the stomach produces more and more to try to get rid of it. The result is inflammation, pain and ulcers.

But research in situations where there's low acid in the stomach has found that a whole host of other bacteria can invade the stomach, causing a very similar inflammation to *Helicobacter*.

This may be most important for people on long-term acid-lowering medication, say for heartburn – they might have smoldering inflammation in the stomach due to bacterial overgrowth.

Just how significant or real this risk might be is yet to be determined.[9]

▼ VULNERABILITY TO HELICOBACTER PYLORI

Since *H. pylori*'s discovery, it's been linked to stomach cancer and even lymphoma of the stomach. So trying to reduce its prevalence in the community could be an important public health measure, but to do that, you've got know the enemy's behaviour a bit better.

H. pylori is mostly acquired sometime in childhood or adolescence, and the longer you have it, the greater the risk of serious complications such as cancer. Having said that, though, the majority of people who walk around with *H. pylori* have no problems at all.

The other finding has been that the poorer your circumstances, the more likely you are to be infected.

A study from the US tried to pin this down further – wanting to see the age in childhood when *H. pylori* infection was most likely.

They followed a group of children from toddler-hood through to about 20 years old. Nearly half of them were black. At the ages of 1 to 3, only about 8 per cent were infected, but that had risen to 1 in 4 (25 per cent) by their 20s. (In blacks in their 20s it was almost 1 in 2: 50 per cent.)

Most of this infection occurred in the first 10 years – in fact it was concentrated around the ages of 7 to 8. Children younger than this were more likely to get rid of the infection themselves, though there weren't many who became negative (that is, who completely eliminated it from their body).

The conclusions here were that kids of primary school age are a major target for *H. pylori* prevention, and that the different results for difference races were most likely due to the effects of poverty.[10]

▼ HELICOBACTER PYLORI TESTING

Indigestion is common. Most specialists would say that someone over 45 who has developed indigestion for the first time should be fully tested – and probably have an endoscopy – to check that there's nothing serious going on. One of the things they'll check is whether or not you're infected with *H. pylori*.

If you're under 45, it is a different story. The chances of the problem being something nasty are very low unless there's something like weight loss or bleeding as well as the indigestion. So what many doctors do is just whack you onto a medication which radically reduces the acid in your stomach – and thus relieves the pain.

The question is whether that's better for you than testing for *H. pylori* – which can be done easily by analysing your breath. (Luckily, it's a machine that does it rather than a person having a sniff. There are some jobs no money would be enough for!)

Anyway, a trial comparing the two strategies in people under 45, where the ulcer germ was treated if discovered, has found that looking for *H. pylori* is worth doing. It allowed symptoms to be more effectively treated in more people, avoided unnecessary endoscopies and reduced the chances of a relapse.[11]

▼ HELICOBACTER PYLORI AS A CARCINOGEN

This has been a suspicion for many years, but a Japanese study nailed it more conclusively.

One of the reasons it took a Japanese team to do this is that they have among the world's highest rates of stomach cancer, and a sophisticated screening programme to detect and treat it early. This means they're already doing hundreds of thousands of endoscopies each year on otherwise healthy people.

The study followed over 1500 people for nearly 8 years, having tested whether they were infected with *H. pylori*. Not a single stomach cancer occurred in anyone who was NOT infected with *H. pylori*. Nor did any occur in people with a duodenal ulcer or those who'd had their *H. pylori* eradicated with treatment, although as a group they were followed up for less time, so it's possible that stomach cancer could turn up later.

The figures suggest that people carrying *H. pylori* have a 1 in 20 chance of developing stomach cancer over a 10 year period. The people at highest risk were those who already had signs of damage to the stomach lining at the beginning of the study. The reason for the low risk in people with a duodenal ulcer is that they tended to have relatively unaffected stomachs.

The message seems to be that *H. pylori* should be thought of in the same way as tobacco, and stomach cancer should be considered a preventable disease.[12]

▼ ... A LINK WITH HEART DISEASE?

Some believe that *Helicobacter pylori* infection is associated with an increased risk of heart disease. One theory is that it might infect blood vessels and so make cholesterol damage more likely. This is controversial, and some studies have shown no link at all, but it hasn't stopped people continuing to look – because if the theory were true, antibiotic treatment could reduce rates of heart attack and stroke.

In the absence of consistent evidence of arterial infection, some have suggested that chronic *H. pylori* infection could raise blood pressure, and that that could be the way that heart disease risk is raised.

A study of over 10,000 people in the Bristol area, who were followed up carefully over a period of years in terms of their *H. pylori* status, found no relationship between *H. pylori* infection and high blood pressure.

What did make a difference to blood pressure was being overweight, older, male and having a high alcohol intake.

What a surprise.[13]

▼ KEYHOLE SURGERY FOR GALL BLADDERS – FIND A GOOD SURGEON

Keyhole surgery to remove gall bladders is nowadays almost universal in Australia, whereas 10 years ago the commonest method for what's known as a cholecystectomy was via a large incision in the abdomen.

So-called minimally invasive surgery uses the laparoscope, a telescope originally designed for gynaecological surgery. The advantages touted are far less pain, and being able to leave hospital and be back on your feet much sooner.

In the early days of laparoscopic cholecystectomy there was a higher injury rate to the bile duct – the tube carrying bile from the liver to the intestines and into which the gall bladder drains – than there'd been with the older method. The surgeon has to make sure he or she steers clear of the bile duct when tying off the gall bladder.

If the bile duct is tied off by mistake, the person can suffer serious liver damage and jaundice. If it leaks, peritonitis can be a problem.

The answer was thought to be more experience, but a review from the Princess Alexandra Hospital in Brisbane, which treats patients for bile duct repairs, suggests that the numbers of bile duct injuries may not be dropping. This raises a question about whether the operation itself is inherently more risky.

The risk of operative damage to the bile duct is, in fact, low, but it is higher than the 'open' operation (the older method). As usual, there is a trade-off. The open surgery has other potential problems: you have to stay in hospital longer, and therefore may have a higher risk of complications such as blood clots and chest infections.

Taking all that into account, keyhole surgery may still be better, but you need to get your GP to check that your selected surgeon has good results and does lots of this kind of surgery.[14]

Drugs and Alcohol

▼ THE PRICE OF HEALTH

There's good news and bad news around about booze, but before I tell you what it is – a brief word about drug abuse of any kind. If you're not smoking or using other drugs by the age of 18 or 19, you're unlikely ever to start. So the key is to stop – or at the very least delay – adolescents taking up the habits. Alas, there isn't much that works. Parents setting a good example is important, and price is a really effective weapon. Put up the cost of a packet of cigarettes and the use by teenagers falls in proportion.

It's the same with alcohol. When beer excise went up after the GST came in, beer consumption reportedly fell. And here's the bad news – in the debate around the time of the introduction of GST, the Democrats and Labor sacrificed (to election politics) claims they might have made for championing public health. After months of lobbying, the beer industry won a lower excise on beer, one of the forms of alcohol most abused by youth. In this case price disincentives were reduced.

And the good news?

Well, if you've actually managed to learn how to drink moderately, yet more research has found benefits. A study in the US has shown that moderate drinkers (between 7 and 14 drinks per week) who have a heart attack are less likely to die from it – so you can live to drink another day.

Cheers.

▼ GRASS – SAFE AND NATURAL? NOT FOR THE PSYCHE

Australian research has undermined the 'green' image of cannabis.

A 7 year study of about 2000 Victorian teenagers found that cannabis is strongly associated with depression and anxiety in young women. The researchers have been following these young men and women since the age of 14; starting, by and large, before they had any mental health problems or were using drugs. The idea was to see whether there was a cause-and-effect relationship between cannabis and depression.

Women who used cannabis daily were 6 times more likely to experience depression and anxiety than non-users and that's after allowing for factors like other drug use, education level, income and family background.

Plus it was dose-related: cannabis above the weekly use was related to more depression and anxiety.

No one knows whether this is due to the marijuana itself or the lifestyle that is associated with heavy use, but the effect is real, probably related to the drug rather than the mental state causing the drug problem.

They couldn't explain the lack of the same effect on boys; they may be more at risk of psychosis from cannabis rather than depression.

The message here is that the safe image of marijuana needs to be dispelled, and preventive measures put in place.[1]

▼ BUT WAIT, THERE'S MORE TO DISPEL THE SAFE CANNABIS MYTH

Smoking cannabis affects the lungs the same way smoking tobacco does; it can create dependence (though not as severe as that caused by tobacco, alcohol or heroin); it's associated with schizophrenia; and, according to an international study involving Australian researchers, in heavy users it's associated with damaged thinking ability.

They compared people who'd been smoking cannabis almost daily for about 24 years with a group who'd been smoking it for 10 years, and with a group of non-smokers. Marijuana users had generally taken it up at around the age of 15, and were regular smokers by the time they were 17, consuming about two joints a day, most days of the month. As I said, these were heavy users, and cannabis was their main drug.

Long-term users had greater problems with recall, time estimation, information processing, learning, attention and retrieval of information. The shorter-term users were pretty much the same as the non-users except that they were showing signs of not being able to estimate time as well.

These deficits could affect their ability to perform academically, do complex jobs well and manage interpersonal relationships. Whether people recover if they stop or reduce their use of marijuana is not known yet.

So while there's some comfort in the fact that if you were drinking at this level for this long you'd be in a far worse state – or dead – it's still a reminder that there's no such thing as a safe drug.[2]

▼ AND TOBACCO RELATES TO MENTAL HEALTH AS WELL

There's more and more interest around the world in why people with mental illness have very high rates of smoking. Is it because of stress, or could it be that tobacco is actually helping them develop the condition? If so, it's a double-edged sword.

One group of researchers carried out a study of people quitting smoking. They compared people with and without schizophrenia, and monitored both groups' thinking ability.

For the people who had schizophrenia, quitting was especially difficult and often didn't last long. In addition, giving up cigarettes made their thinking ability worse, whereas in healthy individuals, thinking ability improved.

This is important for a couple of reasons. Work in Western Australia has shown that people with schizophrenia have significantly shorter life spans than the rest of us, and one reason for this is their high rate of smoking-related illnesses – up to 90 per cent of these people smoke.

The second reason is that smoking may be a form of self-medication. If this is so, then nicotine could be used to treat people with schizophrenia without the carcinogens of tobacco smoke. Patches have been tried and the results have been disappointing, but the research could point to the way to new, innovative medications which could treat both the schizophrenia and relieve the need to smoke.[3]

▼ ... AND ANXIETY

Smoking in adolescence may increase the risk of anxiety disorders.

There's a lot of talk in psychological research about the higher incidence of mental health problems in heavy smokers. Depression and anxiety in particular are more common, and as with the story above, the theory is that nicotine may be a way of unconsciously self-medicating the brain to make you feel better.

And when you try to quit you feel terrible, so you don't persist.

But it may work the other way around as well: smoking may cause mental illness.

A study from New York State has followed adolescents through to their 20s, measuring all sorts of psychological, social and health variables. They found that 22-year-olds who were smoking 20 a day when they were aged 16 had a much higher incidence of anxiety disorders, including panic attacks.

And there was no evidence of such problems before they took up their habit.

The study couldn't be sure about cause and effect, but other work on heroin, cocaine and alcohol has found that heavy use can actually change brain structure and function permanently. So it might be the same with nicotine.

It also gives a more near-term reason for adolescents not to take up the habit.[4]

▼ AND IT CAN MAKE QUITTING SO MUCH HARDER TO DO

It's a gross oversimplification, but in general there are two kinds of smokers: the ones who can give up fairly easily and the ones who are really glued to the drug. Some people simply have a strong physical addiction, but this self-medication concept may be another reason.

One study took a group of heavy smokers (a pack a day or more) who had a history of severe depression yet were fine at the moment and on no medication. They were then put through a smoking cessation programme.

The study wasn't perfect, because quite a few dropped out, but the findings were salutary. For those who'd successfully quit, the risk of relapsing into depression was more than 7 times higher than it was for those who hadn't managed to give up.

Possibly, smokers with depression know that already. What it means is that for these people, giving up the evil weed may need additional assistance. It also raises questions about whether nicotine replacement therapy could be used as an antidepressant.[5]

▼ CELLULOID TOBACCO

The main reason for banning cigarette advertising is its effect on teenagers. Remember, if you don't start smoking by your late teens, you're unlikely ever to begin.

Tobacco companies know this well, and consistently use images and role models targeted at children. These days, there's product placement in movies instead of advertising, and movie makers seem happy to have their heroes smoke their hearts out.

A group of researchers has measured the effects of this on teenagers.

They surveyed over 3500 adolescents aged 10 to 14 who'd never smoked, assessed about 50 films on current release for their smoking content, then a year or two later, followed up the young people to compare which movies they'd seen with whether or not they'd subsequently taken up smoking.

Those who'd seen the most smoking in movies were nearly 3 times as likely to have started – and those figures were corrected for most of the other factors which might have made them prone to smoking. Over half of all teenage smoking initiation could be blamed on celluloid tobacco.

The children most influenced by smoking in films had *non*-smoking parents. Those who did have a smoking mother or father were at risk anyway. Cigarette companies must be pleased to know that movies reach the kids that parental non-smoking doesn't.

It's been estimated that if every movie containing smoking got an R rating, a large number of lives would be extended.[6]

▼ PARTY SMOKE

Even if kids don't smoke, it's highly likely that they're going to be inhaling other people's smoke at parties. Just smell their clothes afterwards.

'Does this matter?' you may ask. 'After all, they're young and healthy.' Well, yes it does, according to a study from Japan.

They used a test which measures endothelial function in the arteries of the heart. The endothelium is the inner lining of arteries. It can influence all sorts of things, from how cholesterol is laid down to whether or not the artery is twitchy and likely to go into spasm. They compared groups of smokers and non-smokers in their 20s. Before they began, the non-smokers had better endothelial function than the smokers.

But when exposed to environmental tobacco smoke, the levels of carbon monoxide in the non-smokers' blood went up, and their endothelial function became indistinguishable from that of the smokers.

The bottom line therefore was that passive smoking in non-smoking young people harmed their coronary arteries.

On a one-off basis, this probably isn't an issue, but repeated exposure could be quite damaging, and could explain why passive smoking increases the risk of heart attacks in non-smokers.[7]

▼ STUDENTS, DRINKING AND VIOLENCE

You've heard about the effects of second-hand smoke, but what about second-hand alcohol?

It's a bit different from second-hand smoking, where you're actually inhaling someone else's cigarette smoke. What I'm talking about are the second-hand effects of other people's alcohol: things like violence and accidents.

Since university is where many learn the art of heavy drinking, researchers at the University of Otago in New Zealand randomly surveyed over 1500 students about their experiences of second-hand effects, including a physical attack of some kind, property damage and having unwanted sexual advances or sexual assault. They also asked about the victim's own drinking habits, to see if that made a difference.

There was no doubt that the heavier a drinker the person was, the more likely they were to experience the effects of other people's alcohol, but plenty of abstainers and moderate drinkers also experienced trouble. One in 10 women and 1 in 5 male students in the survey had been assaulted in the previous 4 weeks and 1 in 5 had property damage. Older students had fewer problems.

Much as we'd like to think New Zealand's different, it's probably wishful thinking. This research suggests that more attention may need to be given to alcohol use in this group of young adults.[8]

▼ HEALTH DRINK??

Here's a sobering tale about a health drink. It comes from Western Australia. A 25-year-old woman collapsed. When the ambulance officers arrived, they found her to be in ventricular fibrillation – that's when the heart quivers rather than beats effectively: it's a fatal arrhythmia unless you can be shocked out of it.

The ambulance officers tried to save her, as did the doctors in the hospital – but they failed.

In the past, she'd seen a heart specialist for palpitations, and he'd found her to have quite a common abnormality of one of the heart valves – around 2 or 3 per cent of the population has it, mostly without ever knowing. She was advised to limit her caffeine intake, which she promised to do by sticking to 1 cup of tea per day.

But at the post mortem they found that the woman had very high caffeine levels in her blood.

It turned out that on the day she died she was given a high-energy health drink containing guarana – made from the seeds of an Amazonian plant. According to the people who'd been with her, she downed almost the whole bottle (55 ml).

Tragically, what she didn't know – but what the West Australian scientists discovered when they tested the guarana drink – was that it contained more than 60 times the amount of caffeine that's in cola drinks or tea and over 10 times as much as is in coffee.

Most of us would just get a bit twitchy, but if our heart's at all dicky and we take such a large hit in one go, the result could be disastrous.

So be careful what you put in your mouth ... what's natural isn't always safe.[9]

▼ ... AND SOFT DRINKS MAY BE HARDER THAN YOU THINK

Here's a medical mystery for you.

A young woman arrived at the Royal Adelaide Hospital with a rather unusual story. For the previous 12 months she'd had diarrhoea, weight loss and muscle weakness. On examination, she could barely stand up.

This is a hard one, even for the experts. The range of possibilities revolve around fairly rare conditions such as the muscular dystrophies, inflammation in the muscles from, say, an autoimmune disease, the after-effects of a severe viral infection, or something toxic.

The woman had blood tests which showed a dangerously low potassium level and signs of muscle and liver damage. The doctors then went looking for a possible toxin that could cause such a result – something like lead. But they didn't need to look far, because the woman told them that for the past year she'd been drinking 8 litres of cola soft drink per day – yes, 8 litres.

What she had was essentially a case of chronic *caffeine* toxicity; this has only rarely been documented before. It seems the woman had had problems with drug dependency in the past and this was a substitute for her.

No one knows how she's doing now, because she discharged herself from hospital and hasn't been seen since the time the paper was published.[10]

▼ ... AND ANOTHER MYSTERY TO BE SOLVED

Here's a story from the front line of surgery ... the things that can happen in the middle of the night, and a salutary tale for those with bad habits.

One night a surgical registrar was called to see a young man in the Emergency Department of Sydney Hospital. For the moment, I appoint you to be a surgeon – without the income. This 28-year-old man had central abdominal pain moving to the right side of the tummy. He found it painful to move, and when the doctor put his hand on the abdomen over the spot on the lower right side, the muscles felt very tense.

Need more information? Well, he had a fever and a high white blood cell count – a sign of inflammation.

You must have it now ... he's got appendicitis, hasn't he?

Well, that's what the registrar thought at 2 am, so he took the patient to theatre. But when he opened the abdomen there was nothing wrong with the appendix. If you weren't scrubbed up you'd have scratched your head.

What he found instead was that part of the colon next to the appendix had died. Most unusual in a young person. They removed the offending – and offensive, by this time – bit of large bowel, and when the sun rose later that morning they started asking questions.

It turned out that the young man was a cocaine user. Cocaine, it seems, can knock off blood vessels – in the brain, in the heart and in the bowel. So what goes up your nose can clearly go down badly elsewhere.[11]

▼ THE NATURE OF HEROIN ADDICTION

Methadone as a treatment for heroin dependence has only been around since the early 1960s, and one of the three pioneers at Rockefeller University in New York was Professor Mary Jeanne Kreek, who's considered a giant in the study of opiate addiction.

The Kreek view is that methadone is a treatment for a chronic disease, and it replaces a biochemical deficiency of natural opiates just as insulin does in a person with diabetes.

Professor Kreek also found disturbing evidence that heroin and cocaine are capable of inducing near-permanent brain changes very quickly – and that these brain changes are what help turn the problem into a long-term relapsing condition. Remember, heroin can kill up to one-third of users in time. The problem may be the high doses injected by people in the early stages of their drug use.

Her lab and others have found several gene changes that may predispose to heroin dependence; they have also found that susceptible people may have an abnormal response to stress that goes back to childhood. There's growing evidence that problems with nurturing or stress in early childhood might affect brain development and increase the output of hormones in reaction to stressful circumstances.

So drug users could be treating their stress biology with narcotics – and of course the stress of drug withdrawal itself is severe, which makes the temptation to relapse greater. This hyper-responsivity even exists in former heroin users who are now drug-free, and it looks similar in cocaine users. It helps to explain why periods of high stress put former drug users at risk of returning to their drugs.

The message is that intravenous drug use is messing with biology as well as psychology, which means that it needs biological treatments such as methadone as well as other approaches.

Environment and Health

▼ PCBs AND PREGNANCY

One of the most persistent and potentially worrying group of pollutants in our environment are the polychlorinated biphenyls (PCBs). They're a collection of over 200 different chemicals, and are found in electrical equipment such as transformers.

When a pregnant woman is exposed to PCBs, they can cross into the foetus, and after birth, may be found in breast milk. High doses of PCBs are known to be toxic to nerves; the question is whether or not the lower amounts normally found around us affect child development.

It's not an easy thing to study, because good parenting, having a mother with a high IQ and being born into a family with a high level of education makes a big difference to a child's development.

A recent study in Germany measured PCB exposure and development from birth to age $3^1/_2$. The families were mostly middle class, the babies were otherwise healthy, and the mothers were relatively young – an average age of 30.

There was indeed a negative effect on the child's development due to PCB exposure both to the mother in pregnancy and to the baby via breast milk, but it was only really noticed from about 30 months on. Overall, though, the positive effect of parenting and family swamped the downside from the PCBs.

So the home environment can make up some of the lost ground, but that doesn't excuse the authorities from putting in place stringent controls on these substances to protect children from adverse effects.[1]

▼ SOCIAL ENVIRONMENT, HEIGHT AND ACHIEVEMENT

There's a curious phenomenon with height.

Tall people tend to do better than short ones. They're more likely to earn more, get the job and – and I say this without the slightest rancour, I assure you – if they're a bloke, get the girl.

But in a study which will have old fogies in gentlemen's clubs around the nation choking on their whiskies, social mobility has partly overcome the height thing; the result is that the well-to-do have become shorter.

The researchers took 10,000 people born in 1958 and compared the social class they were born into with their social class as adults. The height difference in adulthood was greater when you categorised people according to their social class as children, and the explanation was largely upward mobility during life.

People migrating to the higher classes were shorter than those already in them, and those heading downwards were taller than the people in the classes below. The result was a levelling out.

Mind you, the height thing was still there. It was the taller than average people in the working classes who tended to move upwards and the shorter than average people in the middle classes who went down.

The serious policy issue in all this is a reminder that things like education are able to overcome some inequalities in childhood which may at first sight seem to be biological.[2]

▼ White-tail spider innocent

An outrageous injustice has been corrected and a hapless victim's been let off the hook. It's the white-tail spider, widely blamed over the last few years for devastating tissue damage after its bite, which is known as necrotising arachnidism.

But no longer. The white-tail spider is innocent. It was just a beat-up that started with speculation from a scientist followed by dramatic media stories. It's been so well promoted that having a slow-healing skin ulcer is now likely to result in a diagnosis of white-tail spider bite. Sometimes the problem is actually skin cancer, and it's missed in all the fuss.

A carefully collected series of well-documented bites – where the spider had been caught in the act – has found that while white-tail spider bites are often sore and red, they don't cause skin damage.

So what does cause the skin damage so lovingly documented by tabloids? As usual, no one knows. It may be a rarer spider called the recluse, or it could be a common or garden skin infection gone wrong.

Whatever it is ... leave poor white-tails alone.[3]

Exercise and Sport

▼ Sports injuries – the stats

A study from Western Australia has probably the most reliable figures yet for injury rates among adults participating in sport. Not elite athletes, but ordinary klutzes like me.

The researchers followed 1500 people from Australian Rules, basketball, netball and field hockey clubs in Perth: they rang each of the players every month for 2 years. In that time, 75 per cent of them sustained an injury that required treatment or resulted in a missed game or training session. The lower limbs were the most common parts injured, with AFL the worst offender – it produced, on average, 2 injuries per squad per week.

Netball – which has the reputation of keeping knee surgeons in business – was actually the safest sport, with basketball next.

Those who were at higher risk had one or more of the following: they hadn't trained pre-season, were highly competitive on the field, had had a previous injury (especially of the back), were inexperienced at the sport, and (in the case of women) ran with their feet turned inwards – pronated.

So get fit, know the rules, stop running knock-kneed, be sure to behave like a wimp during the game and you'll be fine.[1]

▼ The sprained ankle

Going over on your ankle while exercising, playing sport or just by accident when you're out and about is one of the commonest injuries we experience. The result is often a torn ligament – the one that goes from the outside ankle bone down to the foot. It's painful, swells up and stops us getting around for a while.

The question is, what should you do about it?

There are loads of alternatives, from doing nothing to elastic bandages, to taping, to fancy new semi-rigid splints which go down either side of the ankle and are bound together to provide some support. There are also lace-up supports.

A review of the little evidence available on what's best suggests that if you want to get back on your feet or back to exercise, the semi-rigid splint probably comes out best overall. It gets people back to work and exercise faster, and with less instability than elastic bandages. The lace-up support is probably best at reducing swelling.

It's hard to judge taping, because not many trials properly assessed it. Many sports physios swear by taping, but it does cause skin irritation, and for blokes the hair can be a problem.

The issue with the splints is that they aren't cheap. Elastic bandage may be better than nothing, but there's no evidence that it is.[2]

▼ Tennis elbow

Tennis elbow is a real pain in the ... well, elbow ... and common; probably 3 in every 100 adults gets an attack in any 12 month period.

The fancy name for this is lateral epicondylitis, which means a pain on the outer side of the elbow. Some tennis players get it from counting wads of money which are simply too large for any single individual to contemplate.

For half of us it's nothing to do with tennis. The elbow pain's usually the result of doing too much with that arm, especially if what we're doing involves twisting movements.

If tennis is the problem, there are a few things that sometimes work: fixing your swing to stop your wrists rolling, two-handed actions and changing the equipment. But there's still the issue of treatment, because tennis elbow can last for months.

There are a variety of things available, from non-steroidal painkillers to steroid injections to physiotherapy with ultrasound, massage and graded exercises. And you can bet that whenever there's a big choice of treatments, nothing works well.

A trial in The Netherlands compared physiotherapy, steroid injections and just waiting and seeing, to decide what was the best treatment for someone with tennis elbow.

The results were fascinating. In the first 6 weeks, the steroid injections were best, but over a year, those who'd had injections tended to relapse. The physiotherapy group had more sustained benefits – 9 out of 10 were deemed a success at 1 year, compared with 7 out of 10 for injections. Waiting and seeing was better than injections and not far off the results for physio.

Nature wins again, it seems.[3]

▼ Cycling hazard for women

Spare a thought for female cyclists, because the sport can have long-lasting effects. Sore nipples, nerve damage and saddle sores are par for the course, but what would be far less welcome is what's been described as 'bicyclists' vulva'.

Belgian gynaecologists reported on six elite female cyclists in their 20s and 30s who'd cycled an average of nearly 500 kilometres per week for several years. They all had an irreversible swelling on one side of their vulva. Tests showed it was in fact lymphoedema – the same condition that women can get in their arms after breast surgery.

In the case of the cyclists, though, it wasn't cancer or surgery or the type of saddle or the clothing worn that was to blame; it was damage to the lymph drainage from the pelvis, possibly as a result of repeated bouts of skin inflammation caused by the cycling itself.

This shouldn't be a concern to women who are static cycling in gyms unless they're doing enormous distances.

The advice from the specialists was to treat skin problems in elite cyclists seriously and use cold compresses and physiotherapy judiciously.

I'll let you know when they give us an update on cyclists' scrotum.[4]

▼ Is ephedrine a performance enhancer?

The use of ephedrine and ephedra (the herb from which ephedrine is taken) in dietary supplements to enhance athletic performance or for weight loss has been extremely controversial, with one death of a prominent American athlete reported.

The US Food and Drug Administration asked a group of researchers to review the published scientific literature to see whether or not there was any evidence that ephedrine did the jobs it was fabled to do.

All weight loss trials were of short duration and showed that ephedrine – sometimes with caffeine – did have a small effect on weight loss; there was no evidence about whether or not the weight loss is sustained, because there were no long-term studies.

There was no evidence that sports performance was improved.

The price paid for trying these products was a 2 to 4 times greater chance of palpitations, tummy upset, raised blood pressure or psychiatric problems such as anxiety and depression. The researchers found evidence of several deaths and problems such as heart attacks, strokes and seizures associated with ephedrine-containing products; around 50 per cent of these problems occurred in people aged under 30.

The question for users – especially athletes – is, are the dubious benefits worth the risk? For governments it's whether food supplements need to be more strongly regulated in general – not just in this situation.[5]

▼ Screening athletes for heart disease

There's a (thankfully) rare but upsetting phenomenon on the sports field: the young athlete who drops dead.

There are lots of causes. Brain haemorrhages only represent about 1 per cent. The heart is to blame most of the time: the most common cause is hypertrophic cardiomyopathy – a congenital disease of the heart muscle which can be diagnosed with an electrocardiograph.

So why not screen kids before they take part in sport at a high level? Because it's expensive and cumbersome to do an ECG on everyone, and there'll be lots of wrong diagnoses.

The confusing and ironic thing is that many healthy athletes' hearts can look as though they're diseased. An athletic heart can beat irregularly, and be so muscular that it looks sick, when in reality it's not. So finding those athletes who do have a problem requires significant expertise, and since sudden death is so rare, it may not be practical (or economically viable) on a large scale.

The budding athletes who do need a close check are those with a heart murmur, who may have blacked out, who have a family history of heart problems, or who get chest pain or excessive breathlessness when they exercise.[6]

▼ Spinal injury and sport

Some sports, including horse riding, rugby union and rugby league, involve spinal risk, and recent surveys in Australia have tried to separate fact from fiction about where the risks really are and what can be done about them.

Despite the high-profile injury of Christopher Reeve, probably the least researched sport has been horse riding. A 20 year survey of all horse-related spinal injuries in NSW had interesting observations.

Not a single spinal injury occurred in a rider belonging to a Pony Club, and very few occurred in other reputable riding organisations. The major risk for spinal injury from horse riding came from non-organised and occupational riding.

No one's sure what the factors might be, but the likely culprits are reckless speed, not wearing a helmet, poorly maintained equipment and inadequate supervision.

In terms of football, there's still work to be done. The rate of spinal injury hasn't fallen as much as the experts had hoped, despite the fact that in schoolboy rugby union there have been fewer injuries since referees have controlled the force with which the two teams meet in the scrum. One implication of the disappointing football spinal injury figures is that the sports need to consider more rule changes in relation to tackling in league and rucks in union.[7]

▼ LIVING LONGER YOUNGER

Active people tend to be younger. We take a sitting position more frequently as we age, and while there's plenty of evidence supporting the benefits of increased physical activity in younger people and men – it's mixed or non-existent for older women.

A 12 year study of death rates among more than 9000 women aged 65 or over found that when compared with women who remained sedentary, those who walked, danced, did the garden, swam or went to aerobics had a dose-related benefit from the exercise. In other words, the more exercise they did, the lower their age-related chances of dying of any cause, including heart disease and cancer. The decrease was around 50 per cent, at least up to the age of 75.

If they weren't in good shape at the start of the study, healthwise, the exercise didn't do as much good.

These reduced chances of dying prematurely weren't affected by whether or not the woman smoked, how fat she was, or whether she had been active before the study started or began exercising only in her silver years.

So while you probably didn't realise that there were doubts about the value of exercise in older women, you'll be glad to hear that common sense can still prevail.[8]

▼ How hard do you have to pump?

It's very popular at the moment to encourage exercise among elderly people but that can mean all sorts of things, from a bit of stretching and walking to pumping iron. What works? Well, that depends on what you're trying to achieve.

An Australian group has compared resistance training in elderly people with other forms of exercise that aim at flexibility and a gentle cardiovascular workout.

Resistance training is quite hard work, and gets you to put about 80 per cent of your maximum effort into lifting a weight. For people who've never even thought of raising a dumbbell, that weight could be just their arm to start with.

The benefits the researchers assessed were useful everyday things such as the ability to go from sitting to standing, walking speed, and how far forward the person could lean without toppling over. After 10 weeks of sessions once or twice a week, the people performed significantly better on all these measures than if they had gone through a milder programme focused more on flexibility.

So it seems that whatever your age, if strength's what's needed, there's no substitute for a bit of hard yakka.[9]

▼ The benefits of doing it harder

A study of 73,000 women aged between 50 and 80 has looked at how vigorous exercise needs to be to prevent heart disease.

They found that the more physical activity a woman was involved in, the lower her chances of a heart attack or stroke, and that what counted was how much energy was burnt. The more energy expended, the better off the women were, regardless of whether they smoked, were fat or had high blood pressure.

Women who walked *and* did vigorous exercise – meaning they worked up a sweat and raised their pulse – did better. And if they just walked, those who charged along very briskly had half the risk of heart disease of women who rarely walked or who, when they did, just ambled along.

The message from all this is that while any exercise is good, more is better – without going mad. The current official recommendations for exercise are probably too low. Some experts now suggest that doing exercise every day is best, because some of the beneficial effects are short-lasting. They also think you should be exercising for longer – aim for an hour a day if you have the time.[10]

EYES

▼ Seeing your way

Older people often say they're safer drivers than young ones. Sure enough, men under 25 have the highest crash rate and people over 60 the lowest, but when the calculations are adjusted for the number of kilometres the person drives, people over 60 emerge with almost the same crash rate as the under 25s. They are also more likely to seriously harm themselves. In other words, their crash rate looks lower because they don't drive as much – and if you see my mum behind the wheel, another explanation is that you'd be faster walking.

One reason for the higher risk is thought to be cataracts – where the lens of the eye is clouded, impairing vision. The question is, does removing cataracts make driving safer?

For up to 6 years, researchers followed 300 people who'd had cataract removal with an intraocular lens replacement. Their crash rate had halved compared with people with cataracts who hadn't had surgery.

What had in fact happened was that their rate of decline in driving performance was less – it wasn't really that their driving had improved. And worryingly, people who still had their cataracts didn't realise their driving ability was impaired.

Another excellent reason to keep your eyes peeled on the road.[1]

▼ Bifocals

You and I are too young to know what I'm about to talk about, but you've probably noticed that as people age, they need reading glasses or bifocals. That's because their eyes lose the ability to accommodate.

Accommodation in this case has nothing to do with where you rest your weary head at night. It's about your eyes accommodating to reading print close up. The jargon term for it is presbyopia.

The reason it happens is that the lens inside the eye becomes stiff, and the mechanism for focusing on things near at hand doesn't work as well.

Reliable sources tell me that people with presbyopia hate it, and the awkward ways they have of coping with the condition. Unfortunately, there's no surgery that works. Laser treatment of the cornea isn't any help because the problem's not on the outside.

Putting in an intraocular lens, as they would after a cataract operation, isn't much use because the lens isn't made to change shape. Some researchers are trying to invent intraocular lenses which would fix presbyopia.

There are two main approaches currently in play. One is to make a lens which moves backwards and forwards inside the eye, a bit like playing with a magnifying glass; the other is to develop a special kind of gel which can be put inside the sac which holds the lens, so that the lens would behave just like a normal young one.

Both are promising, but the gel version may in the end be more successful, because it mimics what happens in a normal eye.

Human trial results are a way off, but if they're successful, people might be able to lose their reading glasses once and for all.

A word of warning: if anyone tries to flog you an operation for presbyopia called scleral expansion, politely refuse and find another doctor. It involves inserting bands to make the eye longer. It's experimental, associated with unsatisfying results and has an element of risk.[2]

▼ Clayton's blindness

Is it possible to be blind when there's nothing wrong with your eyes or the seeing part of your brain? Well, given that I have to fill a minute of your time, the answer's bound to be yes.

There's a condition – still under-recognised by the medical profession – that starts with excessive blinking, which can become worse and involve more of the eye than a normal blink does. In some people it progresses to muscle spasms, where the eyes slam shut and won't open for a few seconds. If you're driving, you can imagine that that might be a touch disconcerting.

Occasionally, for some reason, singing or shouting can get the eyes to open, but the eyelid spasms can occur so frequently that effectively the person becomes blind. Often people are treated as though they're hysterical – that it's in their minds – or doctors are just puzzled.

But there is a name and there are effective treatments.

The name for the condition is Benign Essential Blepharospasm, and it was one of the first and effective uses for botulinum toxin injections – botox.

In some people, anti-Parkinson drugs may work; a last resort is surgery to the muscles around the eye.

So if the blinking doctor says there's nothing wrong, get a second opinion.[3]

▼ Window on Alzheimer's?

Certain kinds of cataracts, opacities in the lens of the eye, could be linked to Alzheimer's disease if research findings are correct.

An Australian-led team in Boston has been investigating why a messy protein material called amyloid gums up the nerves in the brains of people with Alzheimer's disease. They think the reason relates to the accumulation of copper and iron as we age. It turns out that when there is a lot of copper and iron around, this amyloid not only interferes with the brain – it reacts strongly with the material that makes up the lens of the eye.

So the researchers moved out of the test tube and examined the eyes of people who had died of Alzheimer's disease. They found that there was a higher than expected incidence of cataracts in those people.

But they weren't the forms of cataract that people usually develop as they age. These ones sat in the edge of the lens rather than the middle. Further work is being done to see whether or not there's a link with common or garden cataracts.

If there is, it could provide – literally – a window on Alzheimer's disease for early diagnosis and treatment.[4]

▼ Is the future written in our eyes?

A decade-long study in the Blue Mountains of NSW following the eye health of people over the age of 50 has found a strong link between visual impairment and the chances of dying prematurely.

The younger the person was, the greater the risk.

Visual impairment is loss of vision; at its most severe, it is blindness. The causes include cataract, macular degeneration (a common but incurable disease of the retina at the back of the eye), glaucoma, which damages the optic nerve that takes visual information to the brain, and diabetic eye disease.

After subtracting the influence of things like diabetes, heart disease and smoking, visual impairment by itself predicted the chances of dying.

The results seem real because other studies have found the same thing. However, the evidence is still not strong enough to say it's direct cause and effect – and if it is causative, no one knows why.

Even so, the safest thing is for people to be promptly treated for things like cataract, diabetic eye disease and glaucoma, and for doctors to look for them. Plus we need scaled-up research into the causes and treatment of macular degeneration.[5]

▼ It's worth treating glaucoma

Modern medicine is filled with acts of faith; doctors doing things because they believe they'll help. One such relates to a common condition called glaucoma, which can lead to blindness. Glaucoma is progressive damage to the nerve leaving the eye, which carries vision to the brain. No optic nerve – no sight. The tragedy of glaucoma is that it's silent until too late – the visual loss creeps up on you and is not reversible.

Some people with this optic nerve damage have had high pressure inside the eye, as measured on the slit lamp in an optometrist or ophthalmologist's rooms. If the pressure's high you're told it needs to be reduced to save your vision and prevent glaucoma. But does it? And what if your pressure's normal but there are already signs of harm?

Till recently, there's not been a lot of evidence to support treatment.

Over the past couple of years major studies have been producing the goods, and now there's little doubt that pressure reduction, by drops or surgery, does prevent or slow glaucoma, whether you have high pressure inside your eye or not.

So it's really worth everyone over the age of 50 having their eye pressure and the back of their eyes checked – earlier if there's glaucoma in the family — and having treatment if the condition is present or emerging.[6]

▼ Loose ties, better eyes

Thanks to medical science, there's another excuse for not wearing a tie, no matter how eye-popping it may be. The reason is that it could be literally eye-popping.

Forty men, half of whom had normal eyes and half of whom had glaucoma, were tested. As mentioned previously, glaucoma is a cause of progressive damage to the optic nerve, often associated with raised pressure inside the eye. The researchers measured the eye pressure of these men: some had open collars, and others had ties on, tightened just to the level of discomfort. They were tested a second time, 3 minutes after loosening the ties.

A tight tie raised intraocular pressure in everyone. When the tie was loosened, the pressure returned to where it had been with an open collar.

This suggests that tight ties could lead to mistaken glaucoma diagnoses or wrong conclusions that glaucoma treatment isn't working.

The good thing is that they didn't do what had been done previously, which is wrap a blood pressure cuff round the neck and inflate it to see what happens to the eyes. There's only so much a volunteer can be asked to do to benefit humankind.[7]

▼ Far-sighted Australians

Which is more common in Australia, long-sightedness or short-sightedness?

Well, in the Anglo population the answer is long-sightedness. Long-sighted people have trouble seeing things up close and sometimes, they have problems with distance too. The trouble is an eyeball which is too short, or a cornea — that's the window over the front of the eye — which is too flat.

Either way, light rays focus behind rather than on the retina — the eye's projection screen.

While laser surgery is quite good for short-sighted people, it hasn't worked well in long-sightedness. That's because instead of shaving the cornea, doctors really need to build it up.

A new technique is being trialled: it involves using radio frequency (RF) energy via a tiny metal probe which heats spots around the cornea. The effect is a bit like a purse string – the cornea ends up bulging in the middle.

Early results are quite positive, with few complications. It takes eye specialists a while to learn how to do it, but there are some in Australia trying it. If you're thinking of having the RF treatment, be aware that it's still experimental and ask how many eyes the specialist has done.

If it's fewer than 10, you're probably still a guinea pig.

▼ Don't be detached about myopia

If you're short-sighted you usually have an eye that's longer than normal, which means that light is focused in front of the retina at the back of the eye, instead of on it.

Spectacles, contact lenses and laser surgery are all designed to refocus the light where it should be.

Those of us who are short-sighted have other crosses to bear.

We're more likely to have a detached retina, for instance. That's where the retina starts to peel off its backing. You get blind spots, flashing lights and increased floaters. If it's not treated early enough, you can go blind in that eye or need fairly major eye surgery. Take it from someone who knows.

But Australian research presented at the last World Congress of Ophthalmology gave those of us who walk into things without our specs on something else to worry about. They reported on a survey of eye health in older people which found that short-sighted people are at greater risk of developing a particularly disabling form of cataract – and the more short-sighted they were, the more at risk they were. Over 3.5 dioptres (a measure of lens strength required for correction), the risk was quadrupled.

Cataracts are opacities in the lens of the eye which block light going to the retina, and while no one knows why short-sightedness may be linked to them, there are a couple of theories. First, the longer eye may mean that the blood supply to the back of the eye is not as good as it should be, which would mean that the lens may not be nourished. Second, there could be more free radical damage from a lack of antioxidants.

The good news is that this form of cataract is easily operated on; the bad news is that you may need it done at a younger age.

Heart and Arteries

▼ Coronary risk – mystery solved

A medical mystery may have been solved.

It's about the missing 50 per cent, and is typified by the story of the non-smoking jogger who dies of a heart attack and who didn't have high cholesterol. It was believed that the risk factors for coronary heart disease – cholesterol, blood pressure, smoking, family history and so on – only explained half of all heart disease. The conclusion, therefore, was that there were risk factors yet to be discovered.

A paper in the *Journal of the American Medical Association* has revealed the answer: there never was a mystery. The known coronary risk factors account for almost everyone who has developed angina or had a heart attack.

There are a few reasons for the confusion. The main one is that there's no such thing as normal when it comes to things like blood pressure and cholesterol. Most people who have a heart attack don't have dramatically high levels. They have a slightly raised cholesterol level, a little bit of blood pressure and so on, and together these factors amplify the total risk.

All this presents a dilemma for the government when it comes to rules for letting doctors prescribe drugs to reduce blood pressure and cholesterol. That's because politicians and bureaucrats, like the rest of us, think of ourselves as having low, normal or high levels of these factors.

But the growing conclusion of people who've analysed the data is that there's no simple rule which says here's the line, and anything higher than this is high.

Your level of risk is a package of things, ranging from your gender to your age, from your family history to whether or not you're obese, smoke or get any exercise.

And unlike your family history or whether or not you have diabetes, which can't be changed, you can reverse your blood fats or your hypertension and make a difference.

On the other side there are people with what might seem to be a high cholesterol level but who have no other risk factors and may need no treatment.

The difficulty is that government prescribing rules are still not flexible enough to cope with these complexities. The result is that money's being wasted on people who don't need medications, and those who do aren't necessarily receiving them.

An international study run from Australia called into question the level of blood pressure that doctors think is high and suggested that a more holistic approach is needed. The study was into people who'd already had either a full-blown stroke or a mini, short-lived stroke (called a transient ischaemic attack). Both situations put people at very high risk of a subsequent stroke.

The researchers gave their patients blood pressure medications whether or not they had high or normal blood pressure. The results showed a significant reduction in risk: for every 11 people treated, 1 person was saved from a stroke, and it didn't matter what level the blood pressure had been at the start.

What it seems to come down to is this. Doctors need to become less obsessed with the level of this or that risk factor for heart disease or stroke and instead build up a picture of each person's *total* risk from all factors.

It turns out that if the total risk of a serious event such as a heart attack or stroke is high, bringing down the cholesterol or blood pressure can make a difference – even if the levels don't seem high.

On the other side of the equation, if all you have is high cholesterol or blood pressure – and absolutely no other risk factors (not a common situation, you'd have to say) – treating that single problem may not be necessary. The implication is that in terms of bang for bucks, taxpayers' money can be targeted where it may count most.

So don't readily believe someone who tells you your blood pressure and cholesterol are normal. Ask: compared with what?[1]

▼ Exercise capacity and coronary risk

Your exercise capacity – the maximum amount of metabolic energy you're forced to produce in a treadmill test – predicts your chances of dying prematurely better than many other risk factors, including smoking. That's according to a study of 6000 men in their late 50s.

When people are pushed to the max on a treadmill exercise ECG test, it's possible to measure their exercise capacity in units called metabolic equivalents (METS). For people with heart disease, it's a fact that the lower your exercise capacity, the higher your chances of dying prematurely. But there's been confusion about its relevance in relatively healthy people, and some experts have been adjusting your capacity for your age, thinking that's a reasonable thing to do.

These middle-aged men were referred for exercise testing – presumably because they'd worried their doctors enough to send them in – and were followed for over 6 years. Just under half of them turned out to have no heart disease.

The results showed that heart disease or not, and heart *medications* or not, exercise capacity was the most predictive factor for death over 6 years. Next in line for normal men was smoking, and in men with heart disease, the severity of their cardiovascular history. While older men were – understandably – more likely to cark it than younger ones, adjusting the findings for age didn't actually make a lot of difference. It was your unadjusted or *absolute* exercise capacity that mattered most. For every single point increase in your METS, there was a 12 per cent survival advantage over 6 years. It also seems that if you change your METS, it can make a difference – other studies have suggested that training to increase your exercise capacity does help.

And women? It's likely to be the same, but they're not sure yet.[2]

▼ IF YOUR DOCTOR ASKS YOU IF YOU HAVE A HISTORY OF HEART DISEASE IN YOUR FAMILY, WHAT WOULD YOU SAY?

It's an important question, because a family history of heart disease is a strong predictor of your chances of getting it too – and realising that there is family tendency could motivate you to change your behaviour in a healthier direction.

But what does it take for you to think there is a family problem?

Having even one first-degree relative (a parent, sibling or child) with a heart problem is enough for you to be concerned, and if that person was under the age of 50 when they had angina, blood vessel disease, a heart attack or a stroke, the level of risk (to you) is possibly even higher.

A group of Scottish researchers surveyed a range of men and women from different backgrounds to see what it took to answer 'yes' to a doctor's inquiry about family history. The answer – perhaps not surprisingly – depended on whether they actually knew much about their close family's health. The more relatives someone had with heart disease, the more likely the person was to say 'yes'. Women were more likely than men to say they had a family history of heart disease. Men needed quite a few relatives with bad tickers before they would say their family had a heart problem history. Blue-collar men were the worst of all.

The study also found that even if there was a family history, some people didn't think it was relevant to them, because they thought they were different in some way, or lived a healthier life.

The moral of this story is don't delude yourself, and don't encourage delusion in your doctor. We're deluded enough already.[3]

▼ THE GOOD OIL

You've probably heard the cholesterol story lots of times by now. How there's the good form (HDL, or high-density lipoprotein cholesterol, which tends to take cholesterol away from the arteries) and the bad form (LDL, or low-density lipoprotein cholesterol, which deposits the stuff in your arterial walls).

Most of the attention has been on LDL – because that's easier to lower than HDL is to raise. The statin drugs lower LDL, as do low-fat diets, but the fact is that you get roughly the same preventive benefits whether you lower LDL or raise HDL, and if you can do both, you double your money.

For example, a study in New York has found that people with high HDL levels have reduced chances of having a stroke. The higher the levels the better and it can almost halve the risk in the over 75s.

The things that raise HDL are exercise, weight loss, vitamin B3 – niacin – and probably alcohol. Some people have believed that antioxidants do it as well.

To test the idea that a double whammy of lowering LDL and raising HDL is worth doing, US researchers did a 3 year trial with people who were at high risk of heart disease and had high LDL levels and low HDL levels. They were put in one of four groups and given one of the following: a statin drug in combination with niacin; a cocktail of antioxidants such as vitamin C, vitamin E and beta carotene; the statin, niacin and antioxidants; or a placebo.

The results showed that the combination of the statin and the niacin gave the most benefit. In fact there was evidence that arterial blockages opened up on this treatment. Antioxidants by themselves actually seemed to work against HDL, and when taken with the statin and niacin, reduced their benefits.

So if you have low HDL levels and high LDL levels, a combination of a statin plus niacin may be worth trying. The only problem is that niacin can cause flushing, which may take some getting used to. The research was, unfortunately, another nail in the coffin for antioxidant supplements when it comes to heart disease prevention, although according to research at Deakin University in Melbourne they may still be of coronary benefit if they are taken in whole foods such as red vegetables, especially if they are cooked in olive oil.[4]

▼ Homocysteine as a risk factor

Homocysteine is an amino acid which is now thought, like cholesterol, to be a risk factor for coronary heart disease. This discovery was first made in Australia about 30 years ago, but later confirmed by research in Framingham, Massachusetts, where the health of the townspeople has been followed for nearly 50 years.

No one's too sure why homocysteine has this effect on the arteries, but they do know that its levels are closely related to folate intake – folate or folic acid being one of the B vitamins. The higher your folate, the lower your homocysteine.

Anyway, as the Framingham population aged, researchers turned their attention to Alzheimer's disease and dementia, and in order to make the findings as reliable as possible, they started their 8 year study of over 1000 people while the people were healthy. The results suggested that the higher the level of homocysteine in their blood, the higher their chances of developing dementia and Alzheimer's disease.

And there was no cut-off: the more homocysteine you have, the greater your chances of Alzheimer's and dementia.

That's a long way from saying that lowering your homocysteine will make a difference; that will require a separate trial. But it is tantalising extra evidence that blood vessel disease and diet may be more important in Alzheimer's than people have thought.

Research at the University of New South Wales has provided some support for the connection between homocysteine and dementia. They've been following a group of healthy elderly people who were aged around 70 at the beginning of the study, doing all sorts of tests, including brain scans. Those with the highest levels of homocysteine in their blood were more likely to show brain atrophy – or brain shrinkage – on the scan; their brains had a similar appearance, in fact, to the brains of people with Alzheimer's disease.

It has to be stressed that these people had absolutely no signs of dementia, so the atrophy could just be a chance finding. On the other hand, the shrinkage may be the first indication that there's a problem brewing – only time will tell.[5]

▼ ... AND IN HEART FAILURE?

There have been suggestions that as well as being toxic to arteries, homocysteine may damage heart muscle directly.

One study was an 8 year follow-up of about 2500 men and women aged about 72 (at the start of the study) who'd never had a heart attack and had no heart failure when the research commenced.

Independent of any other factor – such as smoking or cholesterol levels – those with raised homocysteine levels had double the risk of heart failure.

Again, the question is, does taking folic acid to lower homocysteine levels work? Only more research will give us the answer to that one.[6]

▼ LOWERING HOMOCYSTEINE

A Swiss group has done this in a very high-risk group of people who already had such bad heart disease that they'd needed an angioplasty. That's where a balloon catheter is used to widen a narrowed coronary artery.

They were given either a placebo or a combination of folate and vitamins B6 and B12, which are also thought to lower homocysteine.

This was done for 6 months to see if it would prevent re-blockage and subsequent heart attacks.

At 6 months there was a benefit, and the findings at 1 year showed that those given the 6 months of vitamins had lower rates of re-stenosis, as it's called, of the original problem artery and a trend to fewer heart attacks as well.

The debate now is whether you need the whole cocktail of B vitamins; the role of B12 is dubious, and folate by itself might be just as beneficial.[7]

▼ THE HEART SCAN — NOT A MOTIVATOR

One of the many entrepreneurial medical businesses that has been set up in recent years has been CAT scanning to screen for heart disease. The idea is that heart scans will detect how much calcium there is in the coronary arteries, and because calcium can be a sign of disease, this information may provide a risk measure for a heart attack.

The worst that can happen, say some of the proponents, is that you'll be motivated to change your lifestyle.

There are lots of objections to CAT heart screening. The main one relates to the inaccuracies of the technology: there's a chance that you could be falsely reassured by a negative result or spooked into unnecessary tests and surgery if you come up positive.

A trial has looked at whether having a heart scan with more reliable technology than is generally used in Australia motivates people into a healthier lifestyle.

The results were that heart scans made no difference to whether or not people reduced their coronary risk factors. What did was being taken in hand and intensively managed by a nurse or dietician.

So save your heart scan money and spend it on a diet or exercise guru instead.[8]

▼ BLOOD PRESSURE — YOUR CHANCES

High blood pressure is a bigger public health problem than many people have imagined, if research from the US is right.

High blood pressure – also called hypertension – is when the measurement on the blood pressure machine is more than 140 over 90, assuming you have no other coronary risk factors. If you do, you'd qualify as having high blood pressure at a lower level.

Just in case you've ever wondered what these figures mean, they're the millimetres of mercury in the glass column when the doctor or nurse puffs up the cuff on your arm and then slowly releases the air. The top figure is when they first hear a pulse and the bottom figure is when it either disappears or sounds soft. The top figure is the pressure produced by the heart when it contracts and pushes blood out, and the bottom figure is like the background pressure in the arteries between beats.

The significance of 140 over 90 is that it's a line in the sand, the point where the evidence suggests that your risk of strokes and heart attacks become significant.

So what do you reckon your chances of developing high blood pressure are if you live to say the age of 85? One in 5? One in 4, maybe?

No. According to a 50 year study in Framingham, Massachusetts, your chances are 90 per cent: 9 out of 10 people will develop high blood pressure if they live into their 80s. But far fewer than that will be recognised and treated. There's reasonable evidence that even if you're quite elderly it's worth having your blood pressure reduced.

So the message is that just because you've lived long, you're not necessarily okay when it comes to blood pressure, and you need to keep an eye on things. Better still, if you lose some weight, get regular exercise and keep a lid on the alcohol, you might just prevent high blood pressure in the first place.[9]

▼ BLOOD PRESSURE: THE FIGURES

In 2003, the US released a detailed report on the latest advice on high blood pressure, with findings that may contradict what many doctors still believe and practise.

For example, in people over 50, the top figure of blood pressure (the systolic pressure) counts more than the lower one (the diastolic). Medical schools used to teach that the bottom figure was what mattered.

The key number here, as mentioned above, is 140 millimetres of mercury with systolic pressure.

A person's chances of heart disease actually double for every 20 millimetres of mercury rise in systolic pressure and 10 millimetres rise in the diastolic above a level of 115 over 75. If your blood pressure is even only a little above these levels you should consider yourself in the early stages of high blood pressure – so lose weight, stop smoking, reduce your alcohol intake and get more exercise.

And they repeated the really depressing statistic in the story above: if you're 55 and have normal blood pressure and do nothing about your lifestyle, the chances are 9 out of 10 that you'll develop high blood pressure if you live long enough.

A key message for doctors is that even with the best drugs in the world, it's the people who trust their doctor and are well motivated who will do best in keeping their blood pressure down.[10]

▼ Preventing high blood pressure

The US National High Blood Pressure Education Program has a statement for health professionals and the public about what they think the most reliable ways to prevent people developing high blood pressure are.

This committee has studied the evidence behind various measures and concluded that the following are worth doing:
- Keeping your weight normal (if you know how to do this please let me know);
- Reducing your salt intake to 6 grams a day;
- Limiting males' alcohol intake to 700 ml of beer or 300 ml of wine a day and to half that for women;
- Walking briskly for at least 30 minutes a day (but some say that should be nearer an hour);
- Keeping your potassium intake up over 3.5 grams per day; and
- Eating a diet with lots of fruit and veg, low-fat dairy and low saturated fat.

And, as they say, if that doesn't make you live longer, it'll certainly make you feel as if you are.[11]

▼ The DASH diet for high blood pressure

A trial has shown that what's called the DASH (Dietary Approaches to Stop Hypertension) diet is more effective than just increasing your fruit and vegetable intake at lowering blood pressure.

The essence of the DASH diet is that it contains the recommended proportions of protein, fat and carbohydrate, is low on red meat, high in minerals containing magnesium, potassium and calcium, and low in sodium. While the diet does push fruit and vegetables, it isn't especially low in calories, and doesn't need specialty foods.

Trials have also shown that even on the DASH diet, the more you reduce your sodium intake, the better it is for your blood pressure.[12]

▼ Salt reduction

High blood pressure isn't something you think about when you're young, but it has a habit of creeping up on you. For those of us who aren't traditional-living Papua New Guinea highlanders, blood pressure rises very significantly as we age. New Guinea highlanders' blood pressure goes up too, but not nearly as much.

It isn't because they have a stress-free lifestyle. You only need a passing knowledge of PNG to appreciate that conflict's almost a lifestyle in itself up there. Low levels of obesity are one explanation, but the evidence from around the world also consistently points to salt intake as a culprit.

The processed food industry doesn't like this message and nor do we, because most of us have a taste for sodium chloride.

But if you already have high blood pressure, does reducing salt intake make a difference?

One review of the scientific literature confirmed that if you're over 60, and on blood pressure treatment, reducing salt intake can lower your blood pressure and perhaps allow you to stop taking the medication. But this isn't an easy diet. It requires abandoning processed food and eating low-salt bread. Other measures, such as exercise and lower alcohol intake, are probably easier and may even be more effective.

Few if any of these studies have gone on for very long, and the sceptics wonder whether our bodies get used to the lower salt and our blood pressure creeps up again. Or perhaps we get sick of soups or breads that are barely edible and go back to our salty ways.

Another group of researchers analysed evidence from around the world and concluded that the jury is still out as to whether advising people to reduce salt saves lives or prevents heart attacks and strokes. After between 1 and 3 years, the effect of salt restriction on high blood pressure was fairly small, and that was with a pretty extreme salt-reducing diet.

The good news was that they confirmed the previous findings that a low-salt diet may allow people to stop taking their blood pressure medication.

Even so, if people do want us to reduce our salt intake they're going to have to come up with easier ways of doing it effectively. I mean if God had meant us to live in the PNG highlands, why did she invent soy sauce and French food?[13]

▼ IS IT POSSIBLE TO GIVE UP YOUR BLOOD PRESSURE PILLS? AND IF SO, HOW?

Almost 3 million Australians over the age of 25 are thought to have high blood pressure, and for those who can't get it down by exercising, losing weight and cutting back on salt, medication is needed. No one, however, likes the thought of medication for life, which is usually what you're told.

So can you ever get off the tablets?

According to work done in Melbourne, the answer is yes, but only for some.

They followed 500 elderly people, and found that over a third of those who were taken off their medication still had normal blood pressure a year later. The factors which predicted whether or not someone was a candidate for a trial off medication were: not having diabetes or heart disease, being under 75, having easy-to-control blood pressure, taking only one medication, and – inexplicably – having a fat tummy.

The downside of going off your medication, if you fall into this group, is that you have to change your lifestyle – particularly weight loss and salt restriction – and be monitored regularly.

The question then is whether the cure worse than the treatment.[14]

▼ Are expensive blood pressure tablets the best?

The market for blood pressure medications is huge, and there is enormous competition for the attention of doctors. Every pharmaceutical company, naturally, wants doctors to prescribe its own latest tablet. Over the years these medicines have become more and more sophisticated and, needless to say, more expensive.

The most intense commercial battle is over the person newly diagnosed with high blood pressure. That's because the first drug they're prescribed is likely to be the one they stay on for a long time. The aim of the medication, of course, is to prevent heart disease and stroke.

So which is the best so-called first-line therapy? Well, a careful review of the available evidence from long-term studies concluded that none of the newer medications was any better than one of the oldest and cheapest – a low-dose diuretic: a water tablet.

And low-dose diuretics were in fact more effective at lowering the risk of heart failure, heart attacks and stroke than the newer medications.

There are reasons for using the newer drugs – if you have diabetes or kidney failure, for example – but in otherwise healthy people it seems diuretics should be the opening shot if hearts and minds are what count.[15]

▼ If you're getting on a bit and have high blood pressure, is it worth having it treated?

Doctors have wondered about this too, and have raised fears that if you lower blood pressure in the elderly, you might precipitate other problems – such as stroke – because the blood pressure has dropped too far. But the answer seems to be an emphatic 'yes' – you should be treated, no matter what your age.

A study followed nearly 5000 otherwise healthy people aged over 60 who had what's called systolic hypertension – that's where just the top blood pressure figure was over 160. They were given either a placebo or antihypertensive medications.

The results, in those taking the medications, showed a significant reduction in the risk of heart attacks, strokes and heart failure, regardless of the person's basic level of risk at the start (from, say, their cholesterol level or smoking history).

And the higher the level of those risk factors, the greater the benefit, even though elderly people are more likely to experience side effects from the drugs.

Other studies have shown that if you change your diet, reduce your salt intake and lose weight (if possible), you can lower your dose of the blood pressure drugs and have the same benefit.

So don't give up. Try to live young as long as possible.[16]

▼ YOUR PERSONALITY AND YOUR HEART

Do your psychological characteristics increase your risk of coronary heart disease? The word 'hypertension' often makes people think of stress. In fact it's high blood pressure, but that doesn't mean psychological factors have nothing to do with it.

You've probably heard about the Type A personality and heart disease – the person, usually a bloke, who's aggressive, success oriented, a bit obsessive and certainly driven. A major pain.

Once it was thought that the Type A personality was the culprit ... the driven, aggressive, high-paced high achiever. But that theory has fallen apart over the last few years. There may, however, be aspects of Type A behaviour that matter.

A large study in the US has been investigating this in young to middle-aged people. They've followed about 5000 people since the mid 1980s, when they were aged between 18 and 30.

The main characteristics measured were time urgency/impatience, or TUI; achievement striving/competitiveness, or ASC; and hostility. I'm sure you know someone who has one or other of these – maybe it's you!

It turned out that after allowing for other risk factors, including anxiety and depression, the higher a person's scores on TUI and hostility, the more likely they were to develop hypertension over 15 years.

So take a chill pill and un-TUI yourself.

If only it were so easy.

And in a similar study in London, researchers followed about 1500 men for several years to see which psychological problems might be linked with a fatal heart attack when everything else was as equal as it could be.

They found increased risk in people with obsessionality or obsessional neuroses, and in those whose psychological state was expressed in bodily symptoms. The more severe the symptoms, the higher the coronary risk.

Serious anxiety, interestingly, didn't show up as a factor.

The increase in risk wasn't huge, but it's another reminder that we can't ignore the influence of our psyches on our wellbeing.[17]

▼ FORGET THE SKINNY CAP

I'd just like you to know that I've been vindicated – and maybe you have been too. A couple of years or so ago I got fed up drinking skimmed milk coffee: the taste was appalling and I reckoned life was too short not to enjoy the occasional flat white. So I reverted to full cream milk in my coffee, though with some trepidation. Now, thanks to a consoling piece of research, I think I can relax over that fully expressed espresso.

Nearly 6000 men in Scotland were followed from the early 1970s to see how their health fared against a number of variables – one of which was the amount of milk they drank (this was in the days before you needed a degree in chemistry to decide which carton of milk to buy).

They could find no evidence of raised coronary risk in men who drank a lot of milk – more than a third of a pint per day (remember pints? – a third of a pint is about 200 ml).

In fact, if anything, they had lower chances of stroke and heart attack. Milk drinkers were a healthier group in general at the start of the study, but even after controlling for that, there was no added risk.

When you look at the big picture, at all the studies where milk has featured as a factor, the view is mixed. Quite a few large studies have reckoned that milk intake is beneficial, particularly in stroke reduction. It may be due to the calcium in milk; it may just be a reflection of better childhood nutrition; it may be due to the fact that not all fats are bad for you. Who knows ... and maybe who cares, when someone hands you a coffee that actually tastes the way coffee should.

And before you ask – no, the study wasn't funded by the dairy industry.[18]

▼ Risks and benefits of aspirin

There's been a debate about whether daily aspirin is really as marvellous at preventing heart attacks as doctors say.

Aspirin makes platelets less sticky – platelets are tiny particles that are essential for blood clotting. So what's the argument? Well, it's a rather esoteric discussion about statistics and balancing the risks of bleeding and ulcers against the benefits.

A review of the available evidence clarifies things if you're thinking of going on low-dose aspirin.

If you've already had a stroke caused by a blood clot, a heart attack or angina, the story's clearer. Since the risks of another stroke or heart attack are so high, unless there are reasons not to use aspirin, the benefits of about 75 mg per day significantly outweigh the side effects (such as the risk of bleeding).

It's a different question altogether if you've never had heart disease. The evidence suggests that aspirin is only worth taking if you have a greater than 1 in 100 chance of having heart attack or angina in the coming year.

How on earth would you know that? Your GP should have charts which calculate that by bringing various risk factors together: your sex and age (blokes get heart disease about 10 years earlier than women), whether or not you smoke, your family history, your blood pressure, your cholesterol and so on.

Even modestly raised levels of individual factors can amount to a surprisingly high risk when they're added up.[19]

▼ What about lower-risk people and adding vitamin E?

A 4 year trial compared vitamin E and daily low-dose aspirin in 4500 people with one or more risk factors for heart disease but no history of actual heart disease. The researchers were looking for rates of heart attacks, strokes and deaths from arterial disease.

The findings were that taking aspirin did reduce the chances of death from heart disease and the total number of events such as heart attacks and strokes, but that vitamin E had no effect at all.

For 1 death to be prevented,166 people had to take aspirin daily; 53 people had to take it for 1 event to be avoided. A commentary on the study said that this firmed up the argument that people over 65 and people with coronary risk factors should be offered low-dose aspirin unless they had a reason not to take it. You should talk that over with your doctor.

As for vitamin E – it won't do you much good if it's your heart you're concerned about.[20]

▼ POLYPILL CONTROVERSY

According to a group of British experts in preventive medicine who've analysed the world scientific literature in heart disease and stroke prevention, if every healthy person over 55 took a pill containing six different medications, 1 in 3 would be saved from a heart attack or stroke and could expect a further 11 years of life.

The medications in this so-called polypill would be a statin to bring down cholesterol, three blood pressure drugs at half dose to minimise side effects, low-dose aspirin, and the B vitamin folic acid to reduce the risk factor mentioned earlier, homocysteine.

While aspirin does raise the chances of a brain haemorrhage, these risks are outweighed, say the authors, by the benefits, which include up to an 88 per cent reduction in the risk of a heart attack and a similar fall in stroke risk.

While it'd be nice to say that lifestyle changes would make the same difference, the proponents of the polypill claim that unless healthy living has been lifelong, you won't derive the same benefits as you would from the pill – which, by the way, at the time of writing doesn't exist yet. This is still in the realm of theory.

The authors and the *British Medical Journal*, which published the work, were slammed by critics. Many felt that it was wrong to put forward a medication solution for a lifestyle problem.[21]

▼ WOMEN AND HEART DISEASE

Many women are surprised to find that they're several times more likely to die of a heart attack or stroke than of breast cancer. They think they're protected, but what really happens is that women develop their heart disease about 10 years after men, and when they do, it's often worse.

It used to be thought that oestrogen gave females those extra years before the chest pain kicked in, but that theory's been knocked on the head. Hormone replacement therapy actually increases the risk of heart disease rather than decreasing it, and the role of a woman's own oestrogen before the menopause – her on-board oestrogen, if you like – is also being questioned.

Menopause doesn't actually make any difference to women's heart disease. The rates go up steadily with age, and there's no blip upwards when the on-board oestrogen blips down.

A study comparing Japanese and British women confirmed that and showed that women's heart disease rates keep going up while men's fall as they go into old age (probably because blokes who are going to cark it already have.)

The inescapable issues in women, just as in men, are smoking, cholesterol, exercise, diabetes and blood pressure.

Boring but important.[22]

▼ MISCARRIAGES AND HEART DISEASE

Women who miscarry early in pregnancy may be at slightly increased risk of heart disease later in life. That was the conclusion of an 18 year follow-up study of 130,000 women in Scotland.

Regardless of the mother's age, her level of wealth or poverty, and whether or not she's had other problems in pregnancy (such as high blood pressure), the independent risk from an early miscarriage stood up.

Women who'd had one or two miscarriages had just under 50 per cent increased risk of coronary heart disease later in life; if they'd had three or more miscarriages, the risk was more than doubled.

The tentative explanation is that there's evidence that some women who miscarry have an increased tendency to blood clots – it may be that there are problems in the small blood vessels that knit the embryo to the womb via the placenta, problems that could translate into heart disease later.

Even though those figures sound dramatic, the increased risk for an individual woman isn't high, but if these results are real – and they do need to be confirmed by others – it would mean that women who miscarry may need to pay a little more attention (than other women) to their coronary risk factors.[23]

▼ Teenagers and heart disease

Medicine does macabre pretty well, and one macabre avenue of research for many years has been using autopsies on young people who've died in car accidents, violent crime or wars to observe how atherosclerosis is occurring younger and younger.

A group in the US has reported on 3000 such post mortems on people aged from their teens to their mid 30s.

Obesity was a key factor in the acceleration of atherosclerosis – and even early blockage of coronary arteries – in teenage and young men, but not in young women. Fat young men were also more likely to smoke, have poor control of their blood sugar, high blood pressure and high cholesterol levels, but that only explained about 15 per cent of the story.

Obesity appeared to explain a lot of the rest. Just why isn't known, but it may have something to do with an increased tendency to blood clotting.

There are probably two reasons for this degree of atherosclerosis not showing up in young women. One is that they tend not to have fat on their abdomens, and the other is that, as mentioned above, women are about 10 years behind men when it comes to bunging up their arteries, so it may just not have been visible yet.[24]

▼ Don't eat and run

Don't eat and run, especially if you're elderly, because you might end up keeling over. That's the message from research at Columbia University in New York, where they're trying to prevent falls in the elderly – a common cause of disability and nursing home admission. The problem is called post-prandial hypotension.

It's already known that as we age, our blood pressure tends to drop more as we stand up. That's called orthostatic hypotension. What the Columbia researchers did was see whether adding a meal to standing up – which we all do several times a day – has a greater effect on our blood pressure.

They studied 50 elderly people, putting them on a mechanical tilt table and then turning it upright before and after they'd eaten something – all the time measuring their heart rate and blood pressure and watching for symptoms such as light-headedness.

Almost everyone experienced a fall in blood pressure on going to upright – without having a meal. The interesting thing was that this wasn't a sudden fall. It started soon after going to upright, and got progressively worse over about 45 minutes. Several people felt dizzy and faint.

When the researchers added a meal to the picture the blood pressure fall was even greater, and the number of people who felt they might faint actually doubled.

There are various messages from this. One is that when an elderly person stands up, there isn't necessarily a *sudden* drop in blood pressure. It falls over a period of time. Therefore prolonged standing – during a church ceremony, ANZAC day or waiting in a queue, for instance – isn't a very good idea even without eating.

When you add a meal to the equation, quite simply, a lot of extra care should be taken in the period afterwards.

The effect starts about 15 minutes after eating, peaks at about 45 minutes and has waned by around an hour and a half.

But according to the people involved in the study, it is possible to do something about it in certain individuals. Caffeinated coffee after a meal seems, in some, to reduce the drop in blood pressure. As does the wearing of elastic stockings.

▼ ANGINA TREATMENT: WHOSE MONEY IS IT ANYHOW?

When money's tight in health care, which it is all the time, it doesn't take long for the debate to get down to the expensive and so-called heroic treatments being offered to the elderly. Wouldn't they be best confined to the young, the critics ask?

There are two problems with that argument. One is that who's young and who's old depends on who's doing the talking. Have you noticed how, as the baby boomers age, the term 'middle-aged' seems to refer to older and older people?

Then there are the uncomfortable facts. Facts like 60 per cent of cardiac deaths occur in those over 75 – a traditionally under-researched section of the community. Facts like some of these so-called heroic treatments aren't heroic at all, and give older people a new lease of life and independence which they might otherwise not have had.

A good example is a trial in people over the age of 75 who had chronic angina: chest pain on exertion and sometimes even at rest. Some were given anti-angina drugs and others had their coronary arteries opened up either with a balloon catheter or with bypass surgery. Those who'd had the balloon or operation were more likely to have less severe symptoms and a better quality of life.

Not everyone qualifies to have their blockage relieved, but those who do, and those who are poorly controlled on medication, should be considered for more aggressive treatment.[25]

▼ EMERGENCY STENTS SAVE LIVES

If you're unlucky enough to have a heart attack, what's the best care for you in the first hour or two?

One important message is to get to a hospital fast. If you even imagine you might be having a heart attack, the place to be is an Emergency Department, and you shouldn't be shy about calling an ambulance. No one will sneer if you're wrong. There are no prizes for being stoical and dead.

Aspirin has been shown to help if taken as soon as possible. The question is, what next?

For people with specific, confirmed signs of a heart attack, standard care is to give a clot-busting drug as early as possible, but increasingly specialists have been taking people straight to theatre – threading a catheter through the blockage, opening it up with a balloon and usually inserting a stent – a metal brace to keep the artery open.

Is this better, though? An analysis of the available evidence suggests that the emergency catheter saves more lives, but there are certain provisos. The hospital should be used to doing them, it must happen within 2 hours of the attack, and the specialist must do a lot each year to maintain his or her skills. If the hospital can't tick all three of these boxes, they should probably stick to clot busting.

But what if they don't find anything and you're not someone they'd have expected to have heart problem? What if you have no risk factors?

Most centres in Australia, if they're happy with you will just send you home for follow-up by your GP. Some people argue for a more active approach. A study in Texas compared sending people with chest pain who were at low risk of heart disease for either an exercise treadmill test or a coronary angiogram – an X-ray of the coronary arteries – before discharge.

The angiogram diagnosed 1 in 5 people as having heart disease, the treadmill picked up 7 per cent and the rest had normal results. Fewer people who'd had the angio returned to hospital.

It's an expensive and risky way of providing reassurance and there's no evidence that finding the heart disease changed the way these people were treated. So for the time being, maybe good old Aussie common sense should prevail in the Emergency Department.[26]

▼ ... AND STENTS COMPARED WITH SURGERY?

Several studies have shown stents to be clearly superior to the balloon by itself. But how do they compare with coronary artery graft surgery, where if it's well done and the person looks after him or herself, you can expect it to last 15 years? And how does the stent compare when the person has a potentially life-threatening blockage?

This was studied in a reasonably large group of people who all had a tight narrowing of a critical artery in the heart – in fact the one which is most closely linked to a seriously greater risk of death. Stenting did quite well compared with surgery, which had more side effects in the early days after the procedure. Those who'd been grafted though, were less likely to have heart symptoms such as angina 6 months afterwards.

Some surgeons are arguing that surgery will make a comeback, especially 'beating heart' operations (see below).[27]

▼ Heart attack symptoms

As many as 1 in 5 people having a heart attack – a myocardial infarction – don't have the classical symptoms of crushing central chest pain that goes up into your neck and down your left arm.

Some can have an ache in their jaw, be short of breath, have symptoms which feel more like indigestion, or just have a sense of fatigue and discomfort in the upper body.

Such people tend to be women, older and have had a previous diagnosis of heart failure or diabetes.

Research has supported what many have believed for some time: that people with either no pain or very few of the traditional heart attack symptoms have a higher chance of dying within a year of the episode – even correcting for age, gender and underlying disease.

The reason is most likely to be access to prompt and effective treatment.

Even people with classical chest pain take too much time to seek help, and the delay is even greater and in those whose symptoms are less typical. Delay in getting these clot-busting drugs can mean greater muscle damage to the heart and greater risk all round.

There's also some evidence that the quality of care isn't as good for this group once they're in hospital.

So if you have any symptoms out of the blue that you've never had before, or which become a lot worse, head for help straight away. As mentioned above, good Emergency Departments would rather see people with nothing wrong if it means they also catch more of those in real strife.[28]

▼ Beating heart surgery

Coronary artery bypass grafts – CAGS are what the cognoscenti call them – are still among the most frequent blood vessel operations performed. The traditional way of doing the procedure is to connect you to a pump which puts oxygen into your blood and keeps your circulation going while the blocked artery's being replaced.

The trouble with the pump is that it can knock off bits of your brain. Usually the damage is minor and barely noticeable, if it's there at all, but some people can be quite markedly affected in their thinking, memory and even ability to move around.

That's why some heart surgeons have taken to operating without the pump – on a beating heart. They believe that while the operation is more difficult because it's on a moving target, the overall outcome is better.

This hasn't been tested much scientifically, but a randomised trial from the UK confirmed that off-pump CAGS are safer for your brain than on-pump ones.

So if you need new arteries, pump the surgeon for his or her pump policy, and if it's off-pump, check for shaking hands.[29]

▼ IF YOU'RE HAVING HEART SURGERY, YOU SHOULD 'FESS UP TO BEING ON ALTERNATIVE MEDICINES

That's the message from one of the world's leading cardiac surgical units. The unit at Columbia University in New York surveyed 300 people about to undergo surgery and found that about half of them were taking something which could have affected the outcome.

They didn't criticise the patients for not admitting to their complementary medicine consumption – they were more critical of doctors for creating a climate where people are frightened to confess to using alternatives.

The worry is that some preparations, such as Ginkgo biloba and even vitamin E, can interfere with surgery, causing bleeding and perhaps even affecting the ability of the heart to start after it has been on the bypass pump.

The doctor who conducted the study is actually pro-complementary therapy, and argues that people should feel free to tell their doctor what they're on.

The strongest advice is to doctors: they should not be so judgemental that their patients hide important information from them.

If you are on one of these preparations the news is good – all you have to do is go off them for a few days prior to surgery so they're out of your system.

▼ Which doctor for your heart?

Choosing your specialist is never an easy task, and usually you rely on your GP to get it right. But what criteria should you use – especially when the situation is critical?

One which doctors hate using and often find excuses to avoid is how much regular experience that specialist is getting with that condition. Heart surgeons who don't do many heart operations are on average not as good as surgeons who do lots every week. And cardiologists who don't do many catheter procedures each week are also likely to be ones you may not want to visit if a catheter is what you need.

And another condition can be added to the list: the heart attack. And it's to the credit of heart surgeons and physicians that they've probably exposed their own practices to more scrutiny than any other field of medicine.

A Canadian study has found that you're more likely to survive the first 30 days – and indeed the first year – after a heart attack if you end up with a doctor who regularly sees a lot of people with heart attacks. The doctors whose patients did best were those seeing more than 24 people with a coronary per year.

How would you know, when you're sweating with chest pain? It's not easy, but if a major hospital is not far away you should probably ask the ambulance to head there rather than to the local hospital which is earmarked for closure.[30]

▼ Brain attacks

People don't usually realise that strokes and heart attacks are often the result of the same disease – damaged arteries – and that both deserve emergency attention in the shortest possible time.

People don't feel the same degree of urgency when someone's having a stroke compared to a heart attack. In the latter case, the evidence is that the faster you get to an Emergency Department, the better you're going to fare (see previous article). The same thing is true of stroke. It's really important to recognise the signs so you can call for help straight away. They include the sudden onset of weakness or numbness in one side of the face, the arm or the leg, and/or trouble speaking or understanding speech.

With symptoms like that, don't wait to see what happens – ring for an ambulance. The problem is usually a diseased artery in the neck, which sends off clots up into the brain, which then block tiny but vital arteries up there.

You're at high risk of a stroke if you've had one already, you have heart disease, are a smoker, have high blood pressure or have a family history of stroke.

Prevention works for strokes – lower your cholesterol level and blood pressure, and have proper treatment after a heart attack.

▼ Stroke recovery

Can recovery from strokes and brain damage be improved by getting the brain to improve its act as a car parking attendant?

Fascinating work from Columbia University in New York has found that people who've been born with abnormal collections of blood vessels in their brains have managed to reorganise their brain function – sometimes over to the opposite side from where it normally is!

These lumps of arteries and veins are called arteriovenous malformations. They grow steadily, and tend to only show themselves when someone's in their 30s or so, and has a bleed or is showing signs of high blood pressure.

So the brain has had years to learn to cope.

What about after strokes, though, which are usually sudden events? Is the brain plastic enough to redistribute function when the timeline is hours and days? Well, the answer seems to be yes. In fact, what sometimes occurs is that the brain can take a function like speech and move it somewhere else for a while till the original area heals, then move it back. Researchers know this from scans, and occasionally from the tragic circumstance when the new area also suffers a stroke and the function is lost a second time.

The researchers have also found that Valium-like drugs – the benzodiazepines – can temporarily bring back the disability of a stroke after the person has recovered. This sounds like bad news, but it's actually given the researchers a clue about what might be happening in the brain and the idea that there might be a chemical messenger which speeds the redistribution rather than hampers it.

Another idea is that giving speech therapy and other kinds of assistance as soon as possible after a stroke might encourage the brain to sort itself out more quickly and effectively.

▼ ANTIOXIDANTS AND YOUR HEART

They're flogged as the answer to the Faustian bargain we do with biology in order to survive. The deal with the Devil is that oxygen is an essential part of life but we have to pay mightily for its munificence. Oxygen's byproducts – so-called free radicals, which are highly damaging forms of oxygen – make tissues do the biological equivalent of rust.

So it's obvious, isn't it, that antioxidant vitamins such as C and E would help to prevent this oxidation damage occurring? Well, no. The writing's been on the wall for some time that the news there isn't so good.

A 5 year trial of supplements of beta carotene and vitamins C and E in 20,500 adults aged over 40 who were at high risk of heart disease, showed no benefits in terms of death rates, coronary heart disease, dementia, asthma or even cancer.

In addition, researchers at the prestigious Cleveland Clinic in Ohio have analysed the scientific literature worldwide, looking for benefits from swallowing antioxidants to prevent heart disease – specifically vitamin E and beta carotene.

They were able to analyse data from over 80,000 people taking vitamin E and nearly 140,000 trialled on beta carotene, looking at death rates from heart disease and stroke.

The results showed no benefit from vitamin E and a small but statistically significant *increased* risk in those who took beta carotene.

Another study looked in close detail at vitamin E's supposed antioxidant activity, especially on something called lipid peroxidation, which is essentially rusting in fats. This is one of the essential steps in the development of atherosclerosis.

They tested for lipid peroxidation in three ways, to see whether or not vitamin E made a difference when given in increasing doses. The findings were that even at very high doses, fat oxidation was not reduced.

The good news is that they didn't find, as some have, that vitamin E can actually increase oxidation. However, their research does question whether or not vitamin E supplementation is of any benefit at all.

This suggests that researchers may need to go back to the drawing board over just how cholesterol does its damage and what substances may interfere with that process. With beta carotene the reason for the potential harm is unclear. It may affect blood fats in a bad way – in any event, it's probably best avoided.

It doesn't mean that the free radical story is wrong. It's more likely that the experts have yet to find the right antioxidants.[31]

▼ METALS AND YOUR ARTERIES

There's a theory around that a variety of metals are involved in atherosclerosis, the pathological process that leads to heart disease and stroke.

Some people take this idea further and say that if you leach out these metals – lead, copper, magnesium, zinc, iron and especially calcium – you could halt or reverse heart disease. Leaching out metals is called chelation, and there's an industry out there giving intravenous infusions of EDTA, which is supposed to bind the metals and eliminate them.

In chelation treatment, the so-called good metals are often returned as supplements.

Chelation therapy is expensive though, and while there is a little evidence to suggest that it doesn't have major side effects, the question is whether or not it's worth the time and money. An even bigger issue when you have a potentially life-threatening condition is should you abandon regular and proven therapies for chelation?

The balance of evidence from trials to date has not shown benefit, and one study tried to fix up deficiencies in previous research.

The people in this trial definitely had heart disease – proven on X-ray – or had already had a heart attack or angina. Then both the chelation and the placebo groups were tested repeatedly for their exercise tolerance and the time they took to develop signs of reduced blood going to the heart.

They were all also put on the best medical treatments available. The results showed that everyone improved, but the chelation made no extra difference.

So if you're offered chelation, it's probably best to save your money.[32]

▼ Guggul – myrrh tree resin

When the Three Wise Men turned up in Bethlehem with their pressies for the new baby, myrrh was on the list. Now it's hard to know what was on their minds, because myrrh in those days was both an ingredient of incense and a medicine with various uses.

Heart attacks would have been almost unknown in those days – people didn't live terribly long, and even if they had, the Mediterranean diet and endless walking would have kept their arteries pretty clean. The Romans were a much more realistic risk to wellbeing.

But myrrh's been making a comeback as a cholesterol-lowering agent – or at least as a herbal drug made from one specific myrrh tree resin. The extract is called guggul, and some say it contains substances which could be good for cholesterol levels.

Lots of people are swallowing guggul with this in mind, but there haven't been good studies to back it up.

A randomised trial has suggested that the Three Wise men should have stuck to incense. It showed that guggul raised the bad form of cholesterol by up to 10 per cent and that about 1 in 10 people developed a skin rash from it.

So you'd probably do better on loaves and fishes.[33]

▼ Q10 and heart disease

A natural food supplement which is popular for heart disorders is coenzyme Q10. Some studies have shown that it may protect the heart during cardiac surgery or when someone's at imminent risk of a heart attack.

The reason is thought to be its antioxidant action, but the results of past trials have been controversial – part of the reason being that different preparations of coenzyme Q10 have been used and it's not known whether they're equally effective.

A group in Melbourne compared the levels of coenzyme Q10 in a small group of people given either a preparation in soybean oil or one which comes by itself in an emulsion. Both achieved the same level of enzyme after a week of use and reached what are thought to be therapeutic levels.

Neither had any effect at all on cholesterol levels, which means there's a need for better trials of this substance to see whether or not it really confers the benefits on the heart that people say it does.[34]

▼ Clayton's heart failure?

Heart failure affects tens of thousands of people each year – but you may be surprised to hear that up to 50 per cent of those who have all the symptoms of heart failure don't actually have a heart that's failing. It's a mysterious condition, and the experts aren't too certain what's going on or how to treat it most effectively.

The symptoms of heart failure include breathlessness on exertion or even at rest, swollen ankles, a swollen abdomen and fatigue, and these are usually blamed on a heart that's not pumping blood around the body as forcefully as it used to.

But in many people, the heart's pumping action doesn't seem to be much affected. For want of a better name, cardiologists call it *diastolic* heart failure as opposed to *systolic* heart failure, which is true pump failure.

Systole is when the heart contracts and pushes blood out – the pulse, if you like – and diastole is when the heart relaxes and fills with blood ready for the next heartbeat.

What seems to be happening is that the heart doesn't fill with blood properly so it doesn't have enough to pump out. This could be due to stiff veins taking the blood back to the heart or a stiff heart. The main risk factor for diastolic heart failure is high blood pressure.

The condition's hard to diagnose correctly and the best treatment is not known.

More work is needed on this common but neglected problem.[35]

▼ THE ANEURYSM TIME BOMB

One of the many things you don't want when you're older is an aortic aneurysm.

That's where the main artery from your heart is weakened as it goes through the abdomen, and as a result, it balloons out. The balloon is the aneurysm, and once it reaches over 5 cm in diameter, the chances of it popping catastrophically are quite high.

There are fewer bigger surgical emergencies, but the tragedy is that the pain is often confused with something else. That's one reason why three-quarters of people with a leaking aneurysm die before ever getting to hospital, half of the rest never get to theatre and of those who do, 40 per cent will die. Statistics don't come much worse than that – especially when the risks are very small of having an aneurysm repaired *before* it leaks.

A couple of studies from the UK have found that it's cost effective to screen men (they're more at risk than women) at the age of 65 using a simple, painless ultrasound of the abdomen. If an aneurysm's found it can be monitored and repaired if it's becoming too large.[36]

▼ STEMMING HEART DISEASE

With all this debate about stem cells, it's easy to forget that this therapy's been around for many years and saved a lot of lives.

I'm talking about bone marrow transplantation, which provides stem cells for blood but also contains cells that can become the lining tissue for blood vessels and may be able to induce new arteries to develop and grow.

This is exactly what a Japanese group of researchers have tried with people who had a shortage of blood to their legs – a common complication of smoking and arterial disease. Into one leg they injected the person's own bone marrow and into the other they placed placebo white blood cells.

The legs with the bone marrow were more likely to have an improved blood supply and the people experienced fewer symptoms (such as pain in the calf when walking). Some foot ulcers healed and feet went from blue to pink. And about half the people showed new artery growth on X-ray. A significant number of amputations may have been either delayed or prevented, and the effects seemed to last at least 6 months, with few serious complications.

This was a preliminary study, so the true safety and effectiveness of the procedure isn't known for sure, but it's a potentially cheap and effective way to get people back on their feet who might otherwise not have any to stand on.[37]

INFECTIONS

▼ Coughs, colds and more serious infections

Wouldn't it be great if they found a cure for the common cold?

How often have you heard someone say that? Medical researchers keep trying, because antibiotics certainly don't work. The common cold, by the way, involves a combination of the following: fever, cough, runny nose, sore throat and headache. It is often confused with the flu.

One theory being explored is that the common cold viruses spread so easily through the nose, ears and throat because of the inflammation the infection causes. So what would happen if you tried to interrupt the virus by preventing the inflammation?

A group in Wales tried to do this with a common asthma and hayfever preventer used in children, called cromoglycate. In asthma it's called Intal, and in hayfever, Rynacrom. The trial studied nearly 300 5-year-olds with upper respiratory infections. They were given either cromoglycate sprays up their schnozzes or just straight saline, to see if the real stuff works.

Unfortunately, it didn't. So it's back to lots of fluids and paracetamol if really needed.

Wouldn't it be great if someone found the cure for the common cold?[1]

▼ 'I feel a cold coming on ... must get hold of some vitamin C'

How often have you heard that? How often have you said it yourself?

Linus Pauling, who won a Nobel Prize for nothing to do with vitamin C, championed it for all sorts of ills, from the cold to cancer. Unfortunately, it has no beneficial effect on cancer; there is even some evidence that vitamin C may be a cancer promoter in some circumstances.

When it comes to the common cold there have been several trials. When combined, these trials show that vitamin C doesn't reduce the occurrence of colds in the first place, but people taking a gram of vitamin C a day might reduce the duration of symptoms by about 10 or 11 hours.

Those findings were generally for people who took vitamin C on a regular basis, though. What about those who decide to load up on it at the first signs of a sniffly nose?

A trial conducted in Canberra tested this on 400 healthy volunteers who took either 1 gram a day for 3 days at the start of a cold, 3 grams a day or a placebo.

The results showed no reduction in either length of illness or severity of symptoms. In fact the placebo group tended to get a better deal with their colds than the groups on vitamin C.

It's a shame, because it'd be nice to have such a simple option available. So it's back to the paracetamol and the paper hankies.[2]

▼ ZINC MIGHT BE A DIFFERENT STORY

One of the latest fads in treating the common cold is the zinc lozenge. The theory is that since zinc has anti-viral properties, it should be able to knock off the common cold bug – the rhinovirus.

The first scientific reports of benefits from zinc go back to 1984, and since then there have been various trials to see whether or not it works. One involved 50 volunteers aged about 37. They entered the trial within a day of developing a cough, headache, runny nose, sore throat and the other symptoms we've learned to know and love as part of a cold.

Participants took zinc lozenges or a placebo every 2–3 hours.

The zinc group had 3 fewer days with a cough, about 1 day fewer with a runny nose and generally had a less severe attack than those on the placebo.

A commentary on the trial warned that the study was small, and that when you look at large numbers the benefits may be more modest.

It's actually quite hard to do a properly controlled trial of zinc lozenges. That's because the taste is hard to hide, so people tend to know whether they're on a placebo or the real thing. The critics say when it comes to the bottom line, the differences are really quite small, with 3 cold symptoms being rated as mild in people taking zinc and moderate by those not on the zinc.

Anyway – it's your mouth and your cold – so you choose. Me, I'll stick with my honey tea. It tastes better.[3]

▼ Cough medicines – save your money

Over-the-counter cough and cold medicines are huge business – you just have to look at the space pharmacists give to them on their shelves. But do they work?

Two researchers in Britain reviewed the evidence on whether or not an adult with an acute cough due to an upper respiratory infection is helped by an over-the-counter cough medicine. They analysed results from over 2000 people and found that preparations containing antihistamines were no better than taking a placebo, and combinations involving so called anti-cough medications, decongestants or substances that are supposed to help you hawk up more phlegm showed little if any benefit.

There weren't many risks from the medications; they were generally quite safe. They just didn't seem to work.

Researchers haven't given up on this, though, and more recently have surveyed the world literature to see whether or not antihistamines help if you have the common cold.

The review showed no significant benefit; sometimes, with older antihistamines, the sedative effects made things worse.

Interestingly, another recent study has found that more sociable people were less susceptible to infection with the common cold – even when they were deliberately infected with a cold virus – suggesting that sociability was toughening their immunity.

If you have a cough that is associated with a very high fever and rapid breathing, that could be a sign of pneumonia, and you need to see your GP.

But the message for a common or garden cough and cold is that on the current evidence you'd do just as well taking a cup of tea with honey and a couple of paracetamol – that's the Swan remedy, free of charge. It allows you to save your money for more useful things, like funding your teenage children's social lives.[4]

▼ Radical treatment for strep throat

Could streptococcal infection – the germ that causes the strep throat – be controlled by a harmless enzyme? That's the suggestion from US research. The road to the discovery started with the germ that sickens the germ which makes *us* sick.

If you think we have problems with germs, you might be comforted to know that all bacteria which cause disease have viruses which infect them. They're called bacteriophages, and the idea of using them to treat infection isn't new.

The Russians pioneered phage therapy early in the 20th century – in the pre-antibiotic era. They even have phage institutes and hospitals, but phage therapy doesn't work well, partly because bacteria develop resistance to the phages.

The US research got round this by using the enzyme the virus produces to burst its way out of the streptococcus.

They've found that this enzyme prevents infection when sprayed into the mouths of mice, and can eliminate streptococci from saliva in a matter of seconds – penicillin takes minutes. There's also no resistance so far, and no side effects.

If the technique pans out, the medication would be used to prevent spread in childcare centres and families where there's been strep infection – and, interestingly, on the battlefield, to block the effects of biological warfare.

Sounds as if these army planners know exactly what a threat toddlers can be.

▼ And the same idea with anthrax

With the hysteria over anthrax following September 11, there has been an injection of money and effort in the US to come up with ways of fighting biological terrorism and warfare.

The same researchers working on phage therapy for streptococcal infection have turned their attention to anthrax, and they have preliminary evidence that phage attack could work. They've managed to produce a phage which produces a toxin that detects anthrax bacteria and then kills them.

It could form the basis of both a quick diagnostic test and a treatment that's cheap and easy to manufacture.[5]

▼ Probiotics – a useless fad? Maybe not

Probiotic – living – milk drinks have become very popular in the last few years. If you believe the hype, you too can turn into a 120-year-old mountain dwelling Slav living off fresh goat's milk yoghurt teeming with healthy bacteria.

The most common ones on the market are probiotic milk drinks containing a micro-organism called lactobacillus. There's quite good evidence that they shorten the course of antibiotic-induced and viral diarrhoea and tickle up the immune system. They are thought to work by colonising the bowel with the good bacteria and metabolising food and toxins more effectively.

Researchers in Finland decided to test probiotic milk on a group of children at high risk of infection – those in day care centres, who have an up to 3 times greater chance of developing an upper respiratory or gastrointestinal infection than children at home do.

One group of 1–6-year-olds was given about 200 ml of ordinary milk per day and the other group was given probiotic milk. Those who'd been drinking probiotics had about half a day less absent with illness over the winter months, fewer antibiotics for sore throats and colds, and probably fewer respiratory infections over all.

In other words, the milk seemed to work modestly.

One problem is that not all lactobacilli do the job, and probiotics seem to vary in what they contain. Apparently lactobacillus GG is the one to go for.

So I look forward to your postcard from your new life among the yak herds.[6]

▼ Flu vaccine – worth having?

It certainly seems so in people aged 65 and over. A US study of two groups of about 140,000 people were followed to see what happened to them. Between 50 per cent and 60 per cent were vaccinated. They tended to be those who were sicker to start with, although unvaccinated people were more likely to have dementia or a history of stroke. This, by the way, was what they call an observational study, where researchers observed people's real-world behaviour rather than putting them in a trial.

People who were vaccinated were significantly less likely to be hospitalised for heart disease, stroke, pneumonia or the flu, and in fact had up to a 50 per cent lower risk of dying from all causes. The effects of flu vaccine were the same regardless of the person's age (remembering they were all 65 or over) or how sick they were to start with. The effects, however, were only for the winter months. Flu vaccine didn't have an influence during summer.

So if you're over 65 and your GP's run out of flu vaccine, make sure you're in the queue when it's back in stock, before winter takes hold.[7]

▼ TREATING RUNNY NOSES

Children and runny noses almost go together, don't they?

For some kids the runny nose just won't go away, and it can be pretty frustrating for parents and doctors – not to mention for the child. And for Aboriginal communities it's a real issue.

In some cases it's an allergy in the same family as asthma. In very young children, a nasty-smelling nasal discharge can be from something stuck in the nose. Mostly the cause is unknown, which in turn means there are arguments about the best treatment.

Some people reckon saline drops work; the evidence is that they don't. And there's a debate about antibiotics, because sometimes it's possible to grow unpleasant bacteria from the snot.

A review of the available evidence has found that in children who've had a nasal discharge for 10 days or more, antibiotics of the kind normally used by GPs, if given for at least 10 days, are significantly better than a placebo or saline drops or decongestants. However, 9 children have to be treated for 1 child to benefit.[8]

▼ ANTIBIOTICS FOR SINUSITIS?

Quite a lot of people are afflicted with sinusitis: pain and congestion in the sinuses – the spaces inside the bones of the face. Spring is often when the problem flares up.

Despite there being little evidence that antibiotics help sinusitis any more than just having a steam inhalation, a couple of paracetamol and a decongestant or steroid spray, it's a condition for which GPs often write out an antibiotic script.

Because GPs are increasingly worried about antibiotic resistance, they're writing prescriptions for newer, fancier and more expensive germ killers. Not good for the pharmaceutical bill and not good for the spread of resistance – but okay if they fix up the sinusitis better.

Researchers in the US have followed the records of nearly 30,000 people with acute sinusitis to see whether or not the newer antibiotics are any better than the older, so-called first-line medications such as amoxicillin (Amoxil's one of the trade names) and trimethoprim-sulphamethoxazole (trade names Bactrim and Septrin).

Most people – 9 out of 10 – got better no matter what they were on, and there were no differences in complications, but the cost of treatment was almost double in the group who received the fancier antibiotics.

So if you're convinced by your doctor to have an antibiotic in the first place, ask for the cheapie and save the expensive ones for when you might really need them.[9]

▼ Reducing antibiotic use

Doctors look as though they're doling out fewer antibiotics for coughs and colds.

This is good news for taxpayers because of the money saved, and good news for the people with the coughs and colds because it means they're less likely to develop resistant bacteria and spread them round the community

All colds are caused by viruses, and viruses are not affected by antibiotics; 85 per cent of sore throats are viral too. So in most cases, taking some paracetamol, drinking a lot and waiting for a day or two is the healthiest advice.

There's still evidence, though, that many GPs are overprescribing antibiotics for upper respiratory infections, and that when they do, they frequently use the wrong drugs. Instead of giving basic medications such as penicillin or amoxicillicin – that's Amoxil – they use more advanced drugs, which should be kept in reserve for when they're really needed.

GPs often say that their patients expect antibiotics, and it's true that many people wrongly believe them to be effective.

But *not* prescribing means doctors have to spend more time with their patients, which many doctors are loath to do – they need to build trust, set the right expectations, tell people how to look after themselves and give a realistic view about how long symptoms can last.

It's common for a cough and runny nose to last for 2 weeks; symptoms lasting for that length of time still doesn't mean that antibiotics are needed.[10]

▼ OTHER PEOPLE'S AIR-LINE

Airlines like to boast about how new their planes are, but there is a downside to flying in a modern jet: you have to breathe someone else's air.

About half of the atmosphere in the cabin has passed through someone else's lungs and mouth – those un-worthies up in first class, for instance. You've no idea where they've been.

The aircraft manufacturers save fuel (and therefore both money and weight, which is another form of money in an aircraft) by recirculating air and passing it through filters before sending the gas back for a trip around another passenger's body, but the filters aren't necessarily reliable at stopping viruses.

So what's the chance you'll catch a cold from this recycled air?

Well, according to a recent study, the risk is no greater than it was in old-fashioned planes which contained fresh air. The researchers followed up over 1000 passengers on the same route, half of whom got fresh air to breathe, and half of whom got recirculated stuff.

The results suggested that there was no increased risk of upper respiratory symptoms with recycled air, at least on a flight of less than 2 hours.

What I haven't been able to confirm is whether or not it's true that first class gets a better class of air than you and me in the back. Mind you, they probably need it more.[11]

▼ New viruses – where on earth?

Whenever a new disease – AIDS or SARS, for example – emerges, people scratch their heads and wonder how on earth something like that could happen.

New human diseases rarely emerge without us humans having contributed, often by changing our behaviour or the things we do to the environment.

For instance, there's a family of viruses called the hantaviruses, named after a river in Korea. They've been around for millennia, but it took the Korean War, the influx of thousands of troops with tanks churning up the soil and disturbing the mice which carried the germ, to set in motion a devastating haemorrhagic fever that ran riot through the ground forces, killing several thousand.

As one historian said, whenever we humans change the way we live, new diseases emerge; that is true for the origins of smallpox, measles, heart disease, lung cancer, new forms of food poisoning and even the plague – the Black Death. By gathering in cities, by changing agricultural practices, by smoking weeds, by travelling fast in aeroplanes and by having wars, we create the circumstances for an innovative germ or toxin to do us in.[12]

▼ New respiratory virus

Just when you thought it might be safe to go out again, scientists in The Netherlands found a new lung virus in children a couple of years ago. When they discovered what it was and how to look for it, they realised that the virus has been around for the last 50 years, and has in fact infected almost every child in Holland under the age of 5.

Dubbed the human metapneumovirus, it's probably been around in Australia too. Queensland has the dubious honour of being the second place in the world to find the germ.

It comes from the same family as the Hendra virus – the one which killed horses and the horse trainer Vic Rail in Queensland a few years ago. It's probably not all that new; it's just that they now know how to look for it.

The disease the newly discovered virus causes is similar to a condition called bronchiolitis – a wheezy illness in babies and toddlers.

It's associated with anything from a mild respiratory infection to nasty cases of wheezing and pneumonia that mean the child has to go into hospital – sometimes even needing artificial ventilation. It seems that about 1 in 20 children with bronchiolitis may actually have the metapneumovirus.

There's not much evidence that it's associated with a more severe illness, but the chest X-rays of patients can show signs of pneumonia and there are suggestions that the bug could produce longer-lasting effects on the lungs.

After discovering the virus, the Dutch researchers tested 2000 children with winter respiratory infections which were negative for the usual culprits and concluded that maybe 1 in 10 cases of unexplained respiratory infections in children could be due to this bug – and being a virus, it isn't knocked off by antibiotics.

Where did it come from, you may ask, and when? Comparing the human metapneumovirus with other known viruses, the best guess is that it actually originated in birds and made the jump to humans (perhaps flight would be a better word) over 50 years ago. The reason they give that timeframe is they've tested blood stored from the 1950s and found antibodies to it even then.

Now the challenge is to see whether they can develop a vaccine so that this lung virus can be given the bird.[13]

▼ NEW AIDS ORIGINS?

A fascinating and disturbing theory about the origins of the Human Immunodeficiency Virus (HIV), AIDs and even the spread of hepatitis C puts the blame on modern medicine.

The culprit, according to this theory, is the enormous popularity of the injection in medical treatment and immunisation after World War II. Annual global production of hypodermic needles and syringes in 1900 has been estimated at around 100,000, with each one costing about $50 in today's prices. The demand wasn't there, because there weren't many treatments which required injections.

The invention of penicillin and a wider range of immunisations created an injecting boom, and by 1960, world production had reached a billion syringes per year and the price had come down to a few cents.

In developing countries, though, even a few cents was too much, and repeated use of non-sterile injecting equipment was common. This is what has been blamed for the rapid and devastating spread of hepatitis C in countries such as Egypt.

The theory with AIDS is that as hitherto remote communities in Africa opened up, people who'd been bitten by monkeys and infected with the ancestor of HIV could have passed on the virus rapidly and repeatedly to many others as they received their doses of antibiotics. It's known that this kind of rapid exchange can induce equally fast changes in viruses as they adapt to new immune systems.

The graph of use of injections and the graph of the growth of HIV show remarkable overlap; this still doesn't give us a cause-and-effect relationship, but it is interesting.

It's another reminder of how potent medical practices can be, and how, when introducing new technologies, doctors need to careful about ill going with good.[14]

▼ AIDS NO LONGER A DEATH SENTENCE

Some good news about HIV AIDS for a change.

Several years ago, a new form of treatment called HAART – highly active antiretroviral therapy – was introduced. In this treatment, several drugs were used in combination earlier in the course of infection than had previously been the case. The idea was – and is – to knock the virus on the head and keep it down.

People were being treated before they'd developed the signs of AIDS, and after HAART was introduced the death rate fell dramatically, as did the incidence of AIDS progression among HIV-infected individuals.

The problems in the years since have been side effects, HIV becoming drug resistant and stories of treatment failure. The question is whether those issues have really reversed the early gains.

Using information from a long-term Europe-wide study (it also involved Israel and Argentina), researchers have found that death rates and HIV progression have stayed low despite some bad press for

HAART. The reasons include new drugs becoming available and treatment of HIV complications becoming more sophisticated.

HIV AIDS has truly turned into more of a chronic illness than an early death sentence.[15]

▼ AIDS IN SOUTH AFRICA – A PREVENTABLE TRAGEDY

The best estimates yet of the impact of AIDS on South Africa come from the South African Medical Research Council. The figures are appalling, and defy biology.

Normal biology is that when you get old you die. In South Africa 10 years ago that was true, especially in women. A decade later, in South Africa it's when you get young that you die.

The death rate for South African women in their late 20s is 3.5 times what it was in 1985, and 40 per cent of all deaths in the 15–49-year-old age group are AIDS related.

It is thought that 1 in 5 adults are infected; there may be more people living with HIV in South Africa than in any other country in the world. Blood screening of pregnant women has found that the HIV positive rate has gone from 1 in 100 women in 1990 to 1 in 4 in 2001.

The figures from Durban cemeteries tell the story in a microcosm. In 1996 just over 5000 people were buried or cremated in Durban. Just 3 years later, it was over 13,000.

The nation's government was, until recently, in denial. The President, Mr Mbeki, doesn't believe that HIV causes AIDS, and little has been done about the epidemic on a national scale. So what happens next is utterly predictable.

By 2010 – 6 years from now – the death rate in the under 5s will have doubled. The chances of a 15-year-old dying before the age of 60 will be 80 per cent, the cumulative number of AIDS deaths will have reached 6 million, and 1 million people will be sick, living with HIV. Half of the country's 30–44-year-olds will be carrying the virus and life expectancy will have fallen by 16 years, to around 40.

The Medical Research Council's report makes it clear that lots can be done about it now. The question is whether South African politicians will own the problem.[16]

▼ And the rest of Africa?

A leading health demographer, Professor Jack Caldwell of the Australian National University, claims that the results of 13 years' work in Africa explain why that continent has been so terribly affected by HIV AIDS.

In some countries in sub-Saharan Africa, up to 1 in 3 people are infected, with more women than men being HIV positive: women are infected with HIV about 3 times more easily than men. There are several reasons for this pandemic, says Jack Caldwell.

Traditionally, women in Africa have had more freedom to have sex outside marriage. This has been because men marry late and have several wives, which means a long wait if you're male and young so men used to get through by having sex with female members of their extended family.

Once missionaries arrived, Christianity forbade this custom, and sex before marriage became commercial — men used prostitutes far more. Add to this limits on sex education, no condoms for adolescents, the world's lowest use of condoms in any case, and sexually transmissible diseases which cause ulceration.

But even this isn't enough, claims Professor Caldwell. He argues that it is inescapable fact that the countries – and in fact regions within countries – with the highest rates of infection are where men *do not* circumcise.

No one knows why this should be so, but it seems that if such an important factor were anything other than circumcision it would have been accepted long ago because of the preponderance of evidence.

Can these findings be generalised? Jack Caldwell believes that an African type of epidemic can only be expected in places with the same cultural issues operating. One such country is on our doorstep – Papua New Guinea – and the signs are, he says, that HIV AIDS is already established there.

▼ Hepatitis C – much misunderstood

Because it is misunderstood, people carrying the hepatitis C virus can experience discrimination. So here are some facts which may help.

Hepatitis C isn't a sexually transmissible disease; the risk of spread through sex is minimal. Hepatitis C is transmitted by blood. Most infections are the result of needle and syringe sharing, using blood products (before there was a test for the virus), tattooing, body piercing or having medical or dental treatment in a developing country with poor sterile practices.

It affects over 200,000 Australians, with more than 10,000 being added each year. In most developed countries around 1 per cent of the population is affected; in poorer nations that percentage can be much higher. An acute infection can be silent or cause a fair bit of misery, with tiredness, symptoms of the flu, abdominal pain and feeling nauseous. Jaundice – turning yellow – is more common in hepatitis A than C.

The good news is that 1 in 4 people manage to rid themselves of hepatitis C quite quickly. Some of the remaining 75 per cent will have problems because they have developed a chronic hepatitis, and in some it can lead to liver failure and the need for a liver transplant. Hepatitis C is apparently the commonest reason for a liver transplant in Australia. Out of every 100 people with hepatitis C, between 2 and 5 will have liver damage bad enough to produce cancer or liver failure.

Luckily, there are new – albeit expensive – treatments available, including a form of interferon which is sometimes used alongside an antiviral drug. This manages to get rid of the infection in nearly half the people treated.

Since there's no immunisation available yet, prevention relies on making sure blood products are safe, encouraging safe injecting practices such as needle exchanges, and not sharing injecting gear, razors and toothbrushes.

Normal domestic living behaviour such as sharing dishes and bathrooms poses no risk.[17]

Men's Health

▼ Real men can have breasts

... and sometimes those breasts are a sign of serious disease such as cancer.

Those are the findings from a large study following men with breast enlargement – or gynaecomastia. The average age of the men was 44, and once the true gynaecomastias had been separated from the ones which were due to fat, the clinicians started to search for causes. In 60 per cent none was found. But in the rest the list of causes was long.

Alcohol was a major factor, because liver damage can tip the balance of hormones in a man towards the female side. Medications were another very common culprit, with acid-lowering drugs and some heart tablets (such as diuretics) topping the list. Around 1 in 20 had breast cancer. Such men's sisters and daughters need to take notice, because male breast cancer is associated with one of the breast cancer genes.

A few of these men had testicular cancer, which is known to produce female hormones. Another group had excessive production of a hormone in the brain called prolactin: it's the one which women produce when breastfeeding. This can be due to a tumour or a brain injury – or indeed can occur for no apparent reason.

So in the words of the British breast surgeon who presented the data, if you're a bloke with breasts, get it sorted out.

▼ Real men can rupture

Hernias in the groin are a common problem for men. A hernia is a protrusion in a place where it shouldn't occur. In an inguinal hernia – the jargon term for a hernia in the groin – there's a weakness which allows the bowel or its covering to come down into the canal which leads to the testicle.

There's great debate among surgeons about the best way to repair one of these hernias. These days, most surgeons stitch in mesh to strengthen the area; the argument is over whether it should be an open operation with a significant incision or done through a keyhole with a laparoscope.

The sorts of complications that can occur include the hernia coming back, shrinkage of the testicle, pain, pins and needles, and numbness.

A 5 year trial found that both the open and keyhole mesh methods are safe, but that the laparoscopic technique, in good hands, produces far fewer of these problems.

Whether people decide if they're for the chop is up to them and their doctors, but I would suggest that if you're going to have a keyhole hernia repair, go to someone who's done heaps of them in a hospital that is used to the procedure.[1]

▼ Sperm panic

There's been some angst over the last few years about declining sperm counts and semen quality.

Well, it's turning out that there may be no need to worry. There are serious questions about how real the decline actually is. A Melbourne study, for instance, has shown that nothing much has happened to sperm there.

The theory about the alleged sperm collapse was that environmental oestrogens – say from pesticides – were being absorbed by pregnant women and affecting the development of their unborn sons.

Now if that's true, you'd expect natural oestrogen to have the same or even a greater effect, and there is a way of looking at just that.

Pregnant women carrying twins have higher levels of oestrogen, and those with non-identical twins have higher amounts than those with identical ones.

Danish researchers got male twins of both kinds to give them sperm samples, as well as men who were singletons, as they say. They found that low sperm counts were not related to high oestrogen levels. In fact if anything, it went the other way.

So the panic merchants will have to think of something else to go after.[2]

▼ Fear of heights

I hate going up ladders. My wife's always trying to get me to do handyman jobs around the house – even bought me a drill last Fathers' Day. It's still in the box, untouched.

I also bought a ladder a while ago, but am petrified once I get beyond the third rung. Thanks to a paper in the *Medical Journal of Australia*, I now have an excellent excuse never to get the infernal thing out again.

A group in Melbourne reviewed everyone attending the Emergency Department at the Austin Hospital over a 3 year period because of having fallen off a ladder (often the ladder itself had toppled). The average age was 48. Almost all were men and almost none of these men had a job which involved going up a ladder. So I think it's reasonable to assume that a high proportion of these men were nagged up their ladders, don't you? And look what happened to them. More than 1 in 10 had severe trauma, nearly 1 in 2 was admitted to hospital – the problems included head, chest and spinal injuries.

The group's recommendations were that men who don't work up ladders as a routine should be very careful when they climb up one, and that there needs to be an education campaign about safe ladder use. The only safe ladder in my book is the one untouched in the garage.

Speaking personally, I can also tell you that no one goes up ladders at the ABC – opportunities arise from falls off them.[3]

▼ It's a dog's life for some blokes

Bite the hand that hits you – that's the unspoken message from research in Tasmania if you want some un-Christian revenge.

There's not much difference between dog bites and human bites. They can both be devastating because of the trauma and the infection from the nasty little germs we and our mutts carry in our mouths. Maybe around 1 in 5 bites seen by doctors are from humans.

Two doctors from the plastic surgery department at the Royal Hobart Hospital – who obviously had time on their hands between breasts and noses – studied 5 years of human hand bites treated at the hospital. The reason for studying the hand is that serious infections can so easily take root there.

Anyway, back to Tasmanian fisticuffs: just about every injury was to a clenched fist belonging to a young man, which had made contact with another person's teeth … kind of an involuntary bite, I suppose.

Those who were potentially worst off were the ones with a broken hand bone and who came late for care.

And being young blokes, they weren't very good at complying with treatment.

Hard to know what the message is – but speaking personally, I'm only too happy to protect the youth of Australia by keeping my teeth away from their fists.[4]

Mental Health and Psychology

▼ Feeling low? Try some exercise

... at least in a planned way.

Depression is common in our community; some would say it's getting commoner. There is a long list of drugs which can help, and often they're really necessary, but non-drug treatments can work too. It's known, for example, that a talking therapy called cognitive behavioural therapy – which tries to readjust people's negative frame of thinking – is effective in many people with depression, especially if used with medication.

Exercise has been said to be beneficial, but until the last few years the evidence was unreliable. The theory is that exercise raises the levels of mood-elevating chemicals – like natural opiates – in the brain.

One small study tried to get around problems in previous research and tested exercise in a much more controlled way. They looked at a group of men and women who'd had a diagnosis of serious depression for an average of 35 weeks. Many were not being helped very well by antidepressants. The 10 day training programme involved walking on a treadmill for 30 minutes every day.

The results showed a significant and objective improvement in their depressive symptoms, measured in a variety of ways.

There was no control group, unfortunately.

A more recent trial in elderly people – again, people who weren't doing too well on antidepressants – did have a control group. After 10 weeks, those participating in group exercise classes were more likely to have a modest reduction in their depressive symptoms.[1]

▼ Heart attacks and depression

As you might imagine, it's pretty depressing to have a heart attack, and in fact about 30 per cent of people who've had one already have or develop significant depression. A risk factor for depression in this situation is feeling socially isolated, without much support around you from friends or relatives.

It turns out that if you have the lot – a heart attack, depression and a perceived lack of social support – your chances of having serious complications or another heart attack are higher. If that's so, then fixing up the depression and the support should help.

Well, maybe.

A trial involving nearly 3000 people who had just had a heart attack, in which the researchers gave them cognitive behavioural therapy – for restructuring the person's thinking so that it became more realistic – has found that while it was good at relieving the depression, it didn't prevent subsequent heart problems. People who were given antidepressants were helped more, but that part of the trial wasn't placebo controlled, so the results are less reliable.

These results don't mean that the story about depression being bad for the heart is not true, nor that cognitive behavioural therapy isn't much chop. It's probably just that once you've had a heart attack, it's hard work preventing further events.[2]

▼ ANTIDEPRESSANTS – WHAT VALUE?

There always seems to be controversy around antidepressants. The big question is how do you know whether or not they're worth taking? One study looked at antidepressant prescribing in Australia, asking if these medications actually work in the real world – and if there is an effect, is it the drug or something else?

The measure of 'working' they chose was the suicide rate in various age groups over a 10 year period. They compared that with the sales of antidepressants over the same time. They found that the people with the highest rise in antidepressant use were the ones with the greatest decline in suicides, and they tended to be older. The researchers couldn't find an explanation for the change other than the medications.

The suicide rate went up in young people – a group for whom the rate of antidepressant prescribing is low.

The people who did the study reckoned that antidepressants couldn't take all the credit for the fall in suicides. They felt that seeing the doctor and having some talking therapy, no matter how rudimentary, was part of the story.

The challenge for young people is to see the doctor in the first place.[3]

▼ POSTNATAL DEPRESSION – NOT SO POST

A lot of publicity's been given to postnatal depression – and quite rightly, since it predicts long-term problems for the mother, the baby and the mother's partner. But there's been a growing realisation that postnatal depression doesn't come out of the blue, so to speak.

In fact some researchers believe that it's a slightly artificial diagnosis made just because doctors and nurses look for it more intensively after a baby's been born. Perhaps they do this because that's when the woman's mood becomes more obvious. Research from the UK supports that view.

Rather than studying a depressed population of women, they followed a normal group of women through pregnancy to see what happened to their mood. What they found was that the high point – or perhaps I should say low point – for depression scores was at 32 weeks of pregnancy rather than 8 weeks after the birth. More mothers scored highly on depression during the second trimester of pregnancy than the third trimester and the initial period after birth put together.

The implication is NOT that depression after birth isn't a problem – it is.

The issue is detecting problems before the baby's born, because there are probably more distressed women at that time than later.

Treatment then may have more benefit for both the mother and the baby.[4]

▼ WHAT'S GOING ON IN SAD?

Some people dread winter because it depresses them. Seasonal affective disorder – SAD – involves sadness, lethargy, eating too much carbohydrate, putting on weight, sleeping too much and general loss of interest in the world around you.

There's a lot of evidence that people with SAD have a body clock which doesn't adjust to short winter days. One treatment which works in some people is light therapy, where you sit in front of a light box to simulate the hours of sunlight you're missing in winter.

The question is, what's happening in the brain?

Fascinating research has looked at the biological clock in plants. Plants can theoretically get jet lag, but only Prince Charles would know if they get depressed. Anyway, research has shown that both chlorophyll – the green light-sensitive pigment in plants – and another substance rise and fall during the day.

The most similar chemical in humans is bilirubin. Bilirubin makes you jaundiced if you have too much of it.

It turns out that there's early evidence that, for some unknown reason, people with seasonal affective disorder have very low levels of bilirubin at night. If the theory is proven, it could form the basis of treatment and might explain the bilious personality.[5]

▼ Schools and suicide

Schools come in for a lot of stick and never more so than when a student commits suicide. There are self-recriminations and questions about whether or not the school environment could have been more supportive.

Psychologists in South Australia tried to get to the bottom of this by looking at symptoms of depression in teenagers and relating that to their schools. They asked two questions – first, how much did schools differ in their intake of adolescents with symptoms of depression and second, how had that changed (if at all) after 3 years?

The results showed that high schools did vary in the proportion of students with depressive symptoms at intake, but that there weren't many changes in those proportions afterwards.

There was an influence on symptoms that could be attributed to the schools, but it was small, and the natural variation between individual students – in other words the psychological factors in their own lives outside school – seemed to matter more.

The conclusion was that school-wide changes to schools' social environments wouldn't make as much difference as giving teachers practical psychological skills training so that they could help individual students with their coping styles in the classroom.[6]

▼ Your vote might be fatal

Sensationalist I know, but I've probably won your attention – for a minute, anyway. An Australian study of suicide over the last century found significantly increased rates when conservative governments have been in power compared with Labor. They've taken into account every factor they could think of that could have explained the result, and the relationship persisted. In fact if the same party was in power at both state and federal levels, the effect on suicide rates (either up or down) was even more pronounced.

So convincing were the findings that a British group did an analysis for the UK and found a similar pattern there; there was a big jump, for example, when Margaret Thatcher won government. They estimated 35,000 more deaths than expected from suicide in the UK associated with Conservative rule in the 20th century.

The question is why, especially when there's often not much to choose between the parties. The researchers think it may be something to do with hope, particularly among people who are at the bottom of the pile economically.

The main message is that suicide is a complex phenomenon which involves more than just the mental health of an individual. It's also related to things going on in society at large, which can be hard to dissect.[7]

▼ Hostility: a pain in the chest

The hostile type is someone who gets impatient easily, refuses to believe that others have more important business than their own, and when in the 8-item lane in a supermarket, counts how many items people in front of them have in their trolleys and becomes furious when it's more than 8. In other words, a really nice kind of person. Fine if you're fighting on the Kokoda Trail, but not great to live with.

The consolation – for the rest of us, that is – is that they're prone to coronary heart disease. But why?

It seems that when you are exposed to stress, the natural and healthy variability in how your heart beats reduces. To explain: a healthy heart rhythm is a complex affair, with natural variation in the duration of time between beats. Unhealthy hearts lose this variability and have less complex rhythms. In hostile people, stress seems to make their heart variability fall, and at the same time, the variability in their blood pressure – a bad thing – goes up.

A more recent paper looked at the quality of interactions people have with others and classified them as negative or positive. The more negative interactions someone had, the higher their blood pressure. The factor that seemed to affect the intensity of these negative interactions, and thus also their effect on blood pressure, was level of hostility.

Since it's hard to change personality, what can someone with a hostile temperament do? It turns out that exercise both increases heartbeat variability and reduces blood pressure variation. So the assumption – yet to be proven, remember – is that hostile people who exercise might reduce their risk.

Mind you, it wouldn't be pleasant being on a machine in the gym in front of a hostile person who's waiting to get on.[8]

▼ ... AND FORGIVE AND FORGET?

In a small but fascinating study, a group of US researchers found that people who were prone to forgiveness when betrayed by someone close to them or in a situation of conflict had lower blood pressure, lower heart rate and lower physiological measures of stress.[9]

▼ STRESS AND YOUR SKIN

Could it be that Zen has something to offer the Art of Skin Maintenance?

There's now objective evidence that stress can affect your skin in a potentially harmful way.

Results in both animals and humans have shown that stress can reduce what's called the skin permeability barrier – our protection against the outside world. It confirms the impression of many people with skin conditions that at times of stress their rashes become worse.

In experiments with mice under stress, their skin permeability barrier didn't work as well. They produced more cortisone-like stress hormones and these seemed to be the culprits. When the skin barrier dropped, the immune system responded by whistling up white blood cells – the side effect of which was inflammation.

The researchers then went on to study medical students before, during and after their final exams, comparing their skin responses to objective measures of how much stress they were under. The findings were the same as in mice.

The implications here are that if you have eczema or psoriasis, for instance, then your skin permeability barrier is already abnormal – so it doesn't take much to tip you over the edge.

At least one Zen dermatologist – I kid you not – has tried stress reduction and reckons it helps, and I suppose if it doesn't help your skin it might at least make you relax about it.[10]

▼ WORK-RELATED STRESS

This has often been linked to heart disease. It does seem obvious that your job can affect your heart, but actual evidence for the link hasn't been strong. The sort of stress I'm talking about has several dimensions.

Jobs which place high demands on you but give you little say over how tasks are done or how you use your skills are considered stressful. That's made worse if you put in a lot of effort but don't feel adequately rewarded in a variety of ways: financially, by the career opportunities available to you, by appropriate recognition, and with a sense that your job's safe because you do good work.

A group of Finnish researchers has been following over 800 industrial workers for 25 years, looking at their death rates from heart disease and correlating them with work stress.

High job strain – that's high demand and low control – predicted high cholesterol levels at 5 years and had double the coronary death rate at 25 years. Effort/reward imbalance predicted obesity at 10 years and was associated with nearly 2.5 times the death rate from heart disease at 25 years.

The inescapable conclusion was that reducing work-related stress should be a higher priority for employers.[11]

▼ CAN YOU BLAME YOUR BOSS?

According to some research the answer is 'possibly' – if you're a bloke. A group of researchers in California measured the level of work-related stress in nearly 500 people.

The sort of questions asked were how often you have high demands on you at work, how often your workload has increased, how often you get to leave the office to have lunch, how often you have trouble sleeping because of thinking about work and whether or not concerns about work weigh on your mind at home.

Then over a period of time the participants had ultrasound measurements of the carotid arteries in their necks, looking for the sort of thickening produced by arterial damage. The findings showed that the more arterial damage there was, the more stress a man was experiencing. It didn't show up in women, and in men it didn't actually reach what's called statistical significance, meaning that you can't be sure that the effect was real.

However, it ties in with a lot of other work which shows a higher risk of premature death in people whose work makes high demands on them yet who have little control over how that work is done. In other words, the people most likely to cark it are not the high-powered bosses – it's those in the middle being told what to do.

Sound familiar?[12]

▼ Mental illness and life expectancy

A report from Western Australia has exposed a scandal, and it is almost certainly occurring in the rest of Australia as well.

If the figures from Western Australia *do* apply to the rest of the country, a large proportion of people with mental illness have life expectancies more appropriate to parts of Africa: in their 50s rather than the late 70s or early 80s, like the rest of us, which amounts to 2.5 times the rate of premature death, and the reason isn't just suicide. That's part of it, but far more important are things like heart disease, cancer, injuries and infections.

The reason Western Australia's been able to uncover this is that they're the only state which links the hospital records of all its citizens so that their wellbeing can be followed. They've done this for people attending mental health facilities with moderate to severe mental illnesses such as depression and psychosis, and tracked their physical health.

It turns out that people with mental illness have a higher incidence of heart disease than others – probably mostly because they have higher smoking rates. The real problem is that when they have heart problems or cancer they do much worse than the rest of us. They don't appear to receive the same treatment that you or I would, and they suffer accordingly.

One solution, say the authors, is for GPs to be given more responsibility for people with mental illness, to ensure that their whole body is looked after rather than just their mind.[13]

▼ Young people in distress

Australian research has suggested that doctors really need to assess the psychological state of young people who come to see them, because regardless of what the young people are complaining about, a high proportion may be in some distress.

The study recruited a group of GPs to ask 15–24-year-olds coming to see them (for whatever reason) to fill out questionnaires measuring their mental state, with particular focus on depression and their risk of suicide.

About 3000 were assessed in this way. There were more young women than men, and the average age was about 19.

The results showed that despite the fact that only about 12 per cent came to the doctor with a psychological problem – most were attending with physical complaints of some kind – around 40 per cent had signs of psychological distress and maybe as many as 1 in 5 had had significant suicidal thoughts.

The authors warned that because the GPs were self-selected, these statistics could be exaggerated (higher than they would otherwise be across the whole population, that is). The other thing was not knowing whether or not these young people were using their physical complaint as, if you like, a ticket of entry to the GP when what they really wanted to talk about were their psychological troubles.

Either way it probably means that young people who turn up at the GP should be assessed, however briefly, for their mental state in case they need some help.[14]

▼ THE RISK AND PROTECTIVE FACTORS FOR SUICIDE

For the last 15 years or so there's been groundbreaking work in Western Australia into suicide in young people. Luckily, such suicides are a rare event but when one occurs, the tragedy is enormous. The work in Western Australia has discovered a lot more about what increases the risk of suicide, what might protect a young person from it and how, for example, hospital emergency departments can recognise a person at risk and do the right thing.

One of the key clues, it turns out, is deliberate self-harm. It can be hard to know whether a cut or an accident was actually deliberate, but it helps if the right questions are asked by health professionals in, say, the Emergency Department.

Another risk factor is intoxication with either alcohol or illicit drugs, and the researchers (and others) have found a link with regular cannabis use. It appears that use of cannabis by a young person more than once a week raises the risk of depression and consequently of self-harm and suicide.

Self-harm, by the way, increases the chances that someone will commit suicide 20 times, but despite that dramatic statistic it's still a relatively small number who go on to act in that way.

The solutions in Western Australia have been to try to ensure that Emergency Departments and schools know how to detect teenagers at risk and ask the most effective questions about depression, substance abuse and self-harm. The researchers say that this should uncover 80 per cent of the problems. Luckily the overall rate of teenage suicide has been falling, and the same West Australian researchers are working with programmes for primary school children which they hope will prevent the incidence of depression and substance use later in life.[15]

▼ SWEDES CLAIM SUCCESS WITH ANOREXIA

Anorexia nervosa, while not that common – it affects a maximum of about 0.5 per cent of women over the age of 15 – is a serious problem which disrupts families and kills a proportion of people who suffer from it (about 6 per cent of those with the disease over a 10 year period). And the evidence till recently has been that no treatment works – apart, perhaps, from some family therapy. The statistics are that about half get better, while the other half continue to have difficulties, some of which are severe.

A trial in Sweden has found greater success than has been reported anywhere else.

This team in Stockholm take the view that everything in anorexia nervosa starts with the starvation – from feeling cold, to hyperactivity, to obsessional behaviour. Their approach to treatment is to stop all drugs (because they believe some antidepressants can make eating disorders worse), if necessary remove the young woman from her anorectic environment (95 per cent are female, by the way), retrain her in how to eat reasonable amounts in normal amounts of time by using a computerised device, re-warm her and re-socialise her using teachers, accommodation specialists and even dentists (to fix the teeth of people with bulimia).

The results need to be repeated in other centres, but in Sweden, this approach shows good recovery rates and low numbers of relapses.[16]

▼ THE TRAUMA INDUSTRY – BASED ON WHAT?

There's a veritable industry which thrives on crisis. Someone goes on a rampage or there's a disaster and in go the psychological debriefing teams. It sounds quite persuasive, and indeed humane: if people talk about their trauma and get it off their chest you can stop them internalising the stress and thus prevent Post Traumatic Stress Disorder (PTSD), which involves panic attacks, emotional disturbances and memory flashbacks. The process is sometimes called Critical Incident Stress Debriefing, and some of the techniques were actually developed here in Australia.

But over recent years that received wisdom has been questioned, and a few studies have suggested that these kinds of one-off early debriefing sessions may do more harm than good.

A review of the available evidence found that Critical Incident Stress Debriefing within a month of the event does not, on average, reduce symptoms of post traumatic stress or speed recovery. There was a slight suggestion that it could even have made things worse.

It doesn't mean that traumatised people don't need help; it just means that there's no quick means of preventing PTSD.[17]

▼ Mental cannabis and PTSD

Memories become stronger if the events or things we experience are associated with emotion. For example, good teachers use humour. If we recognise a cooking smell associated with happy childhoods in Grandma's kitchen, all sorts of emotions and images will return.

But some people have memories they hate and they can't get rid of them. They keep coming back, creating anxiety and even panic. Such people sometimes have PTSD: their memories have been laid down during times of extreme emotion, such as when they are afraid that they are about to be killed.

Research has suggested a reason why some people with PTSD use drugs like marijuana. It may be because we have receptors in our brain – lock and key mechanisms – which fit cannabinoids (the active compounds in cannabis) as well as the natural chemical messengers in the brain.

In experiments with rats where researchers either genetically engineer the rats not to have these receptors or give them a drug which blocks them, the rats are unable to extinguish memories associated with fear.

The suggestion is that these cannabinoid receptors are involved in getting rid of memories we don't want. If this is true for humans (as well as rats), then perhaps some people are smoking dope to forget. Whether it's successful for any longer than the last puff is highly doubtful. Drug use by people with PTSD is associated with poor outcomes.[18]

▼ Gulf War Syndrome?

With almost every major war in the recent past, new diseases have emerged. Some were physical, and some have had a large psychological component.

In World War I, shell shock was thought to be a neurological disease caused by shell bursts; in World War II it was called 'going troppo';

and in Vietnam the symptoms were put down to Agent Orange. Now there's a name for it: Post Traumatic Stress Disorder.

And people are still publishing papers on what they call Gulf War Syndrome. There's confusing and inconsistent evidence that it may be related to vaccination of troops against biological warfare agents, but when you study people complaining of Gulf War Syndrome, no regular sets of symptoms emerge; nor is it even specific to the Gulf. Soldiers who served in Bosnia also feel ill, but less commonly than the Gull War veterans. Adding all this up has made many conclude that while the illnesses may be real, there is no such entity as Gulf War Syndrome.

Yet despite this, a survey of British Gulf War veterans found that nearly 1 in 5 believed they had the syndrome. What predicted that belief most strongly was knowing someone who also believed that he or she had it. The belief was associated with psychological distress and lower activity levels.

One important message is usually forgotten at the start of most wars: the mental health of military personnel must be given as much attention as their physical wellbeing.[19]

▼ ... COULD THE REASON BE MARRIAGE BREAKDOWN?

A study of Norwegian military peacekeepers found a 40 per cent increase in their rate of suicide, but when that was statistically adjusted for the marital status of the soldiers, researchers found that the increased rate disappeared. In other words, it was directly related to being unmarried or divorced.

This could have meant that these military personnel had personalities or problems beforehand which both affected their relationships and predisposed them to depression, or that army service overseas is a risk factor in its own right and that more attention should be paid to the service person's closest relationships and more support provided for those relationships.[20]

▼ COSMETIC SURGERY AND MENTAL HEALTH

More and more women are having plastic surgery. In particular, they are having breast augmentations, and there's been a huge controversy about the health effects of breast implants. Studying these women accurately, though, is extremely hard to do.

It's easier in Sweden, which has a superb system of gathering comprehensive health statistics. Researchers followed over 3500 women who'd had breast implants for purely cosmetic reasons for 11 years. They were chasing a suspicion that these women's rate of suicide was higher. The researchers compared these women's death rates and causes of death with the Swedish average for similar women who'd not had breast implants.

They expected 5 suicides in this group but found 15, and they expected 58 deaths overall but found 85.

The cause for the excess numbers of women dying was largely lung cancer, due to a greater prevalence of smoking. The larger number of suicides is less easy to explain; the authors felt that women who were dissatisfied with their lives were more likely to seek out cosmetic surgery and that some weren't happier as a result.

The conclusion is that plastic surgeons should make a careful psychological evaluation of people wanting cosmetic surgery in case they need other help.[21]

▼ HANDWRITING AND THE MIND

Will handwriting analysis make a comeback? There was a time when handwriting experts seemed to be in every second Hollywood courtroom drama, making deep and meaningful judgements on everything from people's identities to their deepest psychological defects. But in reality the research backing it up was either poor or non-existent, and the discipline got a bad reputation.

Even so, some doctors use handwriting to evaluate how well medications are working – in Parkinson's disease, for example, they use handwriting to help decide whether or not the dose should be changed. And with the advent of digital technology, where, with a special writing tablet, the actual process of handwriting can be analysed, there may be more uses.

Obsessive compulsive disorder (OCD) has, in the past, been thought to produce writing abnormalities – possibly from subtle brain changes. OCD in its most extreme form is where someone's life is paralysed by obsessive behaviours such as hand washing or repeated checking that doors are locked and electric utensils turned off.

It seems that in people with OCD, digital handwriting measurement correlates with severity: the speed of writing (it gets slower), the size of the letters (they become smaller) and the way they made each stroke of the pen changed in line with the condition worsening.

These findings may have two benefits: a more objective way for psychologists and psychiatrists to assess how badly someone's affected and whether treatment's working and, perhaps more importantly, a window into the brain to help us see what might be going wrong to create this and other disorders.[22]

▼ Hypnosis – beyond vaudeville

Hypnosis has fascinated both mainstream and complementary medicine since the huge enthusiasm for mesmerism in the 19th century. But it long ago moved from being a vaudeville stage trick to a recognised therapy for pain, anxiety and habits such as smoking and overeating.

Research has looked at what happens in the brains of people who are hypnotised. They did brain scans of people looking at black and white and colour images and watched which parts of the brain lit up. The people were then asked to imagine that the black and white image was coloured. People in a hypnotic state responded to the black and white images in the part of the brain which normally sees colour. So brain activity was foxed by the hypnosis.

This supports understanding of how significant the process of hypnosis can be.

People who are hypnotisable tend to be those who easily get engrossed in a book, a film or a play and lose awareness of the world around them. Fine actors may be in a hypnotic kind of state during an intense performance. People who are good spatially and like their information orally rather than on paper seem to be more hypnotisable as well.

The swinging gold pocket watch is now confined to Hollywood. Modern hypnosis is quick and non-gimmicky – it simply gets people to turn inward and create images for themselves.

The message for anyone wanting to try it, is find someone who's a properly qualified health professional and has had extensive training in hypnosis.[23]

▼ Talked to sleep

The last thing you want when you can't sleep is someone talking to you – but in fact for some of us that may be the answer. One in 20 of the population has what's called primary insomnia – that's jargon for not being able to sleep for no obvious reason. People with primary insomnia have a higher risk of becoming depressed and falling ill and often get landed with sleeping tablets or antidepressants.

Some things are known to work (relaxation exercises, for example), but in some people even these things aren't effective. US sleep researchers trialled cognitive behavioural therapy (CBT), which involved a methodical way of correcting people's misconceptions about sleep and changing their bedtime behaviour.

This included prescribing time in bed. People were told to establish a standard wake up time no matter what; to get up when they couldn't fall asleep; not to use the bedroom for work; to avoid sleeping during the day; and not to go to bed before a certain time – only extending the deadline by 15 minutes per week as the sleep improved. If they were still sleepless, the time in bed was *reduced* by 15 minutes per week.

The CBT was compared with relaxation therapy and a placebo treatment: it resulted in a halving of wake time after sleep onset. That was about 4 times better than relaxation therapy and about 5 times better than no treatment. Sleep time went up to about 6 hours and waking time fell to about 25 minutes – not perfect, but the results seemed to last.

The advice I like, if you're not able to fall asleep in the first place, is to treat it like surfing – learn to catch that first wave of tiredness that sweeps over you, because the next wave could be a while coming.[24]

▼ Language and attitudes of mind

While most of us try to resist stereotyping people from other countries, it's very easy to do, and we're often tempted to conclude that people from other nations think differently from us. If we've learned their language, it's even more tempting to believe that the way their language is structured and the words they have for things must contribute to these seemingly different thought processes.

To take a simple example, different languages have names for a device which either pushes screws, pulls them or turns them. If I were to show you these devices, they'd all look the same, and you'd call them screwdrivers. The question is whether people think about screws differently because the words are different. The same goes for motorway or freeway exits. In some languages they're termed entrances to the new road.

Just how much weight can you place on these idiosyncrasies? It's quite an important debate, because it can affect how we think of people from different cultures. For example, there's a huge controversy over whether you teach Aboriginal kids in their own language or English and some of the above assumptions underlie that debate.

Well, it turns out, from a variety of experiments, that when you take certain tasks which are described differently in various languages and remove the language component by just analysing what people understand in their mind's eye, if you like, the differences disappear. People seem to think the way they do regardless of their language.

All sorts of other things affect behaviour, including our environment and our genes, but it seems that learning French, for instance, isn't going go to turn you into a café habitué with a Gitane habit.[25]

▼ Does prayer have the power to heal?

There have been several studies purporting to show health benefits from religious beliefs and prayer, and in the US at least, there's concern that evangelical doctors are prescribing religion to their patients.

What's the evidence? Well, it's thin. There have been almost no well-conducted studies which would lead you to believe that religion is the answer to a patient's prayers. So given that there's little evidence, is it ethical for doctors to advise religion or prayer?

According to a group of US medical researchers and indeed hospital chaplains, it isn't, for three main reasons. The first is the potential for coercion ... where the doctor uses his or her position of power and authority to coerce a patient into a line of action.

The second is invasion of privacy. It is known, for example, that being married is good for a man's health, but is it any business of a doctor to recommend marriage as a course of action?

And the third is the potential for doing harm. If you believe that religion can save you from disease, the opposite must also be true – namely that lack of religion or spiritual belief *causes* say, cancer, which is complete bulldust and can complicate people's already delicate psychological balance when they're seriously ill.

So if the spirit's willing – keep it to yourself.[26]

▼ But a spot of spirituality might help

A group in New York has looked at people who are terminally ill with cancer and at a phenomenon called end of life despair. Just the thing we all dread. The distressing feeling that it's all hopeless and why bother going on?

The study compared end of life despair with spiritual wellbeing – a confidence or faith, if you like, in the meaning and purpose of life and the ability to take comfort in religious beliefs. They did a battery of psychological tests on people in palliative care with a life expectancy of under 12 weeks.

And this is probably no surprise to anyone, but those with high levels of spiritual wellbeing were less likely to think of suicide or want their death to come sooner, and it seemed to be independent of depression. In fact spiritual wellbeing appeared to soften the effects of depression.

There were a lot of uncertainties in these findings and more work is needed. The big question, if it's true, is what do you do about it? Evangelism in the wards is presumably not the answer.[27]

▼ Urinary phobia

This is one minute where you might want to cross your legs and glance over your shoulder.

It's about a social phobia that many men know only too well, or at least empathise with. Shy bladder syndrome: the inability to have a pee when other people are around. And apparently it affects women too.

The experts say shy bladder syndrome or paruresis can be so disabling that some people with it have been known to avoid going to the bathroom even when on long-distance flights. As a result, the expansion of their bladder presumably starts to interfere with speech.

The treatment, as with most phobias, is therapy involving restructuring your thinking about passing water and gradual exposure to anxiety-provoking situations – leaving the urinals at the footy till last.[28]

NERVOUS SYSTEM

▼ Just how much should you worry about yourself if you faint?

A study of people who have had a fainting spell – the technical term is syncope – suggests that with certain types of syncope you should get properly checked up because there could be serious consequences.

The researchers followed nearly 8000 people in the town of Framingham, Massachusetts, for some years and observed what happened to those who'd had a blackout. Disturbingly, they had about a 30 per cent increased risk of premature death. The good news, though, was that it was possible to say which kinds of faints were the problem.

People who had a straightforward vasovagal attack – that's where there are no other symptoms or signs of trouble and you drop at the sight of blood or in a stuffy, overcrowded room – need not worry: that common or garden faint is not associated with any future problems.

The faints to worry about are those where the doctor can't tell what caused it, so there's no diagnosis, or where there are signs of heart involvement, such as pain or an irregular heartbeat, or it comes out of the blue.

In that case, a referral to a cardiologist would be a very good idea.[1]

▼ Does melatonin work for jet lag?

Some frequent travellers swear by melatonin to reduce their jet lag. Is it in their minds, or does the stuff work?

Melatonin is a hormone produced by the pineal gland in the brain – what the ancients used to call the third eye. They weren't far wrong: the pineal is closely associated with a collection of nerves which transmit light impulses from the eyes to the back of the brain for transformation into images. Melatonin rises and falls during the day and night, and this rhythm is disordered when we move quickly into another time zone.

The idea behind taking melatonin tablets is that they help the body clock reset itself faster, and a review of the available evidence from placebo-controlled trials suggests that it works.

Half of those who take melatonin benefit from it. It seems that you only have to take it after arrival, and that between half a milligram and

5 milligrams is what you need. The nearer you get to 5 mg, the faster you fall asleep and the less tired you feel the next day.

People who take melatonin make fewer errors than those on dummy tablets. However, people with epilepsy, or taking aspirin or anti-coagulants, should take medical advice before using melatonin and it's questionable whether you should give it to children.

As to reliable sources of melatonin – that's where it can become difficult, because it is an alternative medicine product. So buyer be wary.[2]

▼ THE SEROTONIN SYNDROME

A new term has emerged relatively recently. It's the serotonin syndrome, and no, it's not the title of another anti-psychiatry self-help book. The serotonin syndrome is real. It often occurs by accident when several medications or herbs that increase the levels of serotonin, a brain transmitter, are taken at the same time.

The symptoms range from jumpiness and agitation, feeling warm and perspiring to more serious problems such as very high temperatures, muscle rigidity, confusion, fits and – rarely – death.

The problem usually arises when someone inadvertently takes two medications which both affect serotonin. Most anti-depressants do it, as does St John's Wort, a popular herbal remedy for depression. Older-fashioned antidepressants can be quite powerful serotonin drugs too, and there are a couple of painkillers – pethidine and tramadol – which can cause problems. Some illicit drugs, including Ecstasy and LSD, also increase serotonin levels.

If you get into strife, it can be treated – usually by stopping the medications and watching you to check that the symptoms disappear. The best thing, though, is to prevent the serotonin syndrome in the first place by ensuring, with your doctor, that if you're on one serotonin medication, you don't take another accidentally.[3]

▼ PARKINSON'S AND COFFEE

I don't normally cover coffee, so to speak. There's always new research around, but the irritating thing is that for every study saying it's poison there's another saying it's no problem.

In any event, here's some good news for fellow flat white mainliners.

Coffee drinkers look as though they have a 30 per cent lower risk of developing Parkinson's disease. Parkinson's is caused by degeneration in the brain that produces a tremor, then muscle rigidity and eventually a kind of dementia.

There's a little evidence that people destined to develop Parkinson's have sober personalities and don't need the buzz of coffee. If this is true it would make the beneficial association between Parkinson's and coffee an accident of genetics. But the reason is more likely to be that caffeine may somehow protect brain cells against toxins from the environment in people susceptible to Parkinson's disease. That's been shown in mice, who were less damaged by a nerve toxin after they'd been dosed with caffeine.

The question is whether hitting the espresso machine *after* Parkinson's starts makes a difference – no one knows that yet. Interestingly, nicotine offers similar protection, but I'd rather go with a coffee habit.[4]

▼ MAD COW DISEASE – POSSIBLE TREATMENTS

Could some very old tried, true and cheap medications turn out to be effective at treating the human manifestation of Mad Cow Disease?

That's the belief of Professor Stan Prusiner, the Nobel laureate who discovered the infectious particle called the prion which is supposed to underlie both Mad Cow and Creutzfeld-Jakob diseases.

His group at the University of California San Francisco have been carrying out test-tube studies of an old anti-malarial drug called quinacrine and a medication for schizophrenia called chlorpromazine.

I need to give you a quick blast of science to explain. These prions are actually normal proteins found in the body. Prusiner's theory, which has yet to be conclusively proven, is that degenerative brain diseases like Creutzfeld-Jakob (CJD) occur when the prions change shape.

What they do have evidence for is that quinacrine and chlorpromazine seem to block this change from a normal to an abnormal prion protein. Japanese researchers have made similar findings.

Antibodies are also being tried, but they may only be effective for related diseases, such as scrapie.

All this is a very long way from making any comment about whether or not they'll work in real life in humans. A trial of quinacrine was held up because a woman died during treatment in 2001. A small number of people with what's called new variant CJD (vCJD) have been given an experimental therapy involving injections directly into the brain with a substance called pentosan polysulphate – a medication used to prevent scrapie and being trialled in animals for arthritis.[5]

▼ Old infections die hard

Some memories really stay with you. One that stayed with me was when I was a junior doctor. An elderly man who'd had an operation a few days before developed the most awful spasms in the face and upper body. He was still conscious, so it didn't look like epilepsy. We'd never seen anything like it and it took a while to twig to what he had.

It was tetanus, a disease we thought had disappeared – and despite everything, he died. We hadn't checked whether or not he was immunised.

A report from Oxford had a similar story. A 76-year-old lady fell in her garden and cut her leg. The emergency department cleaned the wound and closed it with adhesive strips. One week afterwards she was back with a wound infection. She developed all the signs of tetanus, and 3 weeks after that, despite being in one of the most high-tech hospitals in the world, she was dead.

Wounds at risk of tetanus are ones which have been left for a few hours, are infected, involve soil or manure or a deep puncture (such as from standing on a nail).

Adults need a tetanus booster every 10 years, and if there's doubt, a 3 dose course is advised. If you have a tetanus-prone wound and your tetanus cover is uncertain, you will need anti-tetanus antibodies as well as the immunisation.

Tetanus has not gone away.[6]

▼ Parallel universes up your nose?

'The right hand doesn't know what the left one's doing.' It's a complaint usually invoked to describe the organisations we work for.

Some Californian scientists, presumably with time on their hands, decided to see whether your right nostril knows what your left one's been up to. Your nostrils are actually quite interesting. Each one contains an outgrowth of your brain exquisitely designed to identify substances in the air.

The question is, when you experience a new smell, which part of the brain learns the lesson – the bit in your nostril, or where the information's processed inside the skull? By exposing only one nostril to a unique smell, the researchers discovered that the unexposed nostril quickly learned to recognise it, which suggests that the learning had crossed over inside the brain.

The implications are first, that the brain is still quite plastic in adulthood, and second, you shouldn't be too picky when it comes to your nose.[7]

Pregnancy and Childbirth

▼ Having the baby – where and how

Birthing centres have become almost a compulsory part of obstetric units in Australia: warm and friendly, home-like environments where women at low risk of a problem in labour can have as natural a delivery as possible, knowing that if things go wrong they're only a short distance from expert help.

The question for women is how these centres shape up to traditional labour wards.

Results from trials comparing the two have been combined to get a more reliable answer.

They showed that between 20 per cent and 75 per cent of women in birthing centres end up in the conventional labour ward for one reason or another. Those who remained in the centres to have their babies moved around more, had less pain medication, were more likely to deliver in an upright or semi-upright position and were far more satisfied with the experience.

The downside was small but worrying trend to a higher rate of death among the babies; however, it didn't reach statistical significance. It really just serves as a warning that the foetus and mother do need to be monitored, even in these more 'natural' surroundings.[1]

▼ Wait for the second child

As women have their first babies later in life, it becomes harder to conceive. And with the biological clock ticking away, once you've had that child, there's often great pressure to get going with the second. Women who particularly want another pregnancy fast are those who've lost a baby.

You have to be a little careful, though, because it's been suspected that falling pregnant too soon is not good for the next baby.

However, the research has been confusing, because women who have short intervals between pregnancies are often young, poor, short (in height), not well educated, smokers and single – all of these are risk factors in their own right.

A recent study may have clarified the story. Researchers removed the effects of these factors, and found that falling pregnant within 6 months of the birth of a first child doubled the risk of a premature birth and tripled the chances of the baby dying in the first month.

These risks sound dramatic, but since prematurity and neonatal death are fairly rare, the increase only makes them slightly more likely.

Nonetheless, if you can wait beyond 6 months, it's probably a good idea.[2]

▼ When you're in labour have someone by your side; it counts

Some of the critics of modern health care say it's gone high-tech at the expense of high-touch. In other words the technology has got in the way of person-to-person care, perhaps because the technology has swallowed the human's wages.

Anyway, one place where the personal touch is thought to count a lot is the labour ward – and even there some would say there's not enough high-touch.

According to a review of the available scientific trials from around the world, involving nearly 13,000 women, if there was more high-touch for women in labour, you might not need as much high-tech.

The results showed that women who had continuous support – someone they trusted who was there with them – during labour, starting as early as possible, needed less pain relief, required less intervention when it came to the delivery itself and had far fewer complaints about the whole process.

Interestingly – and presumably comfortingly for hospital bean counters – the effect was greater if the person wasn't a member of staff.

So for those blokes who would rather be in the pub, working off the anxiety – forget it![3]

▼ And what about peering into the future – birth weight and your baby's IQ

Some people believe that birth weight is related to a baby's future IQ, and a study from the US has shown that the heavier a baby was at birth, the higher its IQ.

Let's have a closer look though, because the temptation among parents could be to see promise in children just because of their birth weight. The project followed 3500 babies born at full term who, at age 7, were given an IQ test. The findings were then adjusted to allow for other factors which influence IQ, such as education and poverty.

The results were that in boys only – not girls – for every 100 grams more in birth weight you could add half a point to the IQ.

Now this isn't the stuff of high drama: such differences are unnoticeable if you have one kid who was 3 kg and another who was 3.5 kg at birth. The real implications of this study are that the effects of birth weight on brain development are continuous; they don't stop at some mythical weight. The connection has been known for some time in relation to low birth weight babies (full term babies under 2.5 kg), but these findings suggest that the relationship between brain development and birth weight extends into the so-called 'normal' weight zone.

The study's importance isn't for individual families and individual children, but for whole population groups. When you have whole communities of Aboriginal women having babies with low birth weight, as we do in Australia, then entire generations are being born with less than adequate brain development.

It's an added burden to the already intolerable one they've been given, and it means that greater efforts should be made to find ways of preventing low birth weight in at risk groups in Australia.[4]

▼ AND DO THE EFFECTS OF LOW BIRTH WEIGHT GET PASSED ON TO THE NEXT GENERATION?

Research published in *The Lancet* has undermined one of the most provocative theories about health and wellbeing proposed in the last few years.

The idea was that disadvantage can be passed on biologically from generation to generation through mothers. It's called the Barker (or Foetal Origins) Hypothesis, and arises from observations in the UK and elsewhere that babies with a low birth weight are at increased risk of high blood pressure and a whole host of other problems. Professor Barker, who's at the University of Southampton in the UK, argues that if the baby's a girl, she can pass on the same disadvantage to her offspring.

The theory was that poor maternal nutrition forces the foetus to adapt in a pathological way to the circumstances of pregnancy and that this maladaptation plays out in adulthood as high blood pressure. In other words, the blood vessels and heart have to work harder, and thus become narrower and more muscular, predisposing towards disease.

The implications are enormous, and in some countries the theory has influenced social policy, but the new research has taken a critical look at the evidence and found that low birth weight is not a cause of high blood pressure in adults.

It doesn't mean that mothers' nutrition isn't important – it is, but for other reasons, not for reasons to do with blood pressure or birth weight.[5]

PROSTATE

▼ THE PSA TEST: TO DO OR NOT TO DO

One unsurprising phenomenon in health is that scientific evidence often doesn't change our behaviour. A lot of us eat fatty steaks, put butter on our toast, swallow vast amounts of synthetic vitamins, take herbs with goodness knows what in them and have tests that the authorities frown upon. Even doctors do it.

A survey in Victoria found that a high proportion of both male doctors and men in the general community have the Prostate Specific Antigen (PSA) screening test for prostate disease.

The trouble with the PSA test is that high levels don't necessarily mean there's cancer and low levels don't necessarily mean there isn't. In addition, since no one really knows which early treatment of prostate cancer makes a difference, the official line is to discourage PSA screening.

Despite this, the Victorian survey found that about half of the male population aged between 50 and 70 – medical and non-medical – had had themselves tested.

Most doctors were having it done for reassurance, but there was doubt about whether or not the non-medical men were properly informed about the test.

Given that the male market has shunned the evidence and wants prostate testing, the authors concluded that better ways are needed to help men make informed decisions.

A group at the University of New South Wales has put together an information booklet for men who are wondering whether or not to be tested. The idea is to help them make a decision more confidently. One of the things you need to know is what are the chances of the test correctly identifying you as either not having or having prostate cancer.

It seems that if 1000 men have a PSA test, 900 of them will fall in the normal range. Of that 900, 9 will have been falsely reassured because they will indeed have cancer – missed by the test.

Of the remaining 100 with a positive test, two-thirds will turn out not to have prostate cancer after further investigating, say with a biopsy and ultrasound.

So of the original 1000, 30 with a positive test and 9 with a negative test will turn out to have cancer. The next – and unanswered – question is what to do about it?

Prostate cancer death rates have been falling in many countries and no one knows why. Is it the result of whatever PSA testing's being done? A group of US researchers doubts it.

They compared the effects of prostate cancer screening on two populations of men: one in the Seattle/Puget Sound area in Washington State, where in the early days they had very intensive PSA testing; and the other in Connecticut, where there was far less testing going on.

Men in Seattle were far more likely to be diagnosed with prostate cancer and treated for it, but over the 11 years of follow-up, there were no differences in the numbers of deaths from prostate cancer.

It doesn't prove that PSA testing is pointless. The implication is more that the jury's still out on whether a mass screening campaign is a good use of taxpayers' money.[1]

▼ ENLARGED PROSTATE – WHEN TO HAVE THE KNIFE

There's a significant debate among urologists – medical plumbers – about whether and when men who have problems with their stream, as it's delicately called, should have their prostates operated on.

The symptoms include not having much force behind the urinary stream, dribbling, feeling your bladder's not empty and getting up frequently during the night.

These symptoms are often put down to having a large prostate, but studies have suggested that the severity of symptoms isn't closely related to the size of the gland. In fact it's been suggested that what predicts a better outcome is not the size of your prostate but how bad your symptoms are to start with.

One of the things that's put off men and some doctors about this operation – called a Transurethral Resection of the Prostate (TURP) – is its reputation for damaging men's sexual function. That has encouraged the development of laser therapy for prostate disease. But this worry has been exposed as unfounded by a recent British study.

They compared laser treatment, TURP and no treatment in 340 men, and in fact discovered that before they even started treatment, urinary difficulties were significantly associated with erectile and ejaculatory problems.

It actually turned out that both the surgery and the laser treatment improved erectile function but the operation had a better overall result, because it helped ejaculation too. What they didn't include in their comparison was drug treatment for urinary symptoms – it's not known what effect that has.

So if sex is still important, the advice is to go for the surgery.

An interesting footnote to this story is that the commentary was written by a Professor Timothy Wilt.[2]

▼ Prostate cancer – worth waiting?

Prostate cancer is common, but that doesn't mean men will die of it. Because of their age, they may just die *with* prostate cancer – it will be something else that gets them.

With the advent of the PSA blood test, which can indicate that a man is at high risk, more and more men are being diagnosed with prostate cancer and having the prostate gland taken out. The problem is that there's a high rate of erectile dysfunction and incontinence afterwards. So is it worth watching and waiting rather than jumping in?

A trial's been done – with men aged 64 on average – asking just that.

Over 6–8 years, those who'd received the operation were significantly less likely to die of prostate cancer, but 17 people needed to be treated for 1 death from prostate cancer to be prevented. And because of all the other medical problems they had, they were no more likely to live longer than the men who didn't have the operation.

In addition, there were few differences in the quality of life – the cancer created significant problems for those who did not have it removed. Contrary to assumptions, and impotence and leakage notwithstanding, the quality of life of those who'd had the surgery was actually better than that of the ones who'd decided not to have it.

The reason was that the growing tumour also tended, eventually, to cause erectile dysfunction and incontinence – as well as urinary obstruction, which doesn't happen after the surgery. It also may be that the men in the waiting group felt more distressed by these complications because they hadn't been led to expect them.

The other problem the waiting group had to deal with was a risk of cancer spread double that of those having the operation.

Salutary information at make-your-mind-up time.

This is a really tough area. Young men with localised disease may well be better off with the operation because there's more time for the cancer to affect you, but older men need to weigh things up carefully.[3]

▼ FINASTERIDE AND PROSTATE CANCER PREVENTION

Male hormones play a role in prostate cancer, although no one's too sure exactly what it is. It's known that Asian men have less prostate cancer than African-Americans; they also have lower levels of an enzyme called 5 alpha reductase, which turns testosterone into the more powerful dihydrotestosterone.

Finasteride is a drug that inhibits 5 alpha reductase. It was originally developed to shrink enlarged prostates and thus save men from needing surgery. While it does shrink prostates, finasteride hasn't been terribly popular because it is associated with sexual dysfunction (although it does help baldness – hair grows back a bit).

Given its effect on this enzyme, though, the hope was that finasteride could prevent prostate cancer, and a huge, 7 year trial was commenced. In 9000 men aged over 55, there were 25 per cent fewer prostate tumours in those taking finasteride. The trouble was that in those who did get cancers, the cancers tended to be slightly nastier than the cancers of those on the placebo: 6 out of 100 prostate cancers in men on finasteride were aggressive compared with 5 out of 100 on the placebo. The finasteride men were also more likely to have erectile dysfunction and a reduced libido.

So overall it's unlikely that finasteride will be used for prevention, but the trial has shown for the first time that a reduction in risk is possible.[4]

▼ ... AND FISH?

What causes prostate cancer is a mystery. It's thought that exercise may reduce the risk, and there have been suggestions from time to time that diet may play a role. For example, some researchers believe that saturated fat is toxic to the nether organ.

Now fish is getting a good (w)rap.

Over 6000 Swedish men have been followed for 30 years: those who consumed no fish had a 2 to 3 times higher risk of prostate cancer than men who tucked into their herring and mackerel on a regular basis. Exactly what 'regular' means was not mentioned in the paper. The fish were those high in omega 3 fatty acids – these have been shown in the lab to inhibit the growth of prostatic tumours.

There was no doubt that herring lovers also did more exercise, ate less saturated fat, consumed more vegies and fruit and smoked less, but even taking all that into account statistically, fish eating was still a factor in its own right. The researchers' conclusion was that fatty fish consumption may reduce the risk of prostate cancer.[5]

▼ Prostate cancer and vitamin E

There are a lot of people swallowing antioxidants in the hope that they will prevent something. A few years ago, a trial in Finland among smokers tried to find out whether or not vitamin E prevented lung cancer. It didn't, but they noticed that after several years of use, the men taking vitamin E had a 34 per cent reduction in prostate cancer.

The researchers have gone back to the surviving group of 25,000 men to see what happened after the trial stopped. Unfortunately, after several years the preventive effects of vitamin E had disappeared. Three-quarters of the men were still smoking and only 5 per cent were still taking the vitamin E. There was no difference between the original groups in the number of men with prostate cancer.

You can't take much from this research, though, because it wasn't designed to study prostate cancer. The finding was a side result; to discover whether or not vitamin E really does lower the risk of prostate cancer, a specific trial will need to be done.

There is one underway – the Selenium and Vitamin E Chemoprevention Trial (SELECT) – but it will be years before it reports.[6]

▼ Coping with prostate cancer

Australian research has tried to fill a gap in knowledge about the ways in which men with cancer cope. While much is known about women, especially when they have breast cancer, not much has been done with men. A study carried out in Adelaide has looked at men with prostate cancer and come up with several different coping styles.

Some men respond with a very positive outlook, getting on with things.

The second way of coping is still a positive, active approach, but it tends to self-reliance, where the man wants to take control himself and look for his own solutions. This man is distrustful of doctors and what medicine has to offer and can seek out complementary therapies.

The third way is that the man confronted with a diagnosis of prostate cancer becomes emotionally available; open to support should it be offered, abandoning a lifetime of being strong and silent. This man doesn't go out looking for support but accepts it when people come forward.

The fourth way is when the man becomes quite distressed and despondent, and the fifth way was called 'solace' by the researchers. This man deals with his distress, sometimes with alcohol, but is reasonably phlegmatic, thinking that worse things could have happened to him.

The value in knowing that these patterns exist is that these men's partners and families and health professionals can find better ways of helping them through difficult times.[7]

▼ Vasectomy myths

Cross your legs for this one, lads, because it's about vasectomy – a pair of snips that many of us have found all sorts of excuses for avoiding, the main one being cowardice. But there has been another worry around for a while, and that's an alleged increased risk of prostate cancer after vasectomy.

Although no one's ever provided a sensible biological reason to explain why preventing sperm getting to the outside world should affect the prostate, there have been a couple studies suggesting a problem. According to research from New Zealand, the only excuse we blokes can fall back upon now is being lily-livered, because the researchers have been unable to show any link with prostate cancer.

The researchers compared over 900 men who have prostate cancer with over 1000 healthy men, and could find no increased risk associated with having had a vasectomy up to 25 years beforehand. The only thing that did raise the men's chances of prostate cancer was having a father or brother with the disease. Smoking, alcohol, number of children and ethnicity made no difference.

So, boys, you can't let science stand between you and a pair of scissors. Just lie back and think of New Zealand.[8]

SEX

▼ HIGH-PRESSURE LIBIDO

Men with high blood pressure are often concerned about taking medication because they're worried the drugs could affect their libido or sexual performance. One study has suggested that it could be the high blood pressure itself that's the problem.

The research was carried out in men in their 40s who were newly diagnosed with raised blood pressure. They were otherwise healthy, not on any medication and not obese; they were compared with similar men who didn't have high blood pressure.

Several things emerged.

The hypertensive men had significantly lower levels of sexual activity than men with normal blood pressure. They also had significantly lower levels of testosterone.

A reasonable question is whether or not testosterone and sexual activity are actually linked. Other work – which is controversial – has suggested that testosterone can influence your libido whether you're male or female, and in this study there was quite a close correlation in *both* groups of men between their testosterone levels and the number of times they had had sex (in any form) in the previous few weeks.

The next question is whether or not there's a link between testosterone and hypertension, and if there is, what comes first, the high blood pressure or the lower testosterone?

All sorts of things could flow from the answers to these questions – blood pressure treatment could improve sex or testosterone treatment could improve blood pressure. No one's sure what the answers are, yet.[1]

▼ LIQUORICE AND LIBIDO

You'll no doubt be delighted to hear that licorice has been given a qualified all clear when it comes to men with a low libido.

Before I go on, I should say that licorice isn't just another bit of confectionery. For many years it's been known to have significant effects on different bits of the body. It's a weak treatment for stomach ulcers, and affects the production of the stress hormone cortisone.

The way it does this is by slowing down the action of an enzyme which helps convert the raw material for cortisone into the active chemical. This enzyme is very similar to one in the testes, which helps the production of testosterone.

One study in the past found significant reductions in testosterone levels in men consuming liquorice, and the suggestion was that men complaining of low libido should be asked about whether or not they eat a lot of liquorice – and told to avoid it.

I don't know many liquorice-addicted men – do you? So you do wonder about the public health import of the study. Mind you, I wouldn't have a clue about men's libidos either.

Anyway, if you're a bloke and like gnawing on a stick of sticky black stuff between meals, you can relax, because a group in Texas – where clearly libidos are so big among the cowboys that you could ride all day and never get to the end of one – has done its own research into licorice and testosterone and found no significant association between the two.

So chew away, boys, but just don't show your tongue. That *is* something guaranteed to reduce anyone's libido.[2]

▼ Does Viagra help you die with a smile on your face?

That was initially a worry for doctors and consumers of this drug, who'd all like the smile without the death bit. Viagra – its non-brand name is sildenafil – is used to treat erectile dysfunction (as anyone who's not lived in a cave for the last few years knows).

Since it works by dilating blood vessels, the concern was that it could adversely affect the heart. Sildenafil must not be taken if you're on anti-angina drugs, for example, because you can suffer a life-threatening fall in blood pressure – blood which is need for the brain and heart goes elsewhere.

But what about sildenafil by itself? After all, men taking it are often elderly and at high risk of coronary disease. The other concern was that through no fault of the drug, just getting up after a spell, so to speak, could stress your ticker more than is good for you.

The first 5000 or 6000 men prescribed sildenafil in the UK were followed to see what happened to them, and the news was good. Nearly 9 out of 10 of them were still using the medication 3 months after being originally prescribed it.

And when the researchers calculated the numbers of these men who'd had a heart attack or angina while on sildenafil, they found that the rates of death from coronary disease were actually 30 per cent lower than they would have expected from the age and disease pattern of the group.

While this is comforting, two things need to be said. One is that two of the doctors in this study had had grants from Pfizer, the drug company which makes sildenafil, and two, this population might not be typical of the sildenafil user group in Australia – or even in the UK, were everyone to be followed.

It does indicate, though, that those smiles are likely to be living ones.

But what about sildenafil in men who already have heart disease? One study measured this objectively by putting such men on an exercise machine while monitoring their heart function. The results were good. Sildenafil had no adverse effects over and above the exercise itself.

So the question for potential sildenafil users is more about the effort involved in sexual intercourse. That depends on how athletic a couple like their sex, which in turn relates to physical fitness and whether or not there's some emotional stress as well.

It's said – probably by a bloke – that on average, having sex is the equivalent of climbing 20 stairs in 10 seconds. Some women might ask, why bother? But seriously, if that level of exercise causes difficulties for a man, starting sildenafil-induced sex after a spell probably needs care and probably some cardiac tests.[3]

▼ ... AND WHAT GOES UP MAY COME DOWN

After a medication has been in use for a while, side effects emerge simply because of numbers, and a word of warning has been raised about sildenafil as a result of some case reports. They were of two men who had epileptic seizures within a few hours of taking their first dose of sildenafil.

The first man was 63 and all his heart and brain tests were normal. He was advised that it was probably sildenafil, and was warned off it, but he tried it again a few months later and had another fit. The second case was a man of 54 who also had a convulsion a few hours after taking the erectile dysfunction drug for the first time, and again the tests were normal. Neither of the men was having sex at the time of the seizure.

Apparently the manufacturer of sildenafil had a number of similar reports itself, but they hadn't been as closely linked to the drug as these.

It's seems to be a rare problem, and cause and effect is far from proven. Even so, it means that doctors need to be vigilant with their patients on sildenafil should they have an unexpected seizure.[4]

STAYING YOUNG

▼ CAN HUMANS KEEP ON LIVING LONGER?

What can we expect as we age – well, what can *you* expect as *you* age, since, speaking personally, I've no intention of ageing at all. Governments would like to think we can't keep on getting older because they're terrified about forking out a shrinking tax base on an ever-ageing population. And indeed, some people who specialise in this field reckon there are signs that life expectancy is beginning to taper off and will reach its peak around 2075.

But one analysis should give Treasury the shivers. It provides strong evidence that the line on the graph of life expectancy isn't levelling off.

Female life expectancy, they say, has been rising at the rate of 3 months per year for the last 160 years. It's been happening in men too, but not quite so fast, which is partly because there were significant gains for women when childbirth became safer.

Around the world, the average length of time people live has doubled in the last 200 years. It's a result of all sorts of slow but steady advances in lifestyle, diet, housing, immunisation and medical treatment. And since there's no sign that such progress is slowing, why should increases in life expectancy slow either?

Another dramatic illustration of the change is that in Japan in 1950, a 65-year-old woman had a 1 in 1000 chance of surviving to 100. Today it's 1 in 20. A Japanese baby in 2070 will, according to these researchers, reasonably expect to live to 100. And unless we in Australia have a radical change in our living standards, we won't be far behind.

So for the rest of this century at least, it really does seem that age has no limits.[1]

▼ IF YOU LOOK OLD ON THE OUTSIDE, ARE YOU OLD ON THE INSIDE AS WELL?

In other words, if your face looks like a floor plan of Flinders' Street Station, should they be firing up the kiln now? Some skin researchers tried to answer this by working out a skin ageing score using things like sagging, wrinkling and texture.

Then they analysed the skin age of 360 non-cosmetically enhanced women aged between 18 and 80, to see how it differed from their real age. Overweight women tended to have younger skin than average for their age – no one was sure why. It was more than filling out of wrinkles. Smokers who'd sunned themselves too much had particularly older skin than their age. An incidental finding was that 9 out of 10 women under 40 had signs of acne despite denying that they suffered from the problem.

The variation in skin age compared with chronological age in this group of women was greater than could be explained by environmental influences, suggesting that genes had quite a lot to do with it.

The women's skin age seemed fairly stable till they turned 40. Then there was a rapid slide to wrinkles and sag. Which no doubt explains the queues for botox when 'un certain age' has been reached.[2]

▼ GUESS MY AGE

A study in the UK has bad news for male egos and good news for women's. When trained observers were asked to say how old a person was, they tended to underestimate a woman's age by about 6 months and *over*estimate a man's by 3 months.

The question is why? And does it mean anything? Are those who look older than they are likely to cark it sooner? The people in the study, by the way, were British civil servants under the age of 60. The observers were nurses and doctors who were seeing these people to do tests measuring ageing inside and out – before they opened the notes, they took a guess at the person's age.

When analysed afterwards, what appeared to influence their estimate was whether the person had smoking-damaged or sun-damaged skin, grey hair, and a circle round the cornea of the eye called arcus senilis.

It also turned out that the age estimate was related to cholesterol levels: the older they looked, the higher their blood fats.

So maybe they were ageing faster on the inside too.

If the findings are right, it means that if you want to look young, stop smoking, stay indoors, eat low-fat foods, dye your hair and see a plastic surgeon.

And, as I say more than once in this book, you may not live longer, but it'll sure feel as if you are.[3]

▼ Calorie restriction and longevity – it may be something else

Perhaps the elixir of youth is not an elixir at all but a zip across your mouth, especially if you're a cold kind of person who burns sugar well and has good sexual raw material.

It's long been known that if you restrict the calorie intake of rats they live longer. Since no one cares much about rats, they're trying it in monkeys, and preliminary results suggest that calorie-restricted monkeys have about half the death rate of those given as many bananas as their little primate hearts desire.

Since most of us care more about ourselves than we do about even the cutest of monkeys, the same researchers have also investigated humans. They've done this in a 45 year study which has been following normal human ageing.

The monkeys who did best on calorie restriction were those with the lowest natural body temperature, the lowest insulin levels and the highest levels of a hormone called DHEAS, which is the raw material for testosterone. DHEAS normally declines as we age.

And it turns out that in humans too these three things identified those who were living the longest – but not necessarily those on the least number of calories.

The question is what you can do about it? Well, the value and safety of DHEAS supplements are really not known, but there's no harm in pumping iron, because that can lower your insulin – and maybe you should 'chill out' as well.[4]

▼ Is voting Labour (in the UK) bad for longevity?

That could be your conclusion from a superficial reading of research from Britain where they compared voting patterns in the 1997 general election with the chances of dying at any given age. Being a Labour voter was frequently distinctly less conducive to a long life than being a Tory.

But the story's not so simple.

In the last few years Britain has managed to lower the chances of dying prematurely at a rate of nearly 2 per cent per annum. When you look at voting patterns, though – and Australia is unlikely to be much different – areas with a higher concentration of Labour voters had a significantly lower rate of improvement; in fact for some, the chances of premature death had increased.

Conservative constituencies were the ones which showed the main gains.

This means that in relative terms, since the Blair Government has been in office, the health gap between rich and poor regions in the UK has widened. It dulls the shine on their 1997 slogan, 'Things can only get better'.

What does this mean for Australia? It confirms a century of research which shows that health inequalities closely follow occupational, educational and economic disparity. The wider the gap, the bigger the problem. Spending money on hospitals and doctors isn't the complete solution. Major effects also come from education and other structural factors in the economy.[5]

▼ Keep mental

'Use it or lose it' is a common refrain; the cynics say you have to have whatever *it* is before you can even think of using it.

In other words, perhaps older people who keep themselves active and alert are the ones with the equipment to do it and those in whom the rot has set in don't have a chance.

A 5 year study of leisure activities in nearly 500 people aged over 75 has suggested that mental activities can lower the risk of dementia.

What we're talking about are things which require some mental effort – reading, writing, doing crosswords, playing board games or cards, playing musical instruments or participating in group discussions, for example. The participants were carefully assessed to ensure that there was no decline in thinking and memory at the start.

Allowing for illness and education level (since the more education you've had, the later you develop dementia), reading, board games and playing an instrument seemed to be protective. With physical activities, only dancing stepped up to the mark.

For every day when such activities are done each week, the dementia risk fell by 7 per cent.

To be sure of this, a properly conducted trial will be needed, but meantime, keep shaking those dice.[6]

▼ SIZE DOES MATTER

If Finnish men are anything to go by, their chances of getting married are partly set in the womb.

Finland, like most Scandinavian countries, has excellent health information on its citizens going back decades, and researchers wanted to see if there was a biological explanation for why unmarried men live shorter lives than married ones.

Some have thought that it's the hard work of a good woman which saves them – but maybe, just maybe, the reason for a shorter life is that unmarried men are shorter and heavier, having been shorter and *lighter* at birth.

This was supported by comparing the Finns with English men from Hertfordshire. The conclusion was that men who were small at birth were less likely to marry. It's also been suspected that low birth weight and a degree of deprivation of the mother while pregnant might raise the risk of some diseases in the offspring of that pregnancy.

So if cause and effect can be ascribed to all this, small babies mean a smaller chance of getting married – and, perhaps, a higher risk of heart disease.

The solution may be enhancement – not of body parts, but of women's ability to have normal birth weight babies.

This question about whether or not environmental influences can explain the fact that tall people tend to live longer than short ones has been studied in cemeteries, of all places.

Researchers have studied the bones from 3000 skeletons in a northeast England graveyard which dates back to the 9th century.

In those days men lived longer than women – to about 37 years compared with 31 (meaning that you can take natural childbirth only so far). One thing they found was that the forearm bone length increased by 0.2 cm every 200 years (a long time to wait if you're trying to reach that top shelf). This probably reflects improving nutrition.

When it came to height, they found that the longer your bones, the longer you lived, whether you were living in the 9th or the 19th century – even though the killing diseases in both those times were very different from those we have now. Nutrition must have had something to do with it, but shortness by itself was probably a factor.

If you're short I wouldn't worry, though, because one of the consolations is that we won't have to look up to tall people quite as long as we might have thought.[7]

▼ MALE HORMONE MEDICATION FALTERS

In some places, a popular drug among middle-aged men is androstenedione, which is used by the body to make testosterone. These men take androstenedione in the hope of reversing the decline in male hormones as they age.

So does it work and is it safe?

A small study in Texas, where you'd think that men don't need help for anything, suggested that androstenedione didn't come up with the goods. They measured weight, abdominal girth, blood fat levels and sex hormones before and after a month on the supplement, compared with a month on a placebo.

The results showed that there really wasn't much of a testosterone response. Other hormones did go up, though, making some people believe it could cause harm, but apart from a decrease in the good form of cholesterol – HDL – no other potentially harmful effects were found after this short course. Muscle bulk didn't change much either.

So the bottom line for blokes is that if you're taking androstenedione for rejuvenation, your money might be better spent at a gym and on hair dye.[8]

▼ INTELLIGENCE AND LIVING LONGER

Your IQ at age 11 could predict your chances of surviving to old age – at least according to a study of nearly 3000 people born in Scotland in 1921.

In 1932 there was a huge intelligence survey of all Scottish 11-year-olds, and researchers have now studied what happened to some of them and compared that with their IQ. When they controlled for other factors such as deprivation, the results indicated that there was a very close correlation between a child's mental ability and his or her chances of reaching age 76.

A 15 point drop in the IQ test reduced the chances of reaching that age by about 20 per cent, rising to 40 per cent for a 30 point drop. This was even though they found that men with higher IQs were more likely than men with lower IQs to have died in action in World War II.

These findings support other research in this field. There are various possible reasons.

A low IQ at age 11 might be due to poor nutrition in the mother during pregnancy or physical illnesses in the child.

A high IQ might give the child more mental capacity to withstand diseases like Alzheimer's.

Or a decent IQ might make people more liable to adopt healthy behaviours or able to qualify for safer occupations.[9]

▼ Preventing falls – what works?

Our parents are going to be around much longer than ever before in human history, which means that more of us are going to have to deal with their ageing problems as well as our own.

One of the most difficult of those problems, because of its unpredictability, is the fall. In people aged over 65, 1 in 3 fall per year, and 20 per cent of those need treatment, because older people can do themselves a lot of damage in a fall.

There's now good evidence that something can be done about it.

If you can get access to allied health services such as occupational therapists, they can go into your home and seek out and eliminate potential hazards. In general, having a multidisciplinary team involved in an older person's care is a good thing.

Muscle strengthening and balance training seems to work, as does treating heart arrhythmias and, possibly, removing medications which could have a sedative effect.

Older people can also be taught practical ways of getting themselves up should they fall, so that they don't languish on a cold floor till help comes.

And finally, tai chi appears to work, probably because it improves balance.[10]

▼ HAEMOGLOBIN AND WELLBEING

How often have you gone to the doctor's and been told, 'Don't worry, it's nothing', and been left uncertain that the reassurance was well founded? It seems, from preliminary research findings, that one test result widely accepted to be in the healthy range might not be so normal for older people.

It's your haemoglobin level.

Haemoglobin carries oxygen, and if it's low we're said to be anaemic. Older people often have haemoglobin levels which don't quite qualify as anaemia or are just on the low side and no one does anything about it.

A study at Johns Hopkins University in Baltimore, which investigated 1000 women aged over 65, found that within the normal range of haemoglobin, between 12 and 14, there was a remarkable difference in levels of disability. Women with a haemoglobin of 12 had twice the risk of those with a reading of 14 of having difficulties walking short distances and climbing stairs; if their haemoglobin was 10, the risk was 4 times that of those with a haemoglobin of 14. That was after adjusting for the people who had underlying disease.

The unanswered questions are is the relationship a cause-and-effect one, and does taking iron to boost the haemoglobin make a difference?[11]

▼ FRAILTY

'Frail' is a word often used about older people. If you've ever watched an older person in decline, you'll recognise the word and have an image of what it means. In Australia, a lot of money and effort goes into assisting the frail elderly.

However, research in the US has found that people mean different things when they use the word 'frail'. This could imply that the so-called frail are being misclassified, and not necessarily getting the right kind of help.

A decade-long research programme in the US has progressively wrestled the definition of frailty to the ground. Essentially, it's a progressive inability to deal with physical and psychological stress, and involves three or more things, including weight loss, physical slowdown (not walking as quickly, for example), loss of muscle strength and a sense of exhaustion (losing get up and go).

That's independent of whatever illnesses the person may have.

The question is whether being frail is a sign that you're about to turn up your toes, or can it be prevented or reversed? So far there's not a lot of evidence either way, but the suggestion is that keeping active, having good social contacts and support from the people around you, plus muscle strength training with weights, may be effective.[12]

▼ TRYING TO COUNTER IMMUNE AGEING

As we age, our immune systems work less well. That's the main reason why pneumonia's such a big killer in the elderly. In some studies in older people, vitamins and minerals have been shown to improve immune function when tested on blood samples – but that's a long way from saying that people who take these supplements are better protected against infections.

A trial in The Netherlands gave a placebo or vitamin E or a multivitamin/mineral supplement to several hundred healthy older people. Over 14 or 15 months, there was no difference in the rates of respiratory infection, but in the vitamin E group, the severity of the infections was greater. They had a longer illness, more fever and more symptoms.

There are all sorts of imponderables with a study like this. Would it have been different if the people were malnourished rather than healthy, as these were? Would higher doses have worked better? What about other possible benefits, such as dementia delay?

Even so, large numbers of people take these supplements, and they need to know that there may be hidden risks – more safety reassurances are needed.[13]

WEIGHT LOSS

▼ Atkins Diet – can 10 million people be wrong?

Ten million copies of the Atkin's Diet have been sold. This is not surprising, since nearly 1 in 2 women and 1 in 3 men are either dieting or thinking about dieting.

Doctors have slagged off at Atkin's because of its high fat content and restrictions on fruit and vegetables, and it hasn't helped that the Atkin's diet hasn't been well studied. More recently, though, in a real-world randomised trial researchers compared the Atkin's Diet with a calorie-controlled low-fat diet. By 'real world' I mean that they tried to simulate how most of us attempt to lose weight – namely, by ourselves and without supervision.

At 6 months, the Atkin's diet people had lost 4 per cent more than those on the regular diet – amounting to about 4 kg less on board. They also had a greater rise in the good form of cholesterol (HDL) and a lower triglyceride (an unhealthy blood fat) reading. What didn't move on the Atkin's Diet was the bad cholesterol – LDL. Both diets lowered blood pressure and made the body more sensitive to insulin.

After a year, though, nearly half the participants had dropped out and there was no significant difference between the groups. So Atkin's may not achieve the Holy Grail of ongoing diet success, and no one knows yet the long-term effects of eating little fruit and vegies.[1]

▼ Are garlic and chilli peppers weight loss foods in disguise?

There's growing evidence that populations with high garlic and chilli consumption have lower rates of obesity – these populations are mostly in Asian countries. That's after the higher levels of activity and lower levels of fat and energy intake are allowed for.

If it's true, how do these substances work?

There's been a theory that chilli increases our metabolic rate – our energy consumption. That partly comes from the observation we've all made that chilli makes us sweat; there is also some evidence that it causes greater heat production in the body – a bit like caffeine.

When caffeine and chilli have been studied in real life, though, they seem to work by reducing appetite or making us feel full more readily rather than by boosting energy consumption. However, there is some evidence that chilli helps to break down fat by oxidising it.

One Dutch trial of chilli extract (capsaicin) aimed to see if capsaicin would assist with maintaining weight loss in a group of overweight adults. Researchers found that while there was added fat oxidation, there was no slowing effect on weight gain.

Garlic seems to reduce our fat and carbohydrate intake, which affects weight, of course. (Maybe it's because waiters stay away from us because of our breath.)

Anyway, it's probably too early to make definite recommendations and we're twitchy enough as a society already without pushing caffeine-like substances even more. The place to start is more research into low-obesity communities so that we can tie down the reasons for that much more firmly.

Meantime, you can't do a lot of harm by asking for extra chilli on that stir fry ... just beware of the sparks a few hours later.[2]

▼ MAINTAINING WEIGHT LOSS

The statistics on keeping weight off once you've lost it are depressing. If you've been obese and return to the normal weight for your height, there's a 95 per cent chance your kilos will head north again. People who lose modest amounts of weight often do better, but most still stick it back on. Surveys of successful weight losers show that those who keep their weight under control do so because of the enormous amount of exercise they do: between 60 and 90 minutes a day.

A more practical question for non-dieters is how to slow down our inexorable rise in weight year after year. You see, our obesity epidemic comes from a pathetically tiny number of excess calories a day.

The problem is that, probably for genetic reasons, our appetite and eating are very hard to control. Even cutting out a few calories a day is tough, long term. The other answer is jacking up the energy expenditure. In the State of Colorado they've handed out those little wearable step meters and are challenging people to take an extra 2000 steps a day. So far, they know the meter helps in getting people to step up their exercise. Whether it holds back the weight is yet to be seen.[3]

▼ Big-boned in your genes

We're fat and getting fatter. We're hearing that *ad nauseam*; the question is, why?

You can only pin part of the blame on our environment. At least 40 per cent of our body weight is genetically determined. Most of us who veer to the pudgy have an insidious genetic network conspiring – in my case at least – to make us hoover up the kids' leftovers after dinner.

British researchers have been trying to find single genes which might be at fault, and as a result they've found that there are folk who really can call themselves 'big-boned'.

They've tested about 800 families who have very obese children, and discovered that 5 per cent have a defect in a gene called MC4R, or the melanocortin 4 receptor.

This is a lock and key mechanism for processes which control our metabolism, especially appetite. While MC4R children eat a lot and are obese, they're sometimes hard to pick, because in addition to carrying a lot of fat, they're tall and look strong – they have more muscle as well.

There are no treatments for MC4R yet, but people are testing possible medications.

Mind you, I'm not sure where the front rows of school rugby teams will come from if the drugs work.[4]

▼ Another contender for obesity drug?

Researchers hoping to profit from our desire for thinness don't give up. You might recall hearing about leptin a few years ago. It's a hormone produced by fat cells which made fat rodents lose weight, and was supposed to be the answer. A pharmaceutical company paid millions for the rights, but leptin hasn't panned out in most humans.

Now there's a new contender, with the code name SNAP. It blocks the effects of a brain hormone in areas which regulate appetite and food intake, and when given to rats which have eaten so much they've become fat, the doubtless grateful rodents lose weight.

SNAP seems to have other effects, though. When tested to see whether or not it changed other aspects of rat behaviour, they found that it did: it had an antidepressant and anti-anxiety effect. Apparently they can tell this from the way rats interact and swim when forced to.

The next step is to see whether humans will SNAP to attention the way these poor rats have.

I'll let you know.[5]

▼ MENTAL ILLNESS AND YOUR WEIGHT

There are links between obesity, the epidemic on everyone's lips at the moment, and mental health. But which way does it go? Do fat people become depressed and anxious because they're fat, or does mental illness lead to obesity? And what role, if any, does weight loss play in restoring mental wellbeing?

An Australian study of 7000 people has not found a relationship between anxiety and depression and obesity at all. There was a slight connection in women between physical illness and obesity, though: for a given level of physical illness, it didn't matter to your mental health how fat you were, but being obese increased the risk of other diseases.

Then they adjusted for the effect of physical illness on anxiety and depression, and what bubbled to the surface then was that the men and women whose weight did tend to be linked to mental health were actually *under*weight. They had the worst mental health in the sample.

Can't win, can you?

Anyway, it suggests that losing weight in its own right won't fix up your mental wellbeing; the only time it might would be if it alleviates your physical ailments along the way.[6]

▼ OBESITY AND THE HEART

No one's really been sure why obesity is a coronary risk factor in its own right. It's true that if you're fat you're more likely to develop diabetes, high blood pressure and have too much bad cholesterol floating around. But even after those are taken into account, obesity stands proud as a heart risk by itself. Why?

In a study of obese women, Italian researchers looked closely at atherosclerosis – the progressive blockage of arteries by cholesterol damage. This involves actual inflammation in the artery lining, oxygen reactions a bit like rusting, and the switching on of platelets – little fragments in the blood which are an essential part of blood clotting.

The results showed that women with male-pattern obesity – the fat on the abdomen more than the hips – had significantly higher levels of this inflammation and platelet activation than women with a pear shape: the greater the waist circumference, the bigger the problem.

The good news was that weight loss helped to switch off the problem.[7]

▼ Obesity not as big a barrier to surgery

Many surgeons hate operating on obese people. I remember one wit saying after making his abdominal incision on a particularly heavy person, 'If my feet disappear, please pull me out.'

Surgeons believe that obesity causes all sorts of complications, from wound infections to blood clots, but a group of Swiss surgeons tested this by following over 6000 people undergoing non-emergency abdominal operations.

There was no doubt that the fatter a person was, the more likely he or she was to have heart disease, high blood pressure or diabetes, but it did seem from the statistics that thinner people were more likely to have an operation in the first place. Surgeons also preferred to use keyhole surgery on obese patients.

Even allowing for these differences, the only complications which were greater in obese people were wound infections – and only in people having a large abdominal incision. There were no differences when laparoscopic surgery was performed. In addition, the surgery itself didn't take significantly longer in fatter people.

The factors which counted in terms of complications, regardless of body size, were how major the surgery was and whether or not the abdomen needed to be opened.

The conclusions were that obese people shouldn't be denied operations if they need them or forced to lose weight, but that laparoscopic surgery should be carried out whenever possible.[8]

▼ Asthma link to childhood obesity?

Asthma is becoming more and more common across the world and there are many theories about this. One is that as children grow up in ever more hygienic environments, their immune systems don't get the training they need in the first year of life.

The result is misguided white blood cells and antibodies which overreact to allergy-causing substances in the air. Another theory is that children spend too much time in front of television and computer games, increasing their exposure to delightful things like cockroach poo and house dust mites.

In recent years another idea has emerged: that the rise in asthma is caused by the increase in obesity and being overweight. Several studies have found a link, and a group in Britain tested this further in a large number of children who were followed from 1972 to 1994.

They found that over this time, while both asthma and the incidence of being overweight or obese increased, they weren't linked. Asthma was more common in fatter children, but the obesity seemed to be a marker for something else, not part of the cause.

The real factors could be in the diet – or the TV. Kids who are obese spend more time on front of the telly than thin ones. So get those TV addicts off their bums and out of the house.[9]

Women's Health

▼ PMT AND HORMONES

Hundreds of thousands of Australian women suffer from premenstrual syndrome as defined by a set of physical and psychological symptoms in the second half of their menstrual cycle. Sometimes it's bad enough to need treatment but the question is with what?

One trend has been to use one of a family of female hormones called progestogens. The theory is that the woman isn't producing enough progesterone – the natural form of the hormone – in the latter part of her cycle.

There isn't much evidence to back up that belief but since when has that stopped medics from getting out their prescription pads? A group of gynaecologists has reviewed properly conducted trials testing whether progesterone-type medications work in PMS. They found no support for the practice of prescribing progesterone or progestogens for premenstrual syndrome.

Which means another theory bites the dust and there's one thing fewer to distract researchers in this field who are still struggling to find a reliable, safe therapy. Educating adolescent girls about the menstrual cycle and its symptoms helps, as may some of the newer anti-depressant medications, possibly because of their effects on nerve transmission in the brain.[1]

▼ URINARY LEAKAGE – A VERY COMMON PROBLEM

One of the largest-ever studies into urinary incontinence in women has found a high prevalence – even in young women and those who've never had a baby – and that adolescent bedwetting might be an important and neglected factor.

The two main problems are stress incontinence, which affects younger women more, and means trouble with leakage when laughing, coughing or taking exercise. The other problem – especially in older women – is urge incontinence, which is an intense desire to pass water and trouble holding on.

The University of Newcastle in NSW has been following the health of 42,000 women and one of the things they asked was whether they had any problems holding their water.

They found that out of 100 adult women, around 35 of them will have a problem.

The risk factors were: increased weight – every kilogram adds more pressure to the bladder; childbearing – the first and fourth children are the ones which caused the problem; and adolescent bedwetting. One of the reasons for high rates among young women seemed to be the under-recognised issue of unresolved bedwetting which goes on into adolescence and even early adulthood. It's hidden and neglected.

The cost of incontinence is considerable to these women – hundreds of dollars a year excluding the expense of treatments.

Teaching better bladder control and pelvic floor exercises to young women is thought to be part of the answer, and the Newcastle researchers have had some success with a regimen that takes up less time than is normally required.[2]

▼ BEHAVIOURAL THERAPY FOR INCONTINENCE

In younger women the commonest form is stress incontinence, where exercise, coughing, sneezing and even laughing can cause some urine to leak. Surgery helps, but it's major and the effects can wear off, which is why behavioural therapy has become popular – and it's effective. It involves training women to do pelvic floor exercises, asking them to keep a bladder diary and teaching them ways to control their bladders when they need to.

Another technique is electrical stimulation of the pelvic floor, which has also been shown to work. But is it worth adding to behavioural treatment? A recent trial compared three groups of women. One had a full behavioural programme by itself, a second had the programme plus electrical stimulation, and the third was just given a self-help booklet.

The results showed that the stimulator didn't add anything to the behaviour therapy, although the women who had it were more satisfied. The booklet had a significant effect, but not as great.

The key to pelvic floor training is being prepared to stick with it and work hard.[3]

▼ Cranberry juice wins against probiotics for urinary symptoms

Most women will have a urinary infection at some time in their lives. Quite a few will have more than one, and it's often women in their 20s who suffer most.

It's known that cranberry juice is quite good at preventing urinary infection, but it's been thought that live yoghurt drinks might also help by changing the germs to more harmless ones. The micro-organism which seems to count in these probiotic drinks and foods is called lactobacillus GG.

The Finns did a year-long study comparing the effects of cranberry/lingonberry juice with those of lactobacillus GG drinks, taken daily, on women with recurrent urinary tract infections. 'What's a lingonberry?' you may ask. Well, it's from the same Vaccinium berry family as cranberry.

The result was that the daily cranberry/lingonberry juice mix worked and the lactobacillus GG didn't, although 5 women needed to swallow the juice for 6 months for 1 of them to benefit – so you'd have to like it. Overall, then, the chances of an individual woman preventing a urinary infection were about 20 per cent.

The reason berry juice works is thought to be a natural substance which stops the E coli germ sticking to the sides of the bladder.[4]

▼ Milk and bone loss

A casual walk down the dairy aisle in your supermarket will leave you in no doubt that the osteoporosis prevention market is alive, well and huge.

Researchers from the University of Adelaide studied the use of calcium-fortified milk in women just after the menopause, to see if it had any effect on their bone loss. The significance of being just after the menopause is that that's when women lose bone at the greatest rate. It tends to slow down a bit after that. So if you can prevent some bone loss during those early years after menopause there could be a disproportionate benefit.

Anyway, the study was done in such a way that each woman became her own control. For 1 year she took an extra 3 litres a week of calcium-fortified milk and for 1 year she didn't. The bone loss was measured in each woman's spine and forearm – two vulnerable places for fractures later in life.

The results showed significantly lower bone loss in the spine in women using the calcium-fortified milk, but no change in the forearm bones. They didn't measure bone loss at the hip. Why there is this difference between sites in the body they don't know – but the bottom line is that if you're a healthy woman not at particular risk of osteoporosis, then calcium-fortified milk in decent amounts (so that you're getting over 700 mg of extra calcium per day) is a good idea; and, from other studies, it's even better if you exercise too.[5]

▼ HRT – THE END OF AN ERA

In mid-July 2002, the *Journal of the American Medical Association* express-published the results of an interrupted trial designed to see whether or not hormone replacement therapy (HRT) had real health benefits. The study, called the Women's Health Initiative (WHI), was a large trial of HRT in many thousands of post-menopausal women. It was stopped because the rates of heart disease and invasive breast cancer went up. The worldwide headlines were dramatic: a 26 per cent increase in the risk of breast cancer, a 29 per cent increased risk of heart attack and a 41 per cent increase in the risk of stroke.

Breast cancer support groups said this scared women by giving a misleading view of the figures. It was easy to assume – wrongly – that a 26 per cent increase in risk means that for every 100 women taking HRT, 26 were likely to get breast cancer. But that's not what it meant: it means the risk if you're on HRT is 26 per cent higher than the risk you'd have anyway.

In the WHI, 30 women out of 10,000 women *not* taking HRT developed breast cancer. That rose to 38 women per 10,000 if they were on it – a rise of 8 women per 10,000 taking the medication, which is much less dramatic. Eight is about 26 per cent of 30 – that's where the figure comes from.

However, the extra risk was real, and made many women question whether or not they really needed HRT. Since then more results from WHI have been forthcoming – and none are hugely on the side of HRT.

For instance, the study measured two substances in the blood which are a sign of the kind of inflammation that goes on in damaged arteries. One's called C-reactive protein (CRP) and the other interleukin 6 (IL-6). The theory is that HRT raises CRP and IL-6 and that's why the risk of heart attacks goes up.

While the study showed that HRT did raise CRP levels, it also showed that HRT didn't touch IL-6.

The other – and far more important – finding was that women's risk of a heart attack was more closely related to how high their CRP and IL-6 levels were at the start of the study than whether they were or were not on HRT. In other words, HRT was less of a risk than those signs of inflammation, which, by the way – and here's the good news – tend to decline when you quit cigarettes, eat well and take exercise.

Another reason women take HRT is to improve their quality of life, and the results from WHI included effects on sleep, hot flushes, energy levels, depression and sex.

One year after starting HRT, the biggest improvements were in hot flushes and night sweats. There were small benefits from HRT in sleep, general physical functioning and bodily pain, but after 3 years, these had largely disappeared. There were no effects at any time on mental wellbeing, sexual satisfaction or energy levels when compared with the dummy medication.

Then there are thinking ability, memory and dementia, because studies which observed women, rather than putting them on a controlled trial, had suggested that there is a protective benefit from hormone replacement. Animal studies had also found that oestrogen is good for the brain.

But in the harsh glare of a scientific trial, HRT – sadly – didn't deliver. In fact it may have made things worse: 61 women overall out of 4500 developed dementia over 4 years. About 40 of them came from the HRT group and 20 from those on placebo, which is about double the risk. That translates to an extra 23 women developing dementia out of every 10,000 taking hormone replacements.

Needless to say, they could find no evidence of HRT slowing a decline in thinking ability, or improving it. These results are for combined HRT with progesterone and oestrogen. The trial continues with oestrogen alone to see if that's different.

It's unlikely that there'll ever be another trial of HRT, so these conclusions can probably be taken as it. HRT is best for hot flushes and helps bones but probably not a lot else, especially for use lasting more than 3 years. While there are alternatives for bone density, there isn't much else available to help menopausal women who are seriously affected by their symptoms. It's a challenge for medical science.[6]

▼ Phyto-oestrogens and menopause

Long before the recent problems with hormone replacement therapy, many women preferred more natural ways to minimise menopausal symptoms. Particularly appealing was the belief that fewer women in Asia had hot flushes – or flashes – a benefit attributed to a high soy intake and its oestrogen-like compounds (isoflavones).

Some manufacturers jumped on this and produced supplements containing these phyto-oestrogens, most commonly derived from red clover, but until recently no one has known whether or not they really work. A US trial, funded – to its credit – by the Australian company Novogen (which makes Promensil and Rimostil) studied about 250 post-menopausal women who were having at least 35 hot flashes per week.

After 3 months, everyone, including those on a placebo, had about 40 per cent fewer hot flashes. Those on Promensil had a faster reduction, but there was still no difference after 12 weeks. In general, overweight women had a greater benefit, but the reason was unclear. There were no differences in side effects.

The findings contradict some smaller studies, and it's possible that taking phyto-oestrogens in more frequent higher doses might work. But on the basis of this study, you'd have to say they were no better than a dummy preparation.[7]

▼ The pill and wellbeing – keep off the cigarettes

The oral contraceptive pill has had a bad rap which, unlike HRTs, doesn't seem to be merited. Researchers in the 1960s started following over 17,000 women to see what happened to those on the pill long term. Some recent findings have looked at those women in the original group who had died.

There was no raised risk of death from breast cancer in pill users, but there was a 7-fold increase in the risk of cervical cancer, possibly because using the pill was associated with less condom use. The incidence of cancers of the uterus and ovary fell.

Heart disease and the risk of dying from stroke were not significantly raised unless the women smoked. The chances of dying of a heart attack were more than quadrupled at 15 cigarettes or more a day, and doubled at fewer than that per day. Lung cancer risk, by the way, increased 40-fold!

Overall, women who took the pill tended to be less likely to die prematurely than those who hadn't, allowing for the fact that they were probably healthier in the first place.

The dose of oestrogen that these women had taken in the pill tended to be higher than that in today's formulations, which could mean today's pills are even safer.

The main message is that women should think twice about combining smoking and the pill; given the choice, it's the cigarettes that should go.[8]

▼ IUDs DON'T DESERVE A BAD NAME

Intrauterine devices – IUDs – have a bad name in Australia, and their use for contraception has waned considerably over the years. You may recall high-profile litigation involving the Dalkon Shield and the Copper Seven.

Yet despite this, IUDs are still used by millions of women worldwide. They're a relatively cheap and – many believe – safe form of contraception. The question is, are these millions of women at risk or are Australian women missing out?

One of the main concerns is that IUDs cause pelvic inflammatory disease or, at the very least, make pelvic infections more likely and therefore increase the chances of blocked tubes and infertility. According to a well-conducted study, this is not so.

They compared a group of infertile women with blocked tubes with a group of infertile women with open tubes and with a group of pregnant women – you can't get much better proof of fertility than that. There was no difference in copper IUD use between the groups – which, put another way, means there was no added risk of tubal blockage, regardless of the duration of use of the IUD or of the presence of other gynaecological problems.

What did predict infertility from blocked tubes, in this and other studies, was sexually transmitted *Chlamydia* infection – the commonest germ causing pelvic inflammation.

It is highly likely, said the authors, that the bad press given to copper IUDs in the past was from studies which didn't adequately account for one very important factor: women who use contraception of any kind are doing it because they're having sex, and having unprotected sex (sex without a condom, that is) is a risky business.[9]

▼ WOMEN AND ALCOHOL

A lot of the stories you hear about health benefits from things in your diet come from less than reliable research. The information is usually based on studies where patterns of disease – or of disease absence – are noticed in groups of people with particular lifestyles. Or, they take a group of people with, say, diabetes or colon cancer and compare them with people without the problems.

But this is far short of proof that taking on that habit or rejecting it will guarantee you the good life. What's needed for that is a trial where they actually give people the stuff and see whether it works compared with nothing or a placebo.

That's what they did with alcohol in healthy post-menopausal women. Over 8 weeks these women took 1 or 2 drinks per day to see what the effects were on blood fats called triglycerides, as well as to examine the sensitivity of their bodies to insulin. Insensitivity or resistance to insulin is related to the risk of adult onset diabetes.

Over the 2 months, those women allocated 2 standard drinks per day showed lower triglyceride levels and increased insulin sensitivity.

Which was the good news.

The not-so-good news was that the alcohol also increased the levels of hormones known to be linked to breast cancer.

So there's a balancing act here. Heart disease and diabetes in women are far more common than breast cancer but no one knows whether 2 drinks a day ends up with more upside or more downside.

The link between alcohol consumption and the risk of breast cancer has been controversial, and a review of the available evidence tried to get to the bottom of it.

Analysing all the published papers they could lay their hands on, the researchers concluded that alcohol does seem to be a risk factor for breast cancer. Quantifying the risk is another matter. It looked as though an effect was there at 1 standard drink per day but really kicked in at 3 or more drinks a day, which is quite a lot for women.

If these figures are right, then in a country such as Australia or the US, maybe only 2 per cent of women with breast cancer could put the blame on alcohol. In Italy it might be as high as 15 per cent.

Why might it be so?

Alcohol may affect female hormones, which in turn could drive breast cells to multiply faster. Alcohol may also make breast tissue denser, which would make tumours harder to diagnose. Another theory is that alcohol may interact with vitamins and increase the risk through complex processes in the breast.

The message, then, is that the occasional drink isn't a problem. If you're drinking more than 3 glasses a day, don't, and if you have other reasons to be concerned about breast cancer, you should probably keep off the stuff.[10]

REFERENCES

ASTHMA AND ALLERGIES
1. Matheson M et al. *Internal Medicine Journal*. 2002; 32: 451–56.
2. Powell H & Gibson PG *The Cochrane Library*, Issue 4, 2003.
   Sinuff T *Evidence-Based Medicine*. 2003; 8: 115.
3. Illi S et al. *British Medical Journal* 2001; 322: 390–95.
4. Downs SH et al. *Medical Journal of Australia*. 2001; 175: 10–13.
   Torzillo PJ & Chang AB *Medical Journal of Australia*. 2001; 175: 4–5.
5. Chilvers ER at al. *Journal of the Royal College of Physicians of London*. 2000; 34: 68–74.
   Mecklenburgh K et al. *Monaldi Archives for Chest Disease*. 1999; 54: 345–49.
6. Rijssenbeek-Nouwens LHM et al. *Thorax*. 2002; 57: 784–90.
7. Ownby DR et al. *Journal of the American Medical Association*. 2002; 288: 963–72.
   Platts-Mills TAE *Journal of the American Medical Association*. 2002; 288:1012–14.
8. Custovic A et al. *Lancet*. 2001; 358: 188–93.
9. Lewith GT et al. *British Medical Journal*. 2002; 324: 520–23.
10. Lazarus SC et al. *Journal of the American Medical Association*. 2001; 285: 2583–93.
    Lemanske RF et al. *Journal of the American Medical Association*. 2001; 285: 2594–603.
    Website www.nationalasthma.org.au/
11. McDonald NJ & Bara AI *The Cochrane Library*. Issue 3, 2003.
12. van der Wouden JC et al. *The Cochrane Library*. Issue 3, 2003.
13. Gazarian M et al. *Medical Journal of Australia*. 2001; 174: 394–97.
14. Sawyer MG et al. *Journal of Asthma*. 2001; 38: 279–84.
15. Lack G et al. *New England Journal of Medicine*. 2003; 348: 977–85.
    Metzger H *New England Journal of Medicine*. 2003; 348: 1046–48.
16. *Australian Medicines Handbook*, 2000.
    Therapeutic Guidelines – Antibiotic. 2003: Version 12, Therapeutic Guidelines Limited, Melbourne.

BABIES AND CHILDREN
1. Gillman MW et al. *Journal of the American Medical Association*. 2001; 285: 2461–67.
   Hediger ML et al. *Journal of the American Medical Association*. 2001; 285: 2453–60.
   Li L et al. *British Medical Journal*. 2003; 327: 904–905.
   Victoria CG et al. *British Medical Journal*. 2003; 327: 901–904.
2. Ingram J et al. *Lancet*. 2001; 358: 986–87.
3. Atkinson M and Gale EAM *Journal of the American Medical Association*. 2003; 290: 1771–72.
   Norris JM et al. *Journal of the American Medical Association*. 2003; 290: 1713–20.
   Ziegler A-G et al. *Journal of the American Medical Association*. 2003; 290: 1721–28.
4. Website www.abc.net.au/rn/talks/8.30/helthrpt/stories/s949406.htm
5. Website www.abc.net.au/rn/talks/8.30/helthrpt/stories/s459344.htm
6. Strom BL et al. *Journal of the American Medical Association*. 2001; 286: 807–14.

7 Madjenovic G & Levitsky DA *Journal of Pediatrics*. 2003; 142: 604–10.
   Schwartz RP *Journal of Pediatrics*. 2003; 142: 599–601.
8 Coghlan D & Cranswick NE. *Medical Journal of Australia*. 2001; 175: 223–24.
9 Hiscock H & Wake M *British Medical Journal*. 2002; 324: 1062–65. Available: bmj.com/cgi/content/full/324/7345/1062.
10 Hunt CE et al. *Archives of Pediatrics and Adolescent Medicine*. 2003; 157: 469–74.
11 Emmons KM et al. *Pediatrics*. 2001; 108: 18–24.
12 Lawrence GL et al. *Australian and New Zealand Journal of Public Health*. 2003; 27: 413–18.
13 Centers for Disease Control (CDC). *Morbidity and Mortality Weekly Report*. 2002; 51: 1070–72.
   Salk JE. *Journal of the American Medical Association*. 1953; 151: 1081–.
14 Davies P et al. *Archives of Disease of Childhood*. 2002; 87: 22–25.
15 Thomas SL et al. *Lancet* 2002; 360: 678–82.
16 Paradise JL et al. *New England Journal of Medicine*. 2001; 344: 1179–87.
17 Offringa M & Moyer VA *British Medical Journal*. 2001; 323: 1111–14.
18 Liston C & Kagan J *Nature*. 2002; 419: 896.
19 Website The VCFS Foundation: www.vcfs.com.au
       A useful US website is www.vcfsef.org

BONES, JOINTS AND BAD BACKS

1 Kristin R. Baker et al. *The Journal of Rheumatology*. 2001; 28: 1655–65.
2 Fransen M et al. *The Cochrane Library*. Issue 3, 2003.
3 Dawson J et al. *Journal of Epidemiology and Community Health*. 2003; 57: 823–30.
4 Felson DT & Buckwalter J. *New England Journal of Medicine*. 2002; 347: 132–33.
   Moseley JB et al. *New England Journal of Medicine*. 2002; 347: 81–88.
5 Hinman RS et al. *British Medical Journal*. 2003; 327: 135–38.
6 Sharma L et al. *Journal of the American Medical Association*. 2001; 286: 188–95.
7 Savoia HF et al. *ANZ Journal of Surgery*. 2002; 72: 557–60.
8 Harper CM et al. *British Medical Journal*. 2003; 326: 721–22.
9 Juni P et al. *British Medical Journal*. 2002; 324: 1287–88.
   US Food and Drug Administration, 7 June 2002. Available: www.fda.gov/bbs/topics/ANSWERS/2002/ANS01151.html.
10 Mukherjee D et al. *Journal of the American Medical Association*. 2001; 286: 954–59.
   National Prescribing Service Newsletter 2001; 18. Available: www.nps.org.au.
   Norman RJ *Lancet*. 2001; 358: 1287–88.
   Pall ME et al. *Human Reproduction*. 2001; 16: 1323–28.
11 Van der Linden PD et al. *British Medical Journal*. 2002; 324: 1306–07.
12 Kovacs FM et al. *Lancet*. 2003; 362: 1599–1604.
   McConnell J *Lancet*. 2003; 362: 1594–95.
13 Battié MC et al. *Lancet*. 2002; 360: 1369–74.
14 Paassilta P et al. *Journal of the American Medical Association*. 2001; 285: 1843–49.
15 Pengel LHM et al. *British Medical Journal*. 2003; 327: 323–25.
16 Feder G *Evidence-Based Medicine*. 2001; 6: 145.
   Kendrick D et al. *British Medical Journal*. 2001; 322: 400–405.
17 Ernst E *Medical Journal of Australia*. 2001; 176: 376–80.

18 Ingeborg IB et al. *British Medical Journal*. 2003; 326: 911–14.
19 Gordon Susan J et al. *Australian Journal of Physiotherapy* 2002; 48: 9–15.
20 Khan KM et al. *British Medical Journal*. 2002: 324: 626–27.
21 Winemuller MH et al. *Journal of the American Medical Association*. 2003; 290: 1474–78.
22 Kreder HJ *Evidence-Based Medicine*. 2001; 6: 180.
   Torkki M et al. *Journal of the American Medical Association*. 2001; 285: 2474–80.
23 Denke MA *Journal of the American Medical Association*. 2002; 287: 102–103.
   Fesanich D et al. *Journal of the American Medical Association*. 2002; 287: 47–54.
24 Trivedi DP et al. *British Medical Journal*. 2003; 326: 469–72.

BREASTS

1 Bingham SA et al. *Lancet*. 2003; 362: 212–14.
   Prentice RL *Lancet*. 2003; 362: 182–83.
2 Band PR et al. *Lancet*. 2002; 360:1044–49.
   Russo IH *Lancet*. 2002; 360: 1033–34.
3 Slattery ML *Journal of the American Medical Association*. 2001; 285: 799–800.
   Smith-Warner SA et al. *Journal of the American Medical Association*. 2001; 285: 769–76.
4 Baxter N *Journal of the Canadian Medical Association*. 2001; 164: 1837–46.
5 Gelman KA & Olivotto I *Lancet*. 2002; 359: 904–905.
   Nystrom L et al. *Lancet*. 2002; 359: 909–19.
   Website IARC: www.iarc.fr/
6 Collaborative Group on Hormonal Factors in Breast Cancer *Lancet*. 2001; 358: 1389–99.
7 Davidson NE & Helzlsouer KJ *New England Journal of Medicine*. 2002; 346: 2078–79.
   Marchbanks PA et al. *New England Journal of Medicine*. 2002; 346: 2025–32.
8 IBIS Investigators *Lancet*. 2002; 360: 817–24.
   Kinsinger LS & Harris R *Lancet*. 2002; 360: 813–14.
9 Fisher B et al. *New England Journal of Medicine*. 2002; 347: 567–75.
10 Giordano SH et al. *Annals of Internal Medicine*. 2002; 137: 678–87.
   Perkins GH & Middleton LP *British Medical Journal*. 2003; 327: 239–40.

CANCER

1 Bolin T el al. *Medical Journal of Australia*. 2002; 176: 145–46.
   Levitt M. *The Bowel Book*. Oxford University Press, 2002.
   Mandel JS et al. *New England Journal of Medicine*. 2000; 343: 1603–1607.
   Rich MM & Sandler RS *Evidence-Based Medicine*. 2001; 6: 89.
2 Greenwald P *British Medical Journal*. 2002; 324: 714–18.
3 Humphries SE et al. *Lancet*. 2001; 358: 115–19.
   Wang XL & Mahaney MC *Lancet*. 2001; 358: 87–88.
4 Heeschen C et al. *Nature Medicine*. 2001; 7: 833–39.
   Jain RK *Nature Medicine*. 2001; 7: 775–77.
5 Petticrew M et al. *British Medical Journal*. 2002; 325: 1066–69.
6 Graham J et al. *British Medical Journal*. 2002; 324: 1420–22.
7 Tagliabue E et al. *Lancet*. 2003; 362: 527–33.

8   Campbell FA et al. *British Medical Journal*. 2001; 323: 13–16.
    Kalso E *British Medical Journal*. 2001; 323: 2–3.
    Naef M et al. *Pain*. 2003; 105: 79–88.
    Zajicek J et al. *Lancet*. 2003; 362: 1517–26.
9   Bifulco M & Di Marzo V *Nature Medicine*. 2002; 8: 547–50.
10 Hall EJ *Journal of Radiological Protection*. 2000; 20: 347–48.
    Hall EJ *Pediatric Radiology*. 2002; 32: 225–27.
    Hall EJ *Pediatric Radiology*. 2002; 32: 700–706.
    Hall EJ & Wuu CS *Int J Radiat Oncol Biol Phys*. 2003; 56: 83–88.
11 Travis LB et al. *Journal of the American Medical Association*. 2003; 290: 465–75.
    Yahalom J *Journal of the American Medical Association*. 2003; 290: 529–31.
12 Michaud DS et al. *Journal of the American Medical Association*. 2001; 286: 921–29.

CARS

1   Foss RD et al. *Journal of the American Medical Association*. 2001; 286: 1588–92.
    McCartt AT *Journal of the American Medical Association*. 2001; 286: 1631–32.
    Shope JT et al. *Journal of the American Medical Association*. 2001; 286: 1593–98.
    Website The Health Report:
            www/abc.net.au/rn/talks.8.30/helthrpt/stories/s426341.htm
2   Connor J et al. *British Medical Journal*. 2002; 324: 1125–28.
3   Philip P et al. *British Medical Journal*. 2001; 322: 829.
4   Cullinan M & Merriman T *ANZ Journal of Surgery*. 2001; 71: 554–55.
    Danne P *ANZ Journal of Surgery*. 2001; 71: 507–508.
    Thomson BNJ & Davis SM *ANZ Journal of Surgery*. 2001; 71: 552–53.
5   Ichikawa M et al. *Lancet*. 2002; 359: 43–44.
6   Hawkins RA *Evidence-Based Medicine*. 2001; 6: 76.
    Rosenfeld M et al. *Spine*. 2000; 25: 1782–87.
7   Koepsell T et al. *Journal of the American Medical Association*. 2002; 288: 2136–43.
    Parmet S et al. *Journal of the American Medical Association*. 2002; 288: 2212.
    Runge JW & Cole TB *Journal of the American Medical Association*. 2002; 288: 2172–74.
8   Website www.epworth.org.au
9   McCarthy M *Lancet*. 2003; 361: 2168.
    Redelmeier DA et al. *Lancet*. 2003; 361: 2177–82.

CHRONIC FATIGUE SYNDROME

1   Wessely S *Journal of the American Medical Association*. 2001; 286: 1378–79.
    Whiting P et al. *Journal of the American Medical Association*. 2001; 286: 1360–68.
2   Chronic Fatigue Syndrome clinical practice guidelines *Medical Journal of Australia*. 2002; 175: S17–S56. Available: www.mja.com.au/public/guides/cfs/cfs2.html.
3   Barron DF et al. *Journal of Pediatrics*. 2002; 141: 421–25.
    Bou-Holaigah I et al. *Journal of the American Medical Association*. 1995; 274: 961–67.
    Rowe P *Journal of Pediatrics*. 2002; 140: 387–89.
    Rowe P et al. *Lancet*. 1995; 345: 623–24.
    Rowe P et al. *Journal of Pediatrics*. 1998; 135: 494–99.

Rowe P et al. *Journal of the American Medical Association.* 2001; 285: 52–59.
4   White PD et al. *Lancet* 2001; 358: 1946–54.

DEMENTIA

1   Barberger-Gateau P et al. *British Medical Journal.* 2002; 325: 932–33.
2   Ruitenberg A et al. *Lancet* 2002; 359: 281–86.
3   Wilson RS et al. *Journal of the American Medical Association.* 2002; 287: 742–48.
4   Hendrie HC et al. *Journal of the American Medical Association.* 2001; 285: 739–47.
5   Kivipelto M et al. *British Medical Journal.* 2001; 322: 1447–51.
6   Website The Health Report:
       www.abc.net.au/rn/talks/8.30/helthrpt/stories/s818433.htm
7   Blass JP & Ratan RR *The New England Journal of Medicine.* 2003; 348: 1277–78.
    Vermeer SE et al. *The New England Journal of Medicine.* 2003; 348: 1215–22.
8   Palmer K et al. *British Medical Journal.* 2003; 326: 245–47.
9   *National Prescribing Service Newsletter.* 2001; 16.
    Websites www.alzheimers.org.au
             www.carers.asn.au
             www.nps.org.au
10 Aisen PS et al. *Journal of the American Medical Association.* 2003; 289: 2819–26.
    Breitner JCS & Zandi PP *New England Journal of Medicine.* 2001; 345: 1567–68.
    Launer LJ *Journal of the American Medical Association.* 2003; 289: 2865–67.
    'T Veld et al. *New England Journal of Medicine.* 2001; 345: 1515–21.
11 Malouf R & Areosa Sastre A *The Cochrane Library.* Issue 3, 2000.
12 Solomon PR et al. *Journal of the American Medical Association.* 2002; 288: 835–40.
13 Thorgrimsen L et al. *The Cochrane Library.* Issue 3, 2003.
14 Wilson BA et al. *Journal of Neurology, Neurosurgery and Psychiatry.* 2001; 70: 477–82.
15 Wolfson C et al. *New England Journal of Medicine.* 2001; 344: 1111–16.

DIABETES

1   Beckman et al. *Journal of the American Medical Association.* 2002; 287: 2570–81.
2   Solomon CG et al. *Journal of the American Medical Association.* 2001; 286: 2421–26.
3   Tataranni PA & Bogardus C *New England Journal of Medicine.* 2001; 344: 1390–91.
    Tuomilehto J et al. *New England Journal of Medicine.* 2001; 344: 1343–50.
4   Jiang R et al. *Journal of the American Medical Association.* 2002; 288: 2554–60.

DIGESTION

1   Swank DJ et al. *Lancet.* 2003; 361: 1247–51.
2   Donnelly NJ et al. *Medical Journal of Australia.* 2001; 175: 15–18
    Hugh TB & High TJ *Medical Journal of Australia.* 2001; 175: 7–8.
3   Radford-Smith G.L. et al. *Gut.* 2002; 51: 808–13.
    Website The Health Report:
       www.abc.net.au/rn/talks/8.30/helthrpt/stories/s739531.htm
4   Lassen AT et al. *Lancet.* 2000; 356: 455–60.
    Schwartz MD *Evidence-Based Medicine.* 2001; 6: 47.
    Soo S et al. *The Cochrane Library.* Issue 4, 2003.

5 Mohammed I et al. *Gut.* 2003; 52: 1085–89.
6 Duggan A & Harvey M *Medical Journal of Australia.* 2001; 174: 323–24.
7 Kahrilas PJ *Journal of the American Medical Association.* 2001; 285: 2376–78.
  Spechler SJ et al. *Journal of the American Medical Association.* 2001; 285: 2331–38.
8 Nilsson M et al. *Journal of the American Medical Association.* 2003; 290: 66–72.
9 Sanduleanu S et al. *Aliment Pharmacol Ther.* 2001; 15: 379–88.
  Sanduleanu S et al. *Aliment Pharmacol Ther.* 2001; 15: 1163–75.
  Zavros Y et al. *Am J Gastrointest Liver Physiol.* 2002; 282: G175–83.
  Zavros Y et al. *Gastroenterology.* 2002; 122: 119–33.
  Website The Health Report:
        www.abc.net.au/rn/talks/8.30/helthrpt/stories/s744294.htm
10 Malaty HM et al. *Lancet.* 2002; 359: 931–35.
11 Manes G et al. *British Medical Journal.* 2003; 326: 1118–21.
12 Fox JG and Wang TC *New England Journal of Medicine.* 2001; 345: 829–32.
   Uemura N et al. *New England Journal of Medicine.* 2001; 345: 784–89.
13 Harvey R et al. *British Medical Journal.* 2001; 323: 264–65.
14 Slater K et al. *Australian and New Zealand Journal of Surgery.* 2002; 72: 83–88.

DRUGS AND ALCOHOL

1 Arsenault L et al. *British Medical Journal.* 2002; 325: 1212–13.
  Patton CG et al. *British Medical Journal.* 2002; 325: 1195–98.
  Rey MJ and Tennant CC. *British Medical Journal.* 2002; 325: 1183–84.
  Zammit S et al. *British Medical Journal.* 2002; 325: 1199.
2 Pope HG *Journal of the American Medical Association.* 2002; 287: 1172–74.
  Solowij N et al. *Journal of the American Medical Association.* 2002; 287: 1123–31.
3 George TP et al. *American Journal of Psychiatry.* 2000; 157: 1835–42.
  George TP et al. *Neuropsychopharmacology.* 2002; 26: 75–85.
4 Johnson JG et al. *Journal of the American Medical Association.* 2000; 284: 2348–51.
5 Glassman AH et al. *Lancet.* 2001; 357: 1929–32.
  Niaura R & Abrams DB *Lancet.* 2001; 357: 1900–1901.
6 Dalton MA et al. *Lancet.* 2003; 362: 281–85.
  Glantz SA *Lancet.* 2003; 362: 258–59.
7 Glanz SA & Parmley WW *Journal of the American Medical Association.* 2001; 286: 462–63.
  Otsuka R et al. *Journal of the American Medical Association.* 2001; 286: 436–41.
8 Langley JD *British Medical Journal.* 2003; 327: 1023–24.
9 Cannon ME et al. *Medical Journal of Australia.* 2001; 174: 520–21.
10 Rice JE & Faunt JD *Internal Medicine Journal.* 2001; 31: 317–18.
11 Margovsky A & Grieve DA *ANZ Journal of Surgery.* 2001; 71: 321–22.

ENVIRONMENT AND HEALTH

1 Jacobson JL & Jacobson SW *Lancet* 2001; 358: 1568–69.
  Walkowiak J et al. *Lancet* 2001; 358: 1602–1607.

2   Power C et al. *British Medical Journal*. 2002; 325: 131–34.
3   Isbister GK & Gray MR *Medical Journal of Australia*. 2003; 179: 199–202.
    White J *Medical Journal of Australia*. 2003; 179: 180–81.

EXERCISE AND SPORT

1   Finch C et al. *Australian and New Zealand Journal of Public Health* 2002; 26: 462–67.
2   Kerkhoffs GMMJ et al. *The Cochrane Library*, Issue 3, 2002.
3   Snidt N et al. *Lancet*. 2002; 359: 657–62.
4   Baeyens L et al. *British Medical Journal*. 2002; 325: 138.
    Elston MA *British Medical Journal*. 2002; 325: 138.
5   Fontarosa PB et al. *Journal of the American Medical Association*. 2003; 289: 1568–70.
    Shekelle PG et al. *Journal of the American Medical Association*. 2003; 289: 1537–45.
6   Maron BJ *New England Journal of Medicine*. 2003; 349: 1064–75.
7   Lim J et al. *ANZ Journal of Surgery*. 2003; 73: 567–71.
    Roe J P et al. *ANZ Journal of Surgery*. 2003; 73: 331–34.
    Spinecare Foundation and the Australian Spinal Cord Injury Units *ANZ Journal of Surgery*. 2003; 73: 493–99.
    Taylor TKF & Roe JP *Medical Journal of Australia*. 2003; 176: 402.
8   Gregg EW et al. *Journal of the American Medical Association*. 2003; 289: 2379–86.
9   Barrett C & Smerdely P *Australian Journal of Physiotherapy*. 2002; 48: 215–19.
10 Manson JE et al. *New England Journal of Medicine*. 2002; 347: 716–25.
    Thompson PD *New England Journal of Medicine*. 2002; 347: 755–56.

EYES

1   Klein BEK *Journal of the American Medical Association*. 2002; 288: 885–86.
    Owsley C et al. *Journal of the American Medical Association*. 2002; 288: 841–49.
2   Website The Health Report:
        www.abc.net.au/rn/talks/8.30/helthrpt/stories/s543440.htm
3   Contact The Benign Essential Blepharospasm Support Group can be contacted via the Royal Victorian Eye and Ear Hospital.
    Website www.blepharospasm.org/blephars.html
4   Goldstein L.E. et al. *Lancet*. 2003; 361: 1258–65.
5   Wang JJ et al. *Archives of Ophthalmology*. 2001; 119: 1186–90.
6   Wormald R *British Medical Journal*. 2003; 326: 723–24.
7   Teng C et al. *British Journal of Ophthalmology*. 2003; 87: 946–48.

HEART AND ARTERIES

1   Canto JG & Iskandrian AE *JAMA*. 2003; 290: 947–49.
    Commentary *Lancet*. 2001; 358: 1026.
    Greenland P et al. *JAMA*. 2003; 290: 891–97.
    Hackam DG & Anand SS *JAMA*. 2003; 290: 932–40.
    Jackson RT *Medical Journal of Australia*. 2001; 175: 452–53.
    Khot UN et al. *JAMA*. 2003; 290: 898–904.
    Law MR & Wald NJ *British Medical Journal*. 2002; 324: 1570–76.
    National Heart Foundation of Australia; Cardiac Society of Australia and New Zealand *Medical Journal of Australia*. 2001;175 : S57–85.

Panza JA *New England Journal of Medicine.* 2001; 345: 1337–39.
Progress Collaborative Group *Lancet.* 2001; 358: 1033–41.
Vasan RS et al. *New England Journal of Medicine.* 2001; 345: 1291–97.
Websites www.heartfoundation.com.au
    MRC/BHF Heart Protection Study: www.ctsus.ox.ac.uk/~hps

2. Balady GJ *New England Journal of Medicine.* 2002; 346: 852–53.
Myers J et al. *New England Journal of Medicine.* 2002; 346: 746–801.
3. Hunt K et al. *Lancet.* 2001; 357: 1168–71.
4. Brown BG et al. *New England Journal of Medicine.* 2001; 345: 1583–92.
Freedman JE *New England Journal of Medicine.* 2001; 345: 1636–37.
Sacco RL et al. *Journal of the American Medical Association.* 2001; 285: 2729–35.
5. Sachdev PS et al. *Neurology.* 2002; 58: 1539–41.
Sehadri S et al. *New England Journal of Medicine.* 2002; 346: 476–83.
6. Vasan RS et al. *Journal of the American Medical Association.* 2003; 289: 1251–57.
7. The Swiss Heart Study *Journal of the American Medical Association.* 2002; 288: 973–79.
8. Greenland P *Journal of the American Medical Association.* 2003; 289: 2270–72.
O'Malley PG et al. *Journal of the American Medical Association.* 2003; 289: 2215–23.
9. Vasan RS et al. *Journal of the American Medical Association.* 2002; 287: 1003–1010.
10. Chobanian AV et al. *Journal of the American Medical Association.* 2003; 289: 2560–72.
Kottke TE et al. *Journal of the American Medical Association.* 2003; 289: 2573–75.
11. Whelton PK et al. *Journal of the American Medical Association.* 2002; 288: 1882–88.
Website www.nhlbi.nih.gov/hbp/index.html
12. Blecker D *Evidence-Based Medicine.* 2002; 7: 41.
Moore TJ et al. *Hypertension.* 2001; 38: 155–58.
Website www.nhlbi.nih.gov/health/public/heart/hbp/dash
13. Appel LJ et al. *Archives of Internal Medicine.* 2001; 161: 685–93.
Arroll B. *Evidence-Based Medicine.* 2001; 6: 151.
Hooper L et al. *British Medical Journal.* 2002; 325: 628–32.
14. Nelson MR et al. *British Medical Journal* 2002; 325: 815–17.
15. Kottke TE et al. *Journal of the American Medical Association.* 2003; 289: 2573–75.
Psaty BM et al. *Journal of the American Medical Association.* 2003; 289: 2534–44.
16. Ferrucci L et al. *Circulation* 2001; 104: 1923–26.
Gray J *Evidence-Based Medicine.* 2002; 7: 109.
17. Haines A et al. *Heart.* 2001; 85: 385–89.
Williams RB et al. *Journal of the American Medical Association.* 2003; 290: 2190–92.
Yan LL et al. *Journal of the American Medical Association.* 2003; 290: 2138–48.
18. Ness AR et al. *Journal of Epidemiology and Community Health.* 2001; 55: 379–82.
19. Bates ER *Evidence-Based Medicine.* 2001; 6: 171.
Sanmuganathan PS et al. *Heart.* 2001; 85: 265–71.
20. Collaborative Group of the Primary Prevention Project (PPP) *Lancet.* 2001; 357: 89–95.
Gluckman R *Evidence-Based Medicine.* 2001; 6: 112.
21. Law MR et al. *British Medical Journal.* 2003; 326: 1423.
Law MR et al. *British Medical Journal.* 2003; 326: 1427.

Rodgers A *British Medical Journal.* 2003; 326: 1407–1408.
Wald NJ & Law MR *British Medical Journal.* 2003; 326: 1419.
22 Lawlor DA et al. *British Medical Journal.* 2002; 325: 311–12.
23 Smith GCS et al. *British Medical Journal.* 2003; 326: 423–24.
24 McGill HC et al. *Circulation.* 2002; 105: 2712–18.
25 Aronow WS *Lancet.* 2001; 358: 945–46.
TIME Investigators *Lancet.* 2001; 358: 951–57.
26 Bates ER *Evidence-Based Medicine.* 2003; 8: 108.
DeFilippi CR et al. *Journal of the American College of Cardiology.* 2001; 37: 2042–49.
Keeley EC et al. *Lancet.* 2003; 361: 13–20.
Wyer PC *Evidence-Based Medicine.* 2002; 7: 14.
27 Diegeler A et al. *New England Journal of Medicine.* 2002; 347: 561–66.
28 Dorsch MF et al. *Heart.* 2001; 86: 494–98.
29 Zamvar V et al. *British Medical Journal.* 2002; 325: 1268–71.
30 Tu JV et al. *Journal of the American Medical Association.* 2001; 285: 3116–22.
31 Heart Protection Study Collaborative Group. *Lancet.* 2002; 360: 23–33.
Meagher EA et al. *Journal of the American Medical Association.* 2001; 285: 1178–82.
Vivekananthan DP et al. *Lancet.* 2003; 361: 2017–23.
Yusuf S *Lancet.* 2002; 360: 2-3
32 Knudtson ML et al. *Journal of the American Medical Association.* 2002; 287: 481–86.
33 Szapary PO et al. *Journal of the American Medical Association.* 2003; 290: 765–72.
34 Lyon W et al. *Asia Pacific Journal of Clinical Nutrition.* 2001; 10: 212–15.
35 Vasan RS *British Medical Journal.* 2003; 327: 1181–82.
36 Greenhalgh RM & Powell JT *British Medical Journal.* 2002; 325: 1123–24.
Multicentre Aneurysm Screening Study group *British Medical Journal.* 2002; 325: 1135–38.
Multicentre Aneurysm Screening Study group *Lancet.* 2002; 360: 1531–39.
37 Tateishi-Yuyama E et al. *Lancet.* 2002: 360: 427–35.

INFECTIONS

1 Butler C et al. *Lancet* 2002; 359: 2153–58.
2 Audera C et al. *Medical Journal of Australia.* 2001; 175: 359–62.
3 Little P *Evidence-Based Medicine.* 2001; 6: 46.
Prasad AS et al. *Annals of Internal Medicine.* 2000; 133: 2345–52.
4 Cohen S et al. *Psychological Science.* 2003; 14: 389–95.
De Sutter AIM et al. *The Cochrane Library.* Issue 3, 2003. Oxford: Update Software
Schroeder K & Fahey T *British Medical Journal.* 2002; 324: 329–31.
5 Nelson D et al. *Proceedings of National Academy of Sciences.* 20 March 2001.
Rosovitz MJ & Leppla SH *Nature.* 2002; 418: 825–26.
Schuch R et al. *Nature.* 2002; 418: 884–89.
6 Hataka K et al. *British Medical Journal.* 2001; 322: 1327–29.
Wanke CA *British Medical Journal.* 2001; 322: 1318–19.
7 Nichol KL et al. *New England Journal of Medicine.* 2003; 348: 1322–32.
8 Aaawasthi S *Evidence-Based Medicine.* 2003; 8: 111.
Morris P & Leach A *Cochrane Review.* 2002: no. 4; CD0011094.

9. Piccirillo JF at al. *Journal of the American Medical Association.* 2001; 286: 1849–56.
10. *Therapeutic Guidelines:* Antibiotic version 12.
    National Prescribing Service Survey Clinical Audit, NPS News, June 2000.
11. Nutik Zitter J et al. *Journal of the American Medical Association.* 2002; 288: 483–86.
12. Website The Health Report: www.abc.net.au/rn/talks/8.30/helthrpt/stories/s823632.htm
13. Van den Hoogen BG et al. *Nature Medicine.* 2001; 7: 719–24.
14. Drucker E et al. *Lancet.* 2001; 358: 1989–92.
15. Mocroft A et al. *Lancet.* 2003; 362: 22–29.
16. Website www.mrc.ac.za/bod
17. Website Australian Hepatitis Council: www.hepatititisaustralia.com

MEN'S HEALTH

1. Douek M at al. *British Medical Journal.* 2003; 326: 1012–13.
2. Storgaard L et al. *British Medical Journal.* 2002; 325: 252–53.
3. Tsipouras S et al. *Medical Journal of Australia.* 2001; 174: 516–19.
4. Tonta K & Kimble KW *ANZ Journal of Surgery.* 2001; 71: 467–71.

MENTAL HEALTH AND PSYCHOLOGY

1. Dimoe F et al. *British Journal of Sports Medicine.* 2001; 35: 114–17.
   Mather AS et al. *British Journal of Psychiatry.* 2002; 180: 411–15.
2. Enhancing Recovery in Coronary Heart Disease Patients (ENRICHD) Randomized Trial *Journal of the American Medical Association.* 2003; 289: 3106–16.
   Frasure-Smith N & Lesperance F *Journal of the American Medical Association.* 2003; 289: 3171–73.
3. Hall WD et al. *British Medical Journal.* 2003; 326: 1008–11.
4. Evans J et al. *British Medical Journal.* 2001; 323: 257–60.
5. Oren D et al. *Biological Psychiatry.* 2002; 51: 422–25.
6. Keeves J *Australian Journal of Psychology.* 2001; 53: 134–39.
7. Page A et al. *Journal of Epidemiology and Community Health.* 2002; 56: 766–72.
   Shaw M et al. *Journal of Epidemiology and Community Health.* 2002; 56: 723–25.
8. Brondolo E et al. *Psychosomatic Medicine.* 2003; 65: 1003–11.
   Sloan RP et al. *American Journal of Cardiology.* 1994; 74: 298–300.
   Sloan RP et al. *Psychosomatic Medicine.* 1999; 61: 58–68.
9. Lawler KA et al. *Journal of Behavioral Medicine.* 2003; 26: 373–93.
10. Garg A et al. *Archives of Dermatology.* 2001; 137: 53–59.
11. Kivimäki M et al. *British Medical Journal.* 2002; 325: 857–60.
12. Nordstrom CK et al. *Epidemiology.* 2001; 12: 180–85.
13. Lawrence D, Holman D & Jablensky *A Duty to Care. Preventable physical illness in people with mental illness.* The University of Western Australia, Perth, 2001. Available at: www.dph.uwa.edu.au.
14. McKelvey RS et al. *Medical Journal of Australia.* 2001; 175: 550–52.
15. Hillman SD et al. *Suicide in Western Australia.* Institute for Child Health Research, University of Western Australia, 2000.
    Website www.wa.gov.au/drugwestau

16   Ben-Tovim DI et al. *Lancet.* 2001; 357: 1254–57.
     Bergh C et al. *Proceedings of the National Academy of Sciences.* 2002; 99: 9486–91.
17   Emmerick AAP et al. *Lancet.* 2002; 360: 766–71.
     Gist R & Devilly GJ *Lancet.* 2002; 360: 741–42.
18   Marsicano G et al. *Nature.* 2002; 418: 530–34.
     Sah P *Nature.* 2002; 418: 488–89.
19   Chalder T et al. *British Medical Journal.* 2001; 323: 473–76.
20   Thoresen S et al. *Social Psychiatry and Psychiatric Epidemiology.* 2003; 38: 605–610.
21   Koot VCM et al. *British Medical Journal.* 2003; 326: 527–28.
22   Mavrogiorgou P et al. *Journal of Neurology, Neurosurgery and Psychiatry.* 2001; 70: 605–612.
     Stein DJ. *Lancet.* 2001; 358: 524.
23   Website The Health Report:
          www.abc.net.au/rn/talks/8.30/helthrpt/stories/s549690.htm
24   Edinger JD et al. *Journal of the American Medical Association.* 2001; 285: 1843–49.
25   Lidz J et al. *Cognition.* 2003; 87: 151–78.
     Papafragou A et al. *Cognition.* 2002; 84: 189–219.
     Website The Health Report:
          www.abc.net.au/rn/talks/8.30/helthrpt/stories/s579544.htm
26   Sloan RP et al. *Lancet.* 1999; 353: 664–67.
     Sloan RP et al. *New England Journal of Medicine.* 2000; 342: 1913–16.
27   McClain CS et al. *Lancet.* 2003; 361: 1603–1607.
28   Soifer S et al. *Shy Bladder Syndrome.* New Harbinger Publications, Oakland, 2001.
     Websites www.shybladder.org
          The Health Report:
          www.abc.net.au/rn/talks/8.30/helthrpt/stories/s815781.htm

NERVOUS SYSTEM

1   Elpidoforos S et al. *New England Journal of Medicine.* 2002; 347: 878–85.
2   Herxheimer A & Petrie KJ *The Cochrane Library.* Issue 4, 2003: John Wiley & Sons, Chichester, UK.
    Shapiro CM *Evidence-Based Medicine.* 2001; 6: 186.
3   Hall M & Buckley N *Australian Prescriber.* 2003; 26: 62–63.
4   Martyn C & Gale C *British Medical Journal.* 2003; 326: 561–62.
5   Doh-ura K et al. *Journal of Virology.* 2000; 74: 4894–97.
    Korth C et al. *Proceedings of the National Academy of Sciences.* 2001; 98: 9836–41.
    Koster T et al. *Journal of Veterinary Pharmacology and Therapeutics.* 2003; 26: 315–26.
    Peretz D et al. *Nature.* 2001; 412: 739–43.
6   Cassell OCS *British Medical Journal.* 2002; 324: 1442–43.
7   Mainland JD et al. *Nature.* 2002; 419: 802.

PREGNANCY AND CHILDBIRTH

1   Hodnett ED *The Cochrane Library.* Issue 1, 2002.
    Nikodem C *Evidence-Based Medicine.* 2002; 7: 105.
2   Smith CS et al. *British Medical Journal.* 2003; 327: 313–16.
3   Hodnett ED et al. *The Cochrane Library.* Issue 3, 2003.
4   Matte TD et al. *British Medical Journal.* 2001; 323: 310–14.
5   Huxley R et al. *Lancet.* 2002; 360: 659–65.

PROSTATE

1. Gattellari M & Ward JE *Journal of Medical Screening*. 2003; 10: 27–39.
   Gattellari M & Ward JE *Australian Family Physician*. 2003; 32: 429–30.
   Livingston P et al. *Internal Medicine Journal*. 2002; 32: 215–23.
   Lu-Yao G et al. *British Medical Journal*. 2002; 325: 740 –43.
   Website The Health Report:
   www.abc.net.au/rn/talks/8.30/helthrpt/stories/s809313.htm
2. Brookes ST et al. *British Medical Journal*. 2002; 324: 1059–61.
   Wilt TJ *British Medical Journal*. 2002; 324: 1047–48.
3. Holmberg L et al. *New England Journal of Medicine*. 2002; 347: 781–89.
   Steineck G et al. *New England Journal of Medicine*. 2002; 347: 790–96.
   Walsh P *New England Journal of Medicine*. 2002; 347: 839–40.
4. Scardino PT *New England Journal of Medicine*. 2003; 349: 297–99.
   Thompson I *New England Journal of Medicine*. 2003; 349: 215–24.
5. Terry P et al. *Lancet*. 2001; 357: 1764–66.
6. ATBC Study Group *Journal of the American Medical Association*. 2003; 290: 476–85.
7. Ben-Tovim D et al. *Urology*. 2002; 59: 383–88.
8. Cox B et al. *Journal of the American Medical Association*. 2002; 287: 3110–15.

SEX

1. Fogari R et al. *American Journal of Hypertension*. 2002; 15: 217–21.
2. Josephs RA et al. *Lancet*. 2001; 358: 1613–14.
3. Arruda-Olson AM et al. *Journal of the American Medical Association*. 2002; 287: 719–25.
   Marwick TH *Journal of the American Medical Association*. 2002; 287: 766–67.
   Shakir SA et al. *British Medical Journal*. 2001; 322: 651–52.
4. Gilad R et al. *British Medical Journal*. 2002; 325: 869.

STAYING YOUNG

1. Oeppen J & Vaupel JW *Science*. 2002; 296: 1029–30.
2. Guinot G et al. *Archives of Dermatology*. 2002; 138: 1454–60.
3. Bulpitt CJ et al. *Postgraduate Medical Journal*. 2001; 77: 578–81.
4. Roth GS et al. *Science*. 2002; 297: 811.
5. Dorling D et al. *British Medical Journal* 2001; 322: 1336–37.
6. Coyle JT *New England Journal of Medicine*. 2003; 348: 2489–90.
   Verghese J et al. *New England Journal of Medicine*. 2003; 348: 2508–16.
7. Gunnell D et al. *Journal of Epidemiology and Community Health*. 2001; 55: 505–507.
   Phillips DIW et al. *British Medical Journal*. 2001; 322: 771.
8. Beckham SG & Earnest CP *British Journal of Sports Medicine*. 2003; 37: 212–18.
9. Whalley LJ & Deary IJ *British Medical Journal*. 2001; 332: 819–22.
10. Gillespie LD et al. *The Cochrane Library*, Issue 4, 2003.
11. Chaves PH et al. *Journal of the American Geriatric Society*. 2002; 50: 1257–64.
12. Walston J et al. *Archives of Internal Medicine*. 2002; 162: 2333–41.
13. Graat JM et al. *Journal of the American Medical Association*. 2002; 288: 715–21.

WEIGHT LOSS

1. Foster GD et al. *New England Journal of Medicine.* 2003; 348: 2082–90.
   Ware JH *New England Journal of Medicine.* 2003; 348: 2136–37.
2. Lejeune MP et al. *British Journal of Nutrition.* 2003; 90: 651–59.
   Wahlqvist ML & Wattanapenpalboon N *Lancet.* 2001; 358: 348–49.
3. Website The Health Report:
   www.abc.net.au/rn/talks/8.30/helthrpt/stories/s803463.htm
4. Farooqi IS et al. *New England Journal of Medicine.* 2003; 348: 1085–95.
   O'Rahilly S et al. *Endocrinology.* 2003; 144: 3757–64.
   Website The Health Report:
   www.abc.net.au/rn/talks/8.30/helthrpt/stories/s803457.htm
5. Borowsky B et al. *Nature Medicine.* 2002: 8: 825–30.
6. Jorm AF et al. *Australian and New Zealand Journal of Public Health.* 2003; 27: 434–40.
7. Davi G et al. *Journal of the American Medical Association.* 2002; 288: 2008–14.
8. Dindo D et al. *Lancet.* 2003; 361: 2032–35.
9. Chinn S & Chea RJ *Thorax.* 2001; 56: 845–50.
10. Ben-Tovim DI et al. *Lancet.* 2001; 357: 1254–57.
    Bergh C et al. *Proceedings of the National Academy of Sciences.* 2002; 99: 9486–91.
    Website The Health Report:
    www.abc.net.au/rn/talks/8.30/helthrpt/stories/s883176.htm

WOMEN'S HEALTH

1. Chau JP & Chang AM *Health Education Research.* 1999; 14: 817–30.
   Wyatt K et al. *British Medical Journal.* 2001; 323: 776–80.
2. Doran C et al. *Medical Journal of Australia.* 2001; 174: 456–58.
   National help line 1 800 330 066
3. Goode PS et al. *Journal of the American Medical Association.* 2003; 290: 345–52.
   Resnick NM & Griffths DJ *Journal of the American Medical Association.* 2003; 290: 395–97.
4. Kontiokari T et al. *British Medical Journal.* 2001; 322: 1571–73.
5. Cleghorn DB et al. *Medical Journal of Australia.* 2001; 175: 242–45.
   Henderson NK & Prince RL *Medical Journal of Australia.* 2001; 175: 239–40.
6. Fletcher SW & Colditz GA *Journal of the American Medical Association.* 2002; 288: 366–68.
   Grady D et al. *New England Journal of Medicine.* 2003; 348: May 8 edition.
   Hays J et al. *New England Journal of Medicine.* 2003; 348: May 8 edition.
   Pradhan AD et al. *Journal of the American Medical Association.* 2002; 288: 980–87.
   Rapp et al. *Journal of the American Medical Association.* 2003; 289: 2663–72.
   Shumaker SA at al. *Journal of the American Medical Association.* 2003; 289: 2651–62.
   Women's Health Initiative. *Journal of the American Medical Association.* 2002; 288: 321–33.
   Yaffe K *Journal of the American Medical Association.* 2003; 289: 2617–19.
   Website Lockwood S, The Health Report:
   www.abc.net.au/rn/talks/8.30/helthrpt/stories/s641312.htm

7 Tice JA et al. *Journal of the American Medical Association.* 2003; 290: 107–214.
8 Vessey M et al. *Lancet.* 2003; 362: 185–91.
9 Darney PD *New England Journal of Medicine.* 2001; 345: 608–10.
  Hubacher D et al. *New England Journal of Medicine.* 2001; 345: 561–67.
10 Davies MJ et al. *Journal of the American Medical Association.* 2002; 287: 2559–62.
  Singletary KW & Gapstur SM *Journal of the American Medical Association.* 2001; 286: 2143–51.